JUSTIFICATION AND KNOWLEDGE

PHILOSOPHICAL STUDIES SERIES
IN PHILOSOPHY

Editors:

WILFRID SELLARS, *University of Pittsburgh*

KEITH LEHRER, *University of Arizona*

Board of Consulting Editors:

JONATHAN BENNETT, *University of British Columbia*

ALAN GIBBARD, *University of Pittsburgh*

ROBERT STALNAKER, *Cornell University*

ROBERT G. TURNBULL, *Ohio State University*

VOLUME 17

JUSTIFICATION AND KNOWLEDGE

New Studies in Epistemology

Edited by

GEORGE S. PAPPAS

The Ohio State University

D. REIDEL PUBLISHING COMPANY

DORDRECHT : HOLLAND / BOSTON : U.S.A.

LONDON : ENGLAND

Library of Congress Cataloging in Publication Data

Main entry under title:

Justification and knowledge.

(Philosophical studies series in philosophy ; v. 17)
"Papers . . . were originally presented at a conference held in
April, 1978, at the Ohio State University."
Bibliography: p.
Includes index.
1. Knowledge, Theory of—Congresses. I. Pappas, George
Sotiros, 1942–
BD161.J87   121   79–19447
ISBN 90–277–1023–6
ISBN 90–277–1024–4 pbk.

Published by D. Reidel Publishing Company,
P.O. Box 17, Dordrecht, Holland

Sold and distributed in the U.S.A., Canada, and Mexico
by D. Reidel Publishing Company, Inc.
Lincoln Building, 160 Old Derby Street, Hingham,
Mass. 02043, U.S.A.

Printed in The Netherlands

This volume is dedicated to the memory of

JAMES W. CORNMAN

whose most untimely and premature death in May of 1978 was a great loss to his many friends and to Philosophy.

TABLE OF CONTENTS

PREFACE

With one exception, all of the papers in this volume were originally presented at a conference held in April, 1978, at The Ohio State University. The exception is the paper by Wilfrid Sellars, which is a revised version of a paper he originally published in the *Journal of Philosophy*, 1973. However, the present version of Sellars' paper is so thoroughly changed from its original, that it is now virtually a new paper. None of the other nine papers has been published previously. The bibliography, prepared by Nancy Kelsik, is very extensive and it is tempting to think that it is complete. But I believe that virtual completeness is more likely to prove correct.

The conference was made possible by grants from the College of Humanities and the Graduate School, Ohio State University, as well as by a grant from the Philosophy Department. On behalf of the contributors, I want to thank these institutions for their support.

I also want to thank Marshall Swain and Robert Turnbull for early help and encouragement; Bette Hellinger for assistance in setting up the conference; and Mary Raines and Virginia Foster for considerable aid in the preparation of papers and many other conference matters. The friendly advice of the late James Cornman was also importantly helpful.

April, 1979   GEORGE S. PAPPAS

INTRODUCTION

The papers in this volume deal in different ways with the related issues of epistemic justification or warrant, and the analysis of factual knowledge. Some essays are concerned primarily with the first of these issues, others with the second, and some with both.

In the opening paper Alvin Goldman takes as his central task that of providing a noncircular, informative and accurate naturalistic *explanation* of the notion of justified beliefs. His positive proposal is that whether a belief is justified is a function of the reliability of the processes which cause the belief. His answer, thus, is in keeping with causal accounts of knowledge which he developed in earlier papers. What is of special interest in the present paper, however, is the extended and detailed spelling out of the relevant notion of reliability.

Goldman characterizes his theory as a Genetic or Historical theory, since according to it the justification of a belief is a function of the 'prior history' of the belief. He dubs his theory 'historical reliabilism.' Such historical theories are held to sharply contrast with '*Current Time-Slice*' theories of justification since, on the latter theories, the justification of a belief is wholly dependent on facts pertaining to the knower at the time he or she has the belief, or perhaps comes to have the belief. A number of classical and contemporary epistemologists are classified according to whether they fall in one of these two major groups.

Marshall Swain also holds that the notions of causality and epistemic justification are crucially connected. Moreover, like Goldman, Swain offers a reliability account of epistemically justified beliefs, one which he labels the 'probabilistic-reliability model.'

The major part of Swain's paper concerns what it is for a belief to be *based on* reasons. Swain takes reasons to be *states* of a person, some of which (but only some) are usually belief-states. Other reason-states might be perceptual-states or sensation-states. A person's belief is based on such reason-states, according to Swain's account, when there is some causal relation between the belief and the reason states, or some relation of what he calls 'pseudo-overdetermination'. He thus provides a causal account of the (or a) basing relation.

Swain's reliability theory of justification is also sketched in his paper. One difference between his account and that of Goldman is that Swain utilizes the

xi

George S. Pappas (ed.), Justification and Knowledge, xi–xv.
Copyright © 1979 by D. Reidel Publishing Company.

notion of competition between beliefs while Goldman does not (at least not explicitly). This notion of competition is necessary to turn aside an objection, to Swain's theory, which derives from the lottery paradox.

Knowledge is often said to, at times, be *based on* evidence or reasons. In my paper, several distinct basing relations are considered. A believed proposition, h, is said to be inferentially based on evidence e provided that h is deductively, inductively, or epistemically derivable from e. And it seems quite plausible to say that a person has knowledge on the basis of some evidence only if his belief is inferentially based on the evidence.

It also seems that a person's knowledge is based on evidence only if his *belief*, and not the believed proposition, is based on the evidence or the having of it. A number of different interpretations of belief-basing are thus considered, but for none of them is it found that knowing on the basis of evidence requires belief-basing. This somewhat counterintuitive result is not the opposite of that defended by Swain, however, unless the notion of evidence is replaced by that of reasons.

I also distinguish the notion of one's justification for belief being based on one's evidence. The central suggestion here is that different theories of justification-basing can be scaled according to whether they require that the subject be a *perspicacious* agent or not, and if so, to what degree. That is, roughly, some theories of what it is to be justified on the basis of one's evidence require that the person either know or justifiably believe a great deal about his evidence and its relation to his putatively justified belief, while other theories require considerably less perspicacity, vis-à-vis one's evidence, of the subject. Several accounts of justification-basing are examined, and an account which incorporates a weak perspicacity condition is proposed,

The first three papers are concerned primarily with epistemic justification and basing relations. In the next two papers, by Keith Lehrer and Ernest Sosa, different analyses of factual knowedge are proposed and defended.

Lehrer first advances a distinction between acception and believing it. Many analyses of knowledge, including some earlier endorsed by Lehrer, have stated that knowledge entails belief. Such accounts, Lehrer says, are mistaken; knowledge entails, instead, acceptance.

Lehrer explicates reasonable acceptance of a proposition in terms of competition. Roughly, a proposition is reasonably acceptable by a person just in case the proposition fares well in competition with others. This idea of linking reasonable acceptance and competition (which is also found at the end of Swain's paper) is then put to use in distinguishing several distinct ways of dealing with types of sceptical ploys. Lehrer also defends a specific analysis of factual knowledge by a discussion of Gettier and Gettier-like examples, and by contrasting his analysis with those recently proposed by Risto Hilpinen and Peter Klein.

In his paper, Sosa introduces the notion of epistemic presupposition, which he then uses to help shed light on Gettier-type problems and, as well, on several recent proposals for dealing with Gettier problems (made by Harman, Goldman, and Sosa himself in an earlier paper). These matters are treated, first, informally. Then, in the final section of his paper, Sosa more precisely sets out and clarifies the concept of epistemic presupposition, and incorporates it in a wider theory of factual knowledge and justification.

The remaining five papers deal more specifically with epistemic justification. In his paper, John Pollock first characterizes foundational theories of epistemic justification, and distinguishes several varieties. The variety stems from the fact that basic beliefs can be characterized in different ways and the relationships of non-basic beliefs to basic beliefs in virtue of which the former are justified can be stated in a number of distinct ways. Pollock rejects all such theories, however, on the grounds that most people seldom have the beliefs that are candidates for being basic, yet we do not want to say that they lack other justified beliefs for *that* reason.

Pollock defends a theory he calls 'direct realism', a theory that is closely related to foundationalism. Yet, after helpfully distinguishing several types of coherence theories, Pollock ends up *also* defending a specific theory of the latter group. The apparent inconsistency is avoided with the claim that these are really theories of different subject matters. Direct realism, as Pollock construes it, is a theory of *objective* justification, while the coherence theory he advocates is held to be a theory of *subjective* justification.

In his contribution, Roderick Chisholm revises a theory of justification he had proposed in earlier papers and books. He had earlier argued for a foundational theory according to which each person's knowledge is based upon that person's I–propositions – the propositions a person would express by using the first person as grammatical subject. These I–propositions were held to concern the self-presenting. However, in the present paper, Chisholm presents reasons for thinking that there are no I–propositions, so that his foundational theory needs amendment.

Chisholm provides the needed amendments with a new account of the self-presenting. He goes on to present a battery of definitions. Some of these defined concepts are familiar from earlier writings, but the proposed definitions sometimes differ significantly. And some defined concepts are new, especially the notion of a state of affairs being *epistemically unsupported* for a given person. The set of definitions may be regarded as comprising a quite new Chisholmian version of foundationalism.

Foundationalism is also the topic of the paper by James Cornman. He assumes some version of foundationalism, and queries how *non*-basic statements can be justified solely on the basis of epistemically foundational, basic statements. Non-basic statements are not deductively derivable from basic ones, as Cornman notes. But neither are they inductively derivable, if inductive inferences are enumerative, analogical and best explanation type inductive inferences, Cornman argues. Cornman also criticizes, and rejects, an approach of Chisholm's which involves inferring the indirectly evident (*non*-basic statements) from the the directly evident (basic statements) by means of epistemic principles. Such principles are nondeductive, noninductive principles of inference which, if correct, would permit Cornman to solve his problem. However, Cornman rejects Chisholm's approach, primarily on the strength of certain objections to it proposed by Heidelberger.

It would seem, given the failures of these approaches, that skepticism is the most plausible remaining option. However, Cornman pursues one more line which, he says, succeeds. Roughly, he maintains that some simple observation reports such as that expressed by 'I am now seeing something yellow,' are made probable by evidence consisting of basic statements. There is, Cornman says, a way of understanding 'q makes p probable for s at t' which avoids the problems facing previously considered approaches, faces no vexing new problems of its own, and helps to solve his problem. Of course, as Cornman concedes, this is a modest accomplishment in any case. For in thus inferring simple observation statements, one has done nothing to show how to justify more complex empirical statements.

Mark Pastin considers a great number of issues in his paper, but perhaps one of the most interesting concerns whether epistemology construed in a certain way is *superfluous*. One way of understanding this idea is to suppose that the notion of warrant between statements *supervenes on non*-epistemic facts. Pastin considers one notion of supervenience and then argues that not all relations of warrant between statements supervene on non-epistemic facts, even if some do. This is a task of great scope, since it involves refuting or at least rendering doubtful a number of 'naturalistic' approaches to justification. Pastin provides the outline of two basic arguments designed to accomplish this task.

Pastin defends a theory he calls 'problematic realism.' One essential component of such a theory is that a theory in some *non*-epistemic domain (e.g., perception) must account for the warrant or justification of statements concerning entities in the domain (perceptual statements, for example). Since Pastin takes this to hold for all theorizing in non-epistemic domains, he feels justified in claiming that "epistemology not only is not superfluous but pervades all theorizing concerning non-epistemic." The bulk of Pastin's paper is addressed to filling in details of this positive proposal, and illustrating how matters would go in one non-epistemic area (perception). His paper, thus, is considerably broader in scope than most of the other papers in the volume, despite the fact that its central concern includes the matter of epistemic warrant.

Wilfrid Sellars begins his paper by contrasting theories which, like Chisholm's, utilize the notion of the self-presenting with some theories which do not. The latter Sellars calls 'representational' theories. However, the greater part of Sellars' paper is devoted to an examination of some ideas of Firth's, particularly ideas concerning the nature and status of warrant principles. (Compare the Cornman and Pollock papers.)

Sellars rejects the idea that some basic warrant principles are self-evident, and so reasonably acceptable. He also rejects the claim that such principles must be accepted since otherwise scepticism would result. The reasonability or warrant for such principles is to be found elsewhere.

Sellars proposes what he calls 'epistemic evaluation as vindication' as the answer to the above problem. This proposal, which ties in with earlier papers of Sellars on inductive inference, is embedded in the broader context of practical reasoning and acting so as to achieve certain goals. The use of inductive inferences and specific warrant principles is thus justified relative to certain goals and the best, most effective means of achieving them.

The literature on epistemic justification and factual knowledge in English-language journals and books is vast and growing all the time. The bibliography, prepared by Nancy Kelsik, should be of great assistance to all those who study and work in epistemology.

GEORGE S. PAPPAS

ALVIN I. GOLDMAN

WHAT IS JUSTIFIED BELIEF?

The aim of this paper is to sketch a theory of justified belief. What I have in mind is an explanatory theory, one that explains in a general way why certain beliefs are counted as justified and others as unjustified. Unlike some traditional approaches, I do not try to prescribe standards for justification that differ from, or improve upon, our ordinary standards. I merely try to explicate the ordinary standards, which are, I believe, quite different from those of many classical, e.g., 'Cartesian', accounts.

Many epistemologists have been interested in justification because of its presumed close relationship to knowledge. This relationship is intended to be preserved in the conception of justified belief presented here. In previous papers on knowledge,[1] I have denied that justification is necessary for knowing, but there I had in mind 'Cartesian' accounts of justification. On the account of justified belief suggested here, it *is* necessary for knowing, and closely related to it.

The term 'justified', I presume, is an evaluative term, a term of appraisal. Any correct definition or synonym of it would also feature evaluative terms. I assume that such definitions or synonyms might be given, but I am not interested in them. I want a set of *substantive* conditions that specify when a belief is justified. Compare the moral term 'right'. This might be defined in other ethical terms or phrases, a task appropriate to meta-ethics. The task of normative ethics, by contrast, is to state substantive conditions for the rightness of actions. Normative ethics tries to specify non-ethical conditions that determine when an action is right. A familiar example is act-utilitarianism, which says an action is right if and only if it produces, or would produce, at least as much net happiness as any alternative open to the agent. These necessary and sufficient conditions clearly involve no ethical notions. Analogously, I want a theory of justified belief to specify in non-epistemic terms when a belief is justified. This is not the only kind of theory of justifiedness one might seek, but it is one important kind of theory and the kind sought here.

In order to avoid epistemic terms in our theory, we must know which terms are epistemic. Obviously, an exhaustive list cannot be given, but here are some examples: 'justified', 'warranted', 'has (good) grounds', 'has reason

1

George S. Pappas (ed.), Justification and Knowledge, 1–23.
Copyright © 1979 by D. Reidel Publishing Company.

(to believe)', 'knows that', 'sees that', 'apprehends that', 'is probable' (in an epistemic or inductive sense), 'shows that', 'establishes that', and 'ascertains that'. By contrast, here are some sample non-epistemic expressions: 'believes that', 'is true', 'causes', 'it is necessary that', 'implies', 'is deducible from', and 'is probable' (either in the frequency sense or the propensity sense). In general, (purely) doxastic, metaphysical, modal, semantic, or syntactic expressions are not epistemic.

There is another constraint I wish to place on a theory of justified belief, in addition to the constraint that it be couched in non-epistemic language. Since I seek an explanatory theory, i.e., one that clarifies the underlying source of justificational status, it is not enough for a theory to state 'correct' necessary and sufficient conditions. Its conditions must also be appropriately deep or revelatory. Suppose, for example, that the following sufficient condition of justified belief is offered: 'If S senses redly at t and S believes at t that he is sensing redly, then S's belief at t that he is sensing redly is justified.' This is not the kind of principle I seek; for, even if it is correct, it leaves unexplained *why* a person who senses redly and believes that he does, believes this justifiably. Not every state is such that if one is in it and believes one is in it, this belief is justified. What is distinctive about the state of sensing redly, or 'phenomenal' states in general? A theory of justified belief of the kind I seek must answer this question, and hence it must be couched at a suitably deep, general, or abstract level.

A few introductory words about my *explicandum* are appropriate at this juncture. It is often assumed that whenever a person has a justified belief, he knows that it is justified and knows what the justification is. It is further assumed that the person can state or explain what his justification is. On this view, a justification is an argument, defense, or set of reasons that can be given in support of a belief. Thus, one studies the nature of justified belief by considering what a person might *say* if asked to defend, or justify, his belief. I make none of these sorts of assumptions here. I leave it an open question whether, when a belief *is* justified, the believer *knows* it is justified. I also leave it an open question whether, when a belief is justified, the believer can *state* or *give* a justification for it. I do not even assume that when a belief is justified there is something 'possessed' by the believer which can be called a 'justification'. I do assume that a justified belief gets its status of being justified from some processes or properties that make it justified. In short, there must be some justification-conferring processes or properties. But this does not imply that there must be an argument, or reason, or anything else, 'possessed' at the time of belief by the believer.

I

A theory of justified belief will be a set of principles that specify truth-conditions for the schema ⌈S's belief in p at time t is justified⌉, i.e., conditions for the satisfaction of this schema in all possible cases. It will be convenient to formulate candidate theories in a recursive or inductive format, which would include (A) one or more base clauses, (B) a set of recursive clauses (possibly null), and (C) a closure clause. In such a format, it is permissible for the predicate 'is a justified belief' to appear in recursive clauses. But neither this predicate, nor any other epistemic predicate, may appear in (the antecedent of) any base clause.[2]

Before turning to my own theory, I want to survey some other possible approaches to justified belief. Identification of problems associated with other attempts will provide some motivation for the theory I shall offer. Obviously, I cannot examine all, or even very many, alternative attempts. But a few sample attempts will be instructive.

Let us concentrate on the attempt to formulate one or more adequate base-clause principles.[3] Here is a classical candidate:

(1)   If S believes p at t, and p is indubitable for S (at t), then S's belief in p at t is justified.

To evaluate this principle, we need to know what 'indubitable' means. It can be understood in at least two ways. First, 'p is indubitable for S' might mean: 'S has no *grounds* for doubting p'. Since 'ground' is an epistemic term, however, principle (1) would be inadmissible on this reading, for epistemic terms may not legitimately appear in the antecedent of a base-clause. A second interpretation would avoid this difficulty. One might interpret 'p is indubitable for S' psychologically, i.e., as meaning 'S is psychologically incapable of doubting p'. This would make principle (1) admissible, but would it be correct? Surely not. A religious fanatic may be psychologically incapable of doubting the tenets of his faith, but that doesn't make his belief in them justified. Similarly, during the Watergate affair, someone may have been so blinded by the aura of the Presidency that even after the most damaging evidence against Nixon had emerged he was still incapable of doubting Nixon's veracity. It doesn't follow that his belief in Nixon's veracity was justified.

A second candidate base-clause principle is this:

(2)   If S believes p at t, and p is self-evident, then S's belief in p at t is justified.

To evaluate this principle, we again need an interpretation of its crucial term, in this case 'self-evident'. On one standard reading, 'evident' is a synonym for 'justified'. '*Self*-evident' would therefore mean something like 'directly justified', 'intuitively justified', or 'non-derivatively justified'. On this reading 'self-evident' is an epistemic phrase, and principle (2) would be disqualified as a base-clause principle.

However, there are other possible readings of '*p* is self-evident' on which it isn't an epistemic phrase. One such reading is: 'It is impossible to understand *p* without believing it'.[4] According to this interpretation, trivial analytic and logical truths might turn out to be self-evident. Hence, any belief in such a truth would be a justified belief, according to (2).

What does 'it is *impossible* to understand *p* without believing it' mean? Does it mean '*humanly* impossible'? That reading would probably make (2) an unacceptable principle. There may well be propositions which humans have an innate and irrepressible disposition to believe, e.g., 'Some events have causes'. But it seems unlikely that people's inability to refrain from believing such a proposition makes every belief in it justified.

Should we then understand 'impossible' to mean 'impossible in principle', or 'logically impossible'? If that is the reading given, I suspect that (2) is a vacuous principle. I doubt that even trivial logical or analytic truths will satisfy this definition of 'self-evident'. Any proposition, we may assume, has two or more components that are somehow organized or juxtaposed. To understand the proposition one must 'grasp' the components and their juxtaposition. Now in the case of *complex* logical truths, there are (human) psychological operations that suffice to grasp the components and their juxtaposition but do not suffice to produce a belief that the proposition is true. But can't we at least *conceive* of an analogous set of psychological operations even for simple logical truths, operations which perhaps are not in the repertoire of human cognizers but which might be in the repertoire of some conceivable beings? That is, can't we conceive of psychological operations that would suffice to grasp the components and componential-juxtaposition of these simple propositions but do not suffice to produce *belief* in the propositions? I think we can conceive of such operations. Hence, for any proposition you choose, it will be possible for it to be understood without being believed.

Finally, even if we set these two objections aside, we must note that self-evidence can at best confer justificational status on relatively few beliefs, and the only plausible group are beliefs in necessary truths. Thus, other base-clause principles will be needed to explain the justificational status of beliefs in contingent propositions.

The notion of a base-clause principle is naturally associated with the idea of 'direct' justifiedness, and in the realm of contingent propositions first-person-current-mental-state propositions have often been assigned this role. In Chisholm's terminology, this conception is expressed by the notion of a *'self-presenting'* state or proposition. The sentence 'I am thinking', for example, expresses a self-presenting proposition. (At least I shall *call* this sort of content a 'proposition', though it only has a truth value given some assignment of a subject who utters or entertains the content and a time of entertaining.) When such a proposition is true for person S at time t, S is justified in believing it at t: in Chisholm's terminology, the proposition is 'evident' for S at t. This suggests the following base-clause principle.

(3)   If p is a self-presenting proposition, and p is true for S at t, and S believes p at t, then S's belief in p at t is justified.

What, exactly, does 'self-presenting' mean? In the second edition of *Theory of Knowledge*, Chisholm offers this definition: "h is self-presenting for S at t $=_{df.}$ h is true at t; and necessarily, if h is true at t, then h is evident for S at t."[5] Unfortunately, since 'evident' is an epistemic term, 'self-presenting' also becomes an epistemic term on this definition, thereby disqualifying (3) as a legitimate base-clause. Some other definition of self-presentingness must be offered if (3) is to be a suitable base-clause principle.

Another definition of self-presentation readily comes to mind. 'Self-presentation' is an approximate synonym of 'self-intimation', and a proposition may be said to be self-intimating if and only if whenever it is true of a person that person believes it. More precisely, we may give the following definition.

(SP)   Proposition p is self-presenting if and only if: necessarily, for any S and any t, if p is true for S at t, then S believes p at t.

On this definition, 'self-presenting' is clearly not an epistemic predicate, so (3) would be an admissible principle. Moreover, there is initial plausibility in the suggestion that it is *this* feature of first-person-current-mental-state propositions — viz., their truth guarantees their being believed — that makes beliefs in them justified.

Employing this definition of self-presentation, is principle (3) correct? This cannot be decided until we define self-presentation more precisely. Since the operator 'necessarily' can be read in different ways, there are different forms of self-presentation and correspondingly different versions of principle (3). Let us focus on two of these readings: a *'nomological'* reading and a *'logical'* reading. Consider first the nomological reading. On this definition a proposition is self-presenting just in case it is nomologically necessary that if p is true for S at t, then S believes p at t.[6]

Is the nomological version of principle (3) — call it '(3_N)' — correct? Not at all. We can imagine cases in which the antecedent of (3_N) is satisfied but we would not say that the belief is justified. Suppose, for example, that p is the proposition expressed by the sentence 'I am in brain-state B', where 'B' is shorthand for a certain highly specific neural state description. Further suppose it is a nomological truth that anyone in brain-state B will ipso facto *believe* he is in brain-state B. In other words, imagine that an occurrent belief with the content 'I am in brain-state B' is realized whenever one is in brain-state B.[7] According to (3_N), any such belief is justified. But that is clearly false. We can readily imagine circumstances in which a person goes into brain-state B and therefore has the belief in question, though this belief is by no means justified. For example, we can imagine that a brain-surgeon operating on S artificially induces brain-state B. This results, phenomenologically, in S's suddenly believing – out of the blue – that he is in brain-state B, without any relevant antecedent beliefs. We would hardly say, in such a case, that S's belief that he is in brain-state B is justified.

Let us turn next to the logical version of (3) – call it '(3_L)' – in which a proposition is defined as self-presenting just in case it is logically necessary that if p is true for S at t, then S believes p at t. This stronger version of principle (3) might seem more promising. In fact, however, it is no more successful than (3_N). Let p be the proposition 'I am awake' and assume that it is logically necessary that if this proposition is true for some person S and time t, then S believes p at t. This assumption is consistent with the further assumption that S frequently believes p when it is false, e.g., when he is dreaming. Under these circumstances, we would hardly accept the contention that S's belief in this proposition is always justified. But nor should we accept the contention that the belief is justified when it is *true*. The truth of the proposition logically guarantees that the belief is *held*, but why should it guarantee that the belief is *justified*?

The foregoing criticism suggests that we have things backwards. The idea of self-presentation is that truth guarantees belief. This fails to confer justification because it is compatible with there being belief without truth. So what seems necessary – or at least sufficient – for justification is that belief should guarantee truth. Such a notion has usually gone under the label of '*infallibility*', or '*incorrigibility*'. It may be defined as follows.

(INC)   Proposition p is incorrigible if and only if: necessarily, for any S and any t, if S believes p at t, then p is true for S at t.

Using the notion of incorrigibility, we may propose principle (4).

(4)   If p is an incorrigible proposition, and S believes p at t, then S's belief in p at t is justified.

As was true of self-presentation, there are different varieties of incorrigibility, corresponding to different interpretations of 'necessarily'. Accordingly, we have different versions of principle (4). Once again, let us concentrate on a nomological and a logical version, (4_N) and (4_L) respectively.

We can easily construct a counterexample to (4_N) along the lines of the belief-state/brain-state counterexample that refuted (3_N). Suppose it is no-mologically necessary that if anyone believes he is in brain-state B then it is true that he is in brain-state B, for the only way this belief-state is realized is through brain-state B itself. It follows that ' I am in brain-state B' is a nomologically incorrigible proposition. Therefore, according to (4_N), when-ever anyone believes this proposition at any time, that belief is justified. But we may again construct a brain-surgeon example in which someone comes to have such a belief but the belief isn't justified.

Apart from this counterexample, the general point is this. Why should the fact that S's believing p guarantees the truth of p imply that S's belief is justified? The nature of the guarantee might be wholly fortuitous, as the belief-state/brain-state example is intended to illustrate. To appreciate the point, consider the following related possibility. A person's mental structure might be such that whenever he believes that p will be true (of him) a split second later, then p is true (of him) a split second later. This is because, we may suppose, his believing it brings it about. But surely we would not be compelled in such a circumstance to say that a belief of this sort is justified. So why should the fact that S's believing p guarantees the truth of p *precisely at the time of belief* imply that the belief is justified? There is no intuitive plausibility in this supposition.

The notion of *logical* incorrigibility has a more honored place in the history of conceptions of justification. But even principle (4_L), I believe, suffers from defects similar to those of (4_N). The mere fact that belief in p logically guarantees its truth does not confer justificational status on such a belief.

The first difficulty with (4_L) arises from logical or mathematical truths. Any true proposition of logic or mathematics is logically necessary. Hence, any such proposition p is logically incorrigible, since it is logically necessary that, for any S and any t, if S believes p at t then p is true (for S at t). Now assume that Nelson believes a certain very complex mathematical truth at time t. Since such a proposition is logically incorrigible, (4_L) implies that Nelson's belief in this truth at t is justified. But we may easily suppose that this belief of Nelson is not at all the result of proper mathematical reasoning, or even the result of appeal to trustworthy authority. Perhaps Nelson believes this complex truth because of utterly confused reasoning, or because of hasty and ill-founded conjecture. Then his belief is not justified, contrary to what (4_L) implies.

The case of logical or mathematical truths is admittedly peculiar, since the truth of these propositions is assured independently of any beliefs. It might seem, therefore, that we can better capture the idea of 'belief logically guaranteeing truth' in cases where the propositions in question are *contingent*. With this in mind, we might restrict (4_L) to *contingent* incorrigible propositions. Even this amendment cannot save (4_L), however, since there are counterexamples to it involving purely contingent propositions.

Suppose that Humperdink has been studying logic — or, rather, pseudo-logic — from Elmer Fraud, whom Humperdink has no reason to trust as a logician. Fraud has enunciated the principle that any disjunctive proposition consisting of at least 40 distinct disjuncts is very probably true. Humperdink now encounters the proposition p, a contingent proposition with 40 disjuncts, the 7th disjunct being 'I exist'. Although Humperdink grasps the proposition fully, he doesn't notice that it is entailed by 'I exist'. Rather, he is struck by the fact that it falls under the disjunction rule Fraud has enunciated (a rule I assume Humperdink is not *justified* in believing). Bearing this rule in mind, Humperdink forms a belief in p. Now notice that p is logically incorrigible. It is logically necessary that if anyone believes p, then p is true (of him at that time). This simply follows from the fact that, first, a person's believing anything entails that he exists, and second, 'I exist' entails p. Since p is logically incorrigible, principle (4_L) implies that Humperdink's belief in p is justified. But surely, given our example, that conclusion is false. Humperdink's belief in p is not at all justified.

One thing that goes wrong in this example is that while Humperdink's belief in p logically implies its truth, Humperdink doesn't *recognize* that his believing it implies its truth. This might move a theorist to revise (4_L) by adding the requirement that S 'recognize' that p is logically incorrigible. But this, of course, won't do. The term 'recognize' is obviously an epistemic term, so the suggested revision of (4_L) would result in an inadmissible base-clause.

II

Let us try to diagnose what has gone wrong with these attempts to produce an acceptable base-clause principle. Notice that each of the foregoing attempts confers the status of 'justified' on a belief without restriction on *why* the belief is held, i.e., on what *causally initiates* the belief or *causally sustains* it.

The logical versions of principles (3) and (4), for example, clearly place no restriction on causes of belief. The same is true of the nomological versions of (3) and (4), since nomological requirements can be satisfied by simultaneity or cross-sectional laws, as illustrated by our brain-state/belief-state examples. I suggest that the absence of causal requirements accounts for the failure of the foregoing principles. Many of our counterexamples are ones in which the belief is caused in some strange or unacceptable way, e.g., by the accidental movement of a brain-surgeon's hand, by reliance on an illicit, pseudo-logical principle, or by the blinding aura of the Presidency. In general, a strategy for defeating a noncausal principle of justifiedness is to find a case in which the principle's antecedent is satisfied but the belief is caused by some faulty belief-forming process. The faultiness of the belief-forming process will incline us, intuitively, to regard the belief as unjustified. Thus, correct principles of justified belief must be principles that make causal requirements, where 'cause' is construed broadly to include sustainers as well as initiators of belief (i.e., processes that determine, or help to overdetermine, a belief's continuing to be held.)[8]

The need for causal requirements is not restricted to base-clause principles. Recursive principles will also need a causal component. One might initially suppose that the following is a good recursive principle: 'If S justifiably believes q at t, and q entails p, and S believes p at t, then S's belief in p at t is justified'. But this principle is unacceptable. S's belief in p doesn't receive justificational status simply from the fact that p is entailed by q and S justifiably believes q. If what causes S to believe p at t is entirely different, S's belief in p may well not be justified. Nor can the situation be remedied by adding to the antecedent the condition that S justifiably believes that q entails p. Even if he believes this, and believes q as well, he might not put these beliefs together. He might believe p as a result of some other wholly extraneous, considerations. So once again, conditions that fail to require appropriate causes of a belief don't guarantee justifiedness.

Granted that principles of justified belief must make reference to causes of belief, what kinds of causes confer justifiedness? We can gain insight into this problem by reviewing some faulty processes of belief-formation, i.e., processes whose belief-outputs would be classed as unjustified. Here are some examples: confused reasoning, wishful thinking, reliance on emotional attachment, mere hunch or guesswork, and hasty generalization. What do these faulty processes have in common? They share the feature of *unreliability*: they tend to produce *error* a large proportion of the time. By contrast, which species of belief-forming (or belief-sustaining) processes are intuitively justification-conferring? They include standard perceptual processes, remembering, good reasoning, and introspection. What these processes seem to have in common is *reliability*: the beliefs they produce are generally true. My positive proposal, then, is this. The justificational status of a belief is a function of the reliability of the process or processes that cause it, where (as a first approximation) reliability consists in the tendency of a process to produce beliefs that are true rather than false.

To test this thesis further, notice that justifiedness is not a purely categorical concept, although I treat it here as categorical in the interest of simplicity. We can and do regard certain beliefs as more justified than others. Furthermore, our intuitions of comparative justifiedness go along with our beliefs about the comparative reliability of the belief-causing processes.

Consider perceptual beliefs. Suppose Jones believes he has just seen a mountain-goat. Our assessment of the belief's justifiedness is determined by whether he caught a brief glimpse of the creature at a great distance, or whether he had a good look at the thing only 30 yards away. His belief in the latter sort of case is (*ceteris paribus*) more justified than in the former sort of case. And, if his belief is true, we are more prepared to say he *knows* in the latter case than in the former. The difference between the two cases seems to be this. Visual beliefs formed from brief and hasty scanning, or where the perceptual object is a long distance off, tend to be wrong more often than visual beliefs formed from detailed and leisurely scanning, or where the object is in reasonable proximity. In short, the visual processes in the former category are less reliable than those in the latter category. A similar point holds for memory beliefs. A belief that results from a hazy and indistinct memory impression is counted as less justified than a belief that arises from a distinct memory impression, and our inclination to classify those beliefs as '*knowledge*' varies in the same way. Again, the reason is associated with the comparative reliability of the processes. Hazy and indistinct memory impressions are generally less reliable indicators of what actually happened; so beliefs formed from such impressions are less likely to be true than beliefs formed from distinct impressions. Further, consider beliefs based on inference from observed samples. A belief about a population that is based on random sampling, or on instances that exhibit great variety, is intuitively more justified than a belief based on biased sampling, or on instances from a narrow sector of the population. Again, the degree of justifiedness seems to be a function of reliability. Inferences based on random or varied samples will tend to produce less error or inaccuracy than inferences based on non-random or non-varied samples.

Returning to a categorical concept of justifiedness, we might ask just *how* reliable a belief-forming process must be in order that its resultant beliefs be justified. A precise answer to this question should not be expected. Our conception of justification is *vague* in this respect. It does seem clear, however, that *perfect* reliability isn't required. Belief-forming processes that *sometimes* produce error still confer justification. It follows that there can be justified beliefs that are false.

I have characterized justification-conferring processes as ones that have a 'tendency' to produce beliefs that are true rather than false. The term 'tendency' could refer either to *actual* long-run frequency, or to a 'propensity', i.e., outcomes that would occur in merely *possible* realizations of the process. Which of these is intended? Unfortunately, I think our ordinary conception of justifiedness is vague on this dimension too. For the most part, we simply assume that the 'observed' frequency of truth versus error would be approximately replicated in the actual long-run, and also in relevant counterfactual situations, i.e., ones that are highly 'realistic', or conform closely to the circumstances of the actual world. Since we ordinarily assume these frequencies to be roughly the same, we make no concerted effort to distinguish them. Since the purpose of my present theorizing is to capture our ordinary conception of justifiedness, and since our ordinary conception is vague on this matter, it is appropriate to leave the theory vague in the same respect.

We need to say more about the notion of a belief-forming '*process*'. Let us mean by a 'process' a *functional operation* or procedure, i.e., something that generates a *mapping* from certain states − 'inputs' − into other states − 'outputs'. The outputs in the present case are states of believing this or that proposition at a given moment. On this interpretation, a process is a *type* as opposed to a *token*. This is fully appropriate, since it is only types that have statistical properties such as producing truth 80% of the time; and it is precisely such statistical properties that determine the reliability of a process. Of course, we also want to speak of a process as *causing* a belief, and it looks as if types are incapable of being causes. But when we say that a belief is caused by a given process, understood as a functional procedure, we may interpret this to mean that it is caused by the particular *inputs* to the process (and by the intervening events 'through which' the functional procedure carries the inputs into the output) on the occasion in question.

What are some examples of belief-forming 'processes' construed as functional operations? One example is reasoning processes, where the inputs include antecedent beliefs and entertained hypotheses. Another example is functional procedures whose inputs include desires, hopes, or emotional states of various sorts (together with antecedent beliefs). A third example is a memory process, which takes as input beliefs or experiences at an earlier time and generates as output beliefs at a later time. For example, a memory process might take as input a belief *at* t_1 that Lincoln was born in 1809 and generate as output a belief *at* t_n that Lincoln was born in 1809. A fourth example is perceptual processes. Here it isn't clear whether inputs should include states of the environment, such as the distance of the stimulus from the cognizer, or only events within or on the surface of the organism, e.g., receptor stimulations. I shall return to this point in a moment.

A critical problem concerning our analysis is the degree of generality of the process-types in question. Input—output relations can be specified very broadly or very narrowly, and the degree of generality will partly determine the degree of reliability. A process-type might be selected so narrowly that only one instance of it ever occurs, and hence the type is either completely reliable or completely unreliable. (This assumes that reliability is a function of *actual* frequency only.) If such narrow process-types were selected, beliefs that are intuitively unjustified might be said to result from perfectly reliable processes; and beliefs that are intuitively justified might be said result from perfectly unreliable processes.

It is clear that our ordinary thought about process-types slices them broadly, but I cannot at present give a precise explication of our intuitive principles. One plausible suggestion, though, is that the relevant processes are *content-neutral*. It might be argued, for example, that the process of *inferring p whenever the Pope asserts p* could pose problems for our theory. If the Pope is infallible, this process will be perfectly reliable; yet we would not regard the belief-outputs of this process as justified. The content-neutral restriction would avert this difficulty. If relevant processes are required to admit as input beliefs (or other states) with *any* content, the aforementioned process will not count, for its input beliefs have a restricted propositional content, viz., *'the Pope* asserts *p'*.

In addition to the problem of 'generality' or 'abstractness' there is the previously mentioned problem of the *'extent'* of belief-forming processes. Clearly, the causal ancestry of beliefs often includes events outside the organism. Are such events to be included among the 'inputs' of belief-forming processes? Or should we restrict the extent of belief-forming processes to *'cognitive'* events, i.e., events within the organism's nervous system? I shall choose the latter course, though with some hesitation. My general grounds for this decision are roughly as follows. Justifiedness seems to be a function of how a cognizer deals with his environmental input, i.e., with the goodness or badness of the operations that register and transform the stimulation that reaches him. ('Deal with', of course, does not mean *purposeful* action; nor is it restricted to *conscious* activity.) A justified belief is, roughly speaking, one that results from cognitive operations that are, generally speaking, good or successful. But '*cognitive*' operations are most plausibly construed as operations of the cognitive faculties, i.e., 'information-processing' equipment *internal* to the organism.

With these points in mind, we may now advance the following base-clause principle for justified belief.

(5)　　If S's believing p at t results from a reliable cognitive belief-forming process (or set of processes), then S's belief in p at t is justified.

Since 'reliable belief-forming process' has been defined in terms of such notions as belief, truth, statistical frequency, and the like, it is not an epistemic term. Hence, (5) is an admissible base-clause.

It might seem as if (5) promises to be not only a successful base clause, but the only principle needed whatever, apart from a closure clause. In other words, it might seem as if it is a necessary as well as a sufficient condition of justifiedness that a belief be produced by reliable cognitive belief-forming processes. But this is not quite correct, give our provisional definition of 'reliability'.

Our provisional definition implies that a reasoning process is reliable only if it generally produces beliefs that are true, and similarly, that a memory process is reliable only if it generally yields beliefs that are true. But these requirements are too strong. A reasoning procedure cannot be expected to produce true belief if it is is applied to false premisses. And memory cannot be expected to yield a true belief if the original belief it attempts to retain is false. What we need for reasoning and memory, then, is a notion of '*conditional reliability*'. A process is conditionally reliable when a sufficient proportion of its output-beliefs are true *given that its input-beliefs are true*.

With this point in mind, let us distinguish *belief-dependent* and *belief-independent* cognitive processes. The former are processes *some* of whose inputs are belief-states.[9] The latter are processes *none* of whose inputs are belief-states. We may then replace principle (5) with the following two principles, the first a base-clause principle and the second a recursive-clause principle.

(6$_A$)　　If S's belief in p at t results ('immediately') from a belief-independent process that is (unconditionally) reliable, then S's belief in p at t is justified.

(6B)   If S's belief in p at t results ("immediately") from a belief-dependent process that is (at least) conditionally reliable, and if the beliefs (if any) on which this process operates in producing S's belief in p at t are themselves justified, then S's belief in p at t is justified.[10]

If we add to (6A) and (6B) the standard closure clause, we have a complete theory of justified belief. The theory says, in effect, that a belief is justified if and only it is '*well-formed*', i.e., it has an ancestry of reliable and/or conditionally reliable cognitive operations. (Since a dated belief may be over-determined, it may have a number of distinct ancestral trees. These need not all be full of reliable or conditionally reliable processes. But at least one ancestral tree must have reliable or conditionally reliable processes throughout.)

The theory of justified belief proposed here, then, is an *Historical* or *Genetic* theory. It contrasts with the dominant approach to justified belief, an approach that generates what we may call (borrowing a phrase from Robert Nozick) '*Current Time-Slice*' theories. A Current Time-Slice theory makes the justificational status of a belief wholly a function of what is true of the cognizer *at the time* of belief. An Historical theory makes the justificational status of a belief depend on its prior history. Since my Historical theory emphasizes the reliability of the belief-generating processes, it may be called '*Historical Reliabilism*'.

The most obvious examples of Current Time-Slice theories are 'Cartesian' Foundationalist theories, which trace all justificational status (at least of contingent propositions) to current mental states. The usual varieties of Coherence theories, however, are equally Current Time-Slice views, since they too make the justificational status of a belief wholly a function of *current* states of affairs. For Coherence theories, however, these current states include all other beliefs of the cognizer, which would not be considered relevant by Cartesian Foundationalism. Have there been other Historical theories of justified belief? Among contemporary writers, Quine and Popper have Historical epistemologies, though the notion of 'justification' is not their avowed *explicandum*. Among historical writers, it might seem that Locke and Hume had Genetic theories of sorts. But I think that their Genetic theories were only theories of ideas, not of knowledge or justification. Plato's theory of recollection, however, is a good example of a Genetic theory of knowing.[11] And it might be argued that Hegel and Dewey had Genetic epistemologies (if Hegel can be said to have had a clear epistemology at all).

The theory articulated by (6A) and (6B) might be viewed as a kind of 'Foundationalism,' because of its recursive structure. I have no objection to this label, as long as one keeps in mind how different this 'diachronic' form of Foundationalism is from Cartesian, or other 'synchronic' varieties of, Foundationalism.

Current Time-Slice theories characteristically assume that the justificational status of a belief is something which the cognizer is able to know or determine at the time of belief. This is made explicit, for example, by Chisholm.[12] The Historical theory I endorse makes no such assumption. There are many facts about a cognizer to which he lacks 'privileged access', and I regard the justificational status of his beliefs as one of those things. This is not to say that a cognizer is necessarily ignorant, at any given moment, of the justificational status of his current beliefs. It is only to deny that he necessarily has, or can get, knowledge or true belief about this status. Just as a person can know without knowing that he knows, so he can have justified belief without knowing that it is justified (or believing justifiably that it is justified.)

A characteristic case in which a belief is justified though the cognizer doesn't know that it's justified is where the original evidence for the belief has long since been forgotten. If the original evidence was compelling, the cognizer's original belief may have been justified; and this justificational status may have been preserved through memory. But since the cognizer no longer remembers how or why he came to believe, he may not know that the belief is justified. If asked now to justify his belief, he may be at a loss. Still, the belief *is* justified, though the cognizer can't demonstrate or establish this.

The Historical theory of justified belief I advocate is connected in spirit with the causal theory of knowing I have presented elsewhere.[13] I had this in mind when I remarked near the outset of the paper that my theory of justified belief makes justifiedness come out closely related to knowledge. Justified beliefs, like pieces of knowledge, have appropriate histories; but they may fail to be knowledge either because they are false or because they founder on some other requirement for knowing of the kind discussed in the post-Gettier knowledge-trade.

There is a variant of the Historical conception of justified belief that is worth mentioning in this context. It may be introduced as follows. Suppose S has a set B of beliefs at time t_0, and some of these beliefs are *un*justified. Between t_0 and t_1 he reasons from the entire set B to the conclusion p, which he then accepts at t_1. The reasoning procedure he uses is a very sound one, i.e., one that is conditionally reliable. There is a sense or respect in which we are tempted to say that S's belief in p at t_1 is 'justified'. At any rate, it is tempting to say that the *person* is justified in believing p at t. Relative to his antecedent cognitive state, he did as well as could be expected: the *transition* from his cognitive state at t_0 to his cognitive state at t_1 was entirely sound. Although we may acknowledge this brand of justifiedness – it might be called *'Terminal-Phase Reliabilism'* – it is not a kind of justifiedness so closely related to knowing. For a person to know proposition p, it is not enough that the *final phase* of the process that leads to his belief in p be sound. It is also necessary that some entire history of the process be sound (i.e., reliable or conditionally reliable).

Let us return now to the Historical theory. In the next section of the paper, I shall adduce reasons for strengthening it a bit. Before looking at these reasons, however, I wish to review two quite different objections to the theory.

First, a critic might argue that *some* justified beliefs do not derive their justificational status from their causal ancestry. In particular, it might be argued that beliefs about one's current phenomenal states and intuitive beliefs about elementary logical or conceptual relationships do not derive their justificational status in this way. I am not persuaded by either of these examples. Introspection, I believe, should be regarded as a form of retrospection. Thus, a justified belief that I am 'now' in pain gets its justificational status from a relevant, though brief, causal history.[14] The apprehension of logical or conceptual relationships is also a cognitive process that occupies time. The psychological process of 'seeing' or 'intuiting' a simple logical truth is very fast, and we cannot introspectively dissect it into constituent parts. Nonetheless, there are mental operations going on, just as there are mental operations that occur in *idiots savants*, who are unable to report the computational processes they in fact employ.

A second objection to Historical Reliabilism focuses on the reliability element rather than the causal or historical element. Since the theory is intended to cover all possible cases, it seems to imply that for any cognitive process C, if C is reliable in possible world W, then any belief in W that results from C is justified. But doesn't this permit easy counterexamples? Surely we can imagine a possible world in which wishful thinking is reliable. We can imagine a possible world where a benevolent demon so arranges things that beliefs formed by wishful thinking usually come true. This would make wishful thinking a reliable process in that possible world, but surely we don't want to regard beliefs that result from wishful thinking as justified.

There are several possible ways to respond to this case and I am unsure which response is best, partly because my own intuitions (and those of other people I have consulted) are not entirely clear. One possibility is to say that in the possible world imagined, beliefs that result from wishful thinking *are* justified. In other words we reject the claim that wishful thinking could never, intuitively, confer justifiedness.[15]

However, for those who feel that wishful thinking couldn't confer justifiedness, even in the world imagined, there are two ways out. First, it may be suggested that the proper criterion of justifiedness is the propensity of a process to generate beliefs that are true *in a non-manipulated environment*, i.e., an environment in which there is no purposeful arrangement of the world either to accord or conflict with the beliefs that are formed. In other words, the suitability of a belief-forming process is only a function of its success in '*natural*' situations, not situations of the sort involving benevolent or malevolent demons, or any other such manipulative creatures. If we reformulate the theory to include this qualification, the counterexample in question will be averted.

Alternatively, we may reformulate our theory, or reinterpret it, as follows. Instead of construing the theory as saying that a belief in possible world *W* is justified if and only if it results from a cognitive process that is reliable in *W*, we may construe it as saying that a belief in possible world *W* is justified if and only if it results from a cognitive process that is reliable *in our world*. In short, our conception of justifiedness is derived as follows. We note certain cognitive processes in the actual world, and form beliefs about which of these are reliable. The ones we believe to be reliable are then regarded as justification-conferring processes. In reflecting on hypothetical beliefs, we deem them justified if and only if they result from processes already picked out as justification-conferring, or processes very similar to those. Since wishful thinking is not among these processes, a belief formed in a possible world *W* by wishful thinking would not be deemed justified, even if wishful thinking is reliable *in W* . I am not sure that this is a correct reconstruction of our intuitive conceptual scheme, but it would accommodate the benevolent demon case, at least if the proper thing to say in that case is that the wishful-thinking-caused beliefs are unjustified

Even if we adopt this strategy, however, a problem still remains. Suppose that wishful thinking turns out to be reliable *in the actual world*![16] This might be because, unbeknownst to us at present, there is a benevolent demon who, lazy until now, will shortly start arranging things so that our wishes come true. The long-run performance of wishful thinking will be very good, and hence even the new construal of the theory will imply that beliefs resulting from wishful thinking (in *our* world) are justified. Yet this surely contravenes our intuitive judgment on the matter.

Perhaps the moral of the case is that the standard format of a 'conceptual analysis' has its shortcomings. Let me depart from that format and try to give a better rendering of our aim and the theory that tries to achieve that aim. What we really want is an *explanation* of why we count, or would count, certain beliefs as justified and others as unjustified. Such an explanation must refer to our *beliefs* about reliability, not to the actual *facts*. The reason we *count* beliefs as justified is that they are formed by what we *believe* to be reliable belief-forming processes. Our beliefs about which belief-forming processes are reliable may be erroneous, but that does not affect the adequacy of the explanation. Since we *believe* that wishful thinking is an unreliable belief-forming process, we regard beliefs formed by wishful thinking as unjustified. What matters, then, is what we *believe* about wishful thinking, not what is *true* (in the long run) about wishful thinking. I am not sure how to express this point in the standard format of conceptual analysis, but it identifies an important point in understanding our theory.

III

Let us return, however, to the standard format of conceptual analysis, and let us consider a new objection that will require some revisions in the theory advanced until now. According to our theory, a belief is justified in case it is caused by a process that is in fact reliable, or by one we generally believe to be reliable. But suppose that although one of S's beliefs satisfies this condition, S has no reason to believe that it does. Worse yet, suppose S has reason to believe that his belief is caused by an *un*reliable process (although *in fact* its causal ancestry is fully reliable). Wouldn't we deny in such circumstances that S's belief is justified? This seems to show that our analysis, as presently formulated, is mistaken.

Suppose that Jones is told on fully reliable authority that a certain class of his memory beliefs are almost all mistaken. His parents fabricate a wholly false story that Jones suffered from amnesia when he was seven but later developed *pseudo*-memories of that period. Though Jones listens to what his parents say and has excellent reason to trust them, he persists in believing the ostensible memories from his seven-year-old past. Are these memory beliefs justified? Intuitively, they are not justified. But since these beliefs result from genuine memory and original perceptions, which are adequately reliable processes, our theory says that these beliefs are justified.

Can the theory be revised to meet this difficulty? One natural suggestion is that the actual reliability of a belief 's ancestry is not enough for justified-ness; in addition, the cognizer must be *justified in believing* that the ancestry of his belief is reliable. Thus one might think of replacing (6$_A$), for example, with (7). (For simplicity, I neglect some of the details of the earlier analysis.)

(7)   If S's belief in p at t is caused by a reliable cognitive process, and S justifiably believes at t that his p-belief is so caused, then S's belief in p at t is justified.

It is evident, however, that (7) will not do as a base clause, for it contains the epistemic term 'justifiably' in its antecedent.

A slightly weaker revision, without this problematic feature, might next be suggested, viz.,

(8)   If S's belief in p at t is caused by a reliable cognitive process, and S believes at t that his p-belief is so caused, then S's belief in p at t is justified.

But this won't do the job. Suppose that Jones believes that his memory beliefs are reliably caused despite all the (trustworthy) contrary testimony of his parents. Principle (8) would be satisfied, yet we wouldn't say that these beliefs are justified.

Next, we might try (9), which is stronger than (8) and, unlike (7), formally admissible as a base clause.

(9)   If S's belief in p at t is caused by a reliable cognitive process, and S believes at t that his p-belief is so caused, and this meta-belief is caused by a reliable cognitive process, than S's belief in p at t is justified.

A first objection to (9) is that it wrongly precludes unreflective creatures — creatures like animals or young children, who have no beliefs about the genesis of their beliefs — from having justified beliefs. If one shares my view that justified belief is, at least roughly, *well-formed* belief, surely animals and young children can have justified beliefs.

A second problem with (9) concerns its underlying rationale. Since (9) is proposed as a substitute for (6$_A$), it is implied that the reliability of a belief 's own cognitive ancestry does not make it justified. But, the suggestion seems to be, the reliability of a *meta-belief*'s ancestry confers justifiedness on the first-order belief. Why should that be so? Perhaps one is attracted by the idea of a 'trickle-down' effect: if an n+1-level belief is justified, its justification trickles down to an n-level belief. But even if the trickle-down theory is correct, it doesn't help here. There is no assurance from the satisfaction of (9)'s antecedent that the meta-belief itself is *justified*.

To obtain a better revision of our theory, let us re-examine the Jones case. Jones has strong evidence against certain propositions concerning his past. He doesn't *use* this evidence, but if he *were* to use it properly, he would stop believing these propositions. Now the proper use of evidence would be an instance of a (conditionally) reliable process. So what we can say about Jones is that he *fails* to use a certain (conditionally) reliable process that he could and should have used. Admittedly, had he used this process, he would have 'worsened' his doxastic states: he would have replaced some true beliefs with suspension of judgment. Still, he couldn't have known this in the case in question. So, he failed to do something which, epistemically, he should have done. This diagnosis suggests a fundamental change in our theory. The justificational status of a belief is not only a function of the cognitive processes *actually* employed in producing it; it is also a function of processes that could and should be employed.

With these points in mind, we may tentatively propose the following revision of our theory, where we again focus on a base-clause principle but omit certain details in the interest of clarity.

(10)   If S's belief in p at t results from a reliable cognitive process, and there is no reliable or conditionally reliable process available to S which, had it been used by S in addition to the process actually used, would have resulted in S's not believing p at t, then S's belief in p at t is justified.

There are several problems with this proposal. First, there is a technical problem. One cannot use an additional belief-forming (or doxastic-state-forming) process *as well as* the original process if the additional one would result in a different doxastic state. One wouldn't be using the original process at all. So we need a slightly different formulation of the relevant counterfactual. Since the basic idea is reasonably clear, however, I won't try to improve on the formulation here. A second problem concerns the notion of *'available'* belief-forming (or doxastic-state-forming) processes. What is it for a process to be 'available' to a cognizer? Were scientific procedures 'available' to people who lived in pre-scientific ages? Furthermore, it seems implausible to say that all 'available' processes ought to be used, at least if we include such processes as gathering *new* evidence. Surely a belief can sometimes be justified even if additional evidence-gathering would yield a different doxastic attitude. What I think we should have in mind here are such additional processes as calling previously acquired evidence to mind, assessing the implications of that evidence, etc. This is admittedly somewhat vague, but here again our ordinary notion of justifiedness is vague, so it is appropriate for our analysans to display the same sort of vagueness.

This completes the sketch of my account of justified belief. Before concluding, however, it is essential to point out that there is an important use of 'justified' which is not captured by this account but can be captured by a closely related one.

There is a use of 'justified' in which it is not implied or presupposed that there is a *belief* that is justified. For example, if S is trying to decide whether to believe p and asks our advice, we may tell him that he is 'justified' in believing it. We do not thereby imply that he *has* a justified *belief*, since we know he is still suspending judgement. What we mean, roughly, is that he *would* or *could* be justified if he were to believe p. The justificational status we ascribe here cannot be a function of the causes of S's believing p, for there is no belief by S in p. Thus, the account of justifiedness we have given thus far cannot explicate *this* use of 'justified'. (It doesn't follow that this use of 'justified' has no connection with causal ancestries. Its proper use may depend on the causal ancestry of the cognizer's cognitive state, though not on the causal ancestry of his believing p.)

Let us distinguish two uses of 'justified': an *ex post* use and an *ex ante* use. The *ex post* use occurs when there exists a belief, and we say *of that belief* that it is (or isn't) justified. The *ex ante* use occurs when no such belief exists, or when we wish to ignore the question of whether such a belief exists. Here we say of the *person*, independent of his doxastic state vis-à-vis p, that p is (or isn't) suitable for him to believe.[17]

Since we have given an account of *ex post* justifiedness, it will suffice if we can analyze *ex ante* justifiedness in terms of it. Such an analysis, I believe, is ready at hand. S is *ex ante* justified in believing p at t just in case his total cognitive state at t is such that from that state he could come to believe p in such a way that this belief would be *ex post* justified. More precisely, he is *ex ante* justified in believing p at t just in case a reliable belief-forming operation is available to him such that the application of that operation to his total cognitive state at t would result, more or less immediately, in his believing p and this belief would be *ex post* justified. Stated formally, we have the following:

(11)   Person S is *ex ante* justified in believing p at t if and only if there is a reliable belief-forming operation available to S which is such that if S applied that operation to his total cognitive state at t, S would believe p at t-plus-delta (for a suitably small delta) and that belief would be *ex post* justified.

For the analysans of (11) to be satisfied, the total cognitive state at t must have a suitable causal ancestry. Hence, (11) is implicitly an Historical account of *ex ante* justifiedness.

As indicated, the bulk of this paper was addressed to *ex post* justifiedness

This is the appropriate analysandum if one is interested in the connection between justifiedness and knowledge, since what is crucial to whether a person *knows* a proposition is whether he has an actual *belief* in the proposition that is justified. However, since many epistemologists are interested in *ex ante* justifiedness, it is proper for a general theory of justification to try to provide an account of that concept as well. Our theory does this quite naturally, for the account of *ex ante* justifiedness falls out directly from our account of *ex post* justifiedness.[18].

NOTES

[1] 'A Causal Theory of Knowing,' *The Journal of Philosophy* **64**, 12 (June 22, 1967): 357–372; 'Innate Knowledge,' in S. P. Stich, ed., *Innate Ideas* (Berkeley: University of California Press, 1975); and 'Discrimination and Perceptual Knowledge,' *The Journal of Philosophy* **73**, 20 (November 18, 1976), 771–791.

[2] Notice that the choice of a recursive format does not prejudice the case for or against any particular theory. A recursive format is perfectly general. Specifically, an explicit set of necessary and sufficient conditions is just a special case of a recursive format, i.e. one in which there is no recursive clause.

[3] Many of the attempts I shall consider are suggested by material in William P. Alston, 'Varieties of Privileged Access,' *American Philosophical Quarterly* **8** (1971), 223–241.

[4] Such a definition (though without the modal term) is given, for example, by W. V. Quine and J. S. Ullian in *The Web of Belief* (New York: Random House, 1970), p. 21. Statements are said to be self-evident just in case "to understand them is to believe them".

[5] Englewood Cliffs, N.J.: Prentice-Hall, Inc., 1977, p. 22.

[6] I assume, of course, that 'nomologically necessary' is *de re* with respect to '*S*' and '*t*' in this construction. I shall not focus on problems that may arise in this regard, since my primary concerns are with different issues.

[7] This assumption violates the thesis that Davidson calls 'The Anomalism of the Mental'. Cf. 'Mental Events,' in L. Foster and J. W. Swanson, eds., *Experience and Theory* (Amherst: University of Massachusetts Press, 1970). But it is unclear that this thesis is a necessary truth. Thus, it seems fair to assume its falsity in order to produce a counter-example. The example neither entails nor precludes the mental–physical identity theory.

[8] Keith Lehrer's example of the gypsy lawyer is intended to show the inappropriateness of a causal requirement. (See *Knowledge*, Oxford: University Press, 1974, pp. 124–125.) But I find this example unconvincing. To the extent that I clearly imagine that the lawyer fixes his belief solely as a result of the cards, it seems intuitively wrong to say that he *knows* – or has a *justified belief* – that his client is innocent.

[9] This definition is not exactly what we need for the purposes at hand. As Ernest Sosa points out, introspection will turn out to be a belief–dependent process since sometimes the input into the process will be a belief (when the introspected content is a belief). Intuitively, however, introspection is not the sort of process which may be merely conditionally reliable. I do not know how to refine the definition so as to avoid this difficulty, but it is a small and isolated point.

[10] It may be objected that principles (6_A) and (6_B) are jointly open to analogues of the lottery paradox. A series of processes composed of reliable but less-than-perfectly-reliable processes may be extremely unreliable. Yet applications of (6_A) and (6_B) would confer justifiedness on a belief that is caused by such a series. In reply to this objection, we might simply indicate that the theory is intended to capture our ordinary notion of justifiedness, and this ordinary notion has been formed without recognition of this kind of problem. The theory is not wrong *as* a theory of the ordinary (naive) conception of justifiedness. On the other hand, if we want a theory to do more than capture the ordinary conception of justifiedness, it might be possible to strengthen the principles to avoid lottery-paradox analogues.

[11] I am indebted to Mark Pastin for this point.

[12] Cf. *Theory of Knowledge*, Second Edition, pp. 17, 114–116.

[13] Cf. 'A Causal Theory of Knowing,' *op. cit.* The reliability aspect of my theory also has its precursors in earlier papers of mine on knowing: 'Innate Knowledge,' *op. cit.* and 'Discrimination and Perceptual Knowledge,' *op. cit.*

[14] The view that introspection is retrospection was taken by Ryle, and before him (as Charles Hartshorne points out to me) by Hobbes, Whitehead, and possibly Husserl.

[15] Of course, if people in world W learn *inductively* that wishful thinking is reliable, and regularly base their beliefs on this inductive inference, it is quite unproblematic and straightforward that their beliefs are justified. The only interesting case is where their beliefs are formed *purely* by wishful thinking, without using inductive inference. The suggestion contemplated in this paragraph of the text is that, in the world imagined, even pure wishful thinking would confer justifiedness.

[16] I am indebted here to Mark Kaplan.

[17] The distinction between *ex post* and *ex ante* justifiedness is similar to Roderick Firth's distinction between *doxastic* and *propositional* warrant. See his 'Are Epistemic Concepts Reducible to Ethical Concepts?', in Alvin I. Goldman and Jaegwon Kim, eds., *Values and Morals, Essays in Honor of William Frankena, Charles Stevenson, and Richard Brandt* (Dordrecht: D. Reidel, 1978).

[18] Research on this paper was begun while the author was a fellow of the John Simon Guggenheim Memorial Foundation and of the Center for Advanced Study in the Behavioral Sciences. I am grateful for their support. I have received helpful comments and criticism from Holly S. Goldman, Mark Kaplan, Fred Schmitt, Stephen P. Stich, and many others at several universities where earlier drafts of the paper were read.

MARSHALL SWAIN

JUSTIFICATION AND THE BASIS OF BELIEF

Whether a person, S, has knowledge that h depends upon the reasons for which S believes that h. The reasons for which a person believes something constitute that upon which the person's belief is *based*.[1] It often happens that a person's belief that h is based upon a set of reasons R when believing that h on the basis of R is not justified for that person. This can happen even though the person has other reasons such that if the belief had been based upon those reasons, then the belief would have been justified. In such a case, S cannot be said to have knowledge. Consider, for example, Raquel and Laura, both of whom are tellers in a large bank, and both of whom are incredibly beautiful and vivacious. It is the stated policy of the bank that employees who are efficient and responsible can expect to be promoted after a sufficient time, and this policy has been carefully explained to Raquel and Laura. However, Raquel does not believe that decisions to promote are actually a function of efficiency and responsibility. Rather, she believes, quite irrationally, that the president of the bank is infatuated with her beauty and that she will be promoted because of this infatuation. Laura, on the other hand, believes that she, too, will be promoted, but her belief is based upon her belief that she is efficient and responsible and upon her belief that it is the policy of the bank to promote people such as herself. Assuming that both tellers will be promoted, we may say, of Laura, that she knows she will be promoted, but we certainly may not say this of Raquel. The explanation of this difference lies in the fact that Laura's belief is based upon justifying reasons, while Raquel's belief is not so based. This example indicates that the following may be taken to express necessary conditions for knowledge:

(K)   A person, S, has knowledge that h at time t only if there is some set of reasons, R, such that

(1) S's belief that h is based upon R at t; and

(2) S's believing that h on the basis of R is justified at t.

It is possible, indeed quite common, for a person to have a set of reasons such that some subset, R, taken by itself is a set of reasons upon which a belief that h would be justified, but such that believing h on the basis of the entire set (of which R is a subset) would not be justified. If this is the case,

25

George S. Pappas (ed.), Justification and Knowledge, 25–49.
Copyright © 1979 by D. Reidel Publishing Company.

then S cannot be said to have knowledge. Thus, we must add the following necessary condition to those expressed above:

(3)   If, at t, S has any other reasons, R', that are relevant to justifiably believing that h, then S would be justified in believing that h on the basis of $R \cup R'$ at t.

While these three conditions are necessary for knowledge, they are not sufficient. For one thing, there is nothing in these conditions to guarantee the truth of h. For another, there is nothing in these conditions to guarantee that our subject, S, is not the victim of the kind of knowledge-defeating circumstances that have been the subject of so much discussion during the 'Post-Gettier' period.[2] I believe that the above conditions can be augmented with two additional conditions, and that the resulting set of conditions are both necessary and sufficient for knowledge. The two conditions are these:

(4) h;
(5) S has the set of reasons R as a result of at least one nondefective causal ancestry.

Together these conditions constitute a causal account of knowledge. It is not my purpose in this paper to defend this account of knowledge, for I have done that at some length in other papers.[3] Rather, in this paper I want to consider conditions (1) and (2) of the causal analysis (K).

More specifically, I want to suggest a detailed account of condition (1), and, in the very last section of the paper, I want to suggest a general sketch of a theory of justified belief. By far the greater portion of the paper will be devoted to the first of these tasks.

1. THE BASIS OF BELIEF

What are the conditions under which a person's belief is based upon a set of reasons? Like the account of knowledge expressed in (K), the account of basing that I want to develop is a causal account. This account can be given a very general formulation as follows:

(B) S's belief that h is based upon the set of reasons R at t if and only if:

(1) S believes that h at t; and
(2)   for every member r_j of R, there is some time tn (which may be identical with or earlier than t) such that
         (a) S has (or had) r_j at tn; and
         (b) there is an appropriate causal connection between S's having r_j at tn and S's believing that h at t.

Although this account of the basing relation is a causal one, it is not necessary to give such an account if one wants to defend a causal theory of knowing. Moreover, one need not defend a causal theory of knowing if one also adopts a causal account of the basing relation. Neither account is required by the other. Many philosophers object to causal accounts of knowledge, and many object to causal accounts of the basing relation. It is important, I believe, not to confuse these two issues.

The conditions in (B) require further elucidation. For one thing, we must be clear about the kinds of things that are, or can be, members of a set of reasons R. For another, we must be clear about the kinds of causal connections that are 'appropriate' for the basing relation, as required by clause (2b). I turn now to a consideration of these questions.

1.1. Reason States

According to (B), a person's belief that h is based upon a set of reasons R if there is an appropriate causal connection between each member of R and the belief state in question. I shall take all forms of belief states to be causally efficacious; that is, they are states of a person that can be caused and can be causes of other states. Since I am here constructing a causal account of the basing relation, I am committed to holding that the members of the set of reasons, R, upon which a belief is based are *also* causally efficacious. This means that the members of R must be events (or states),[4] and this is a fact that leads immediately to a point over which it is very easy to become confused.

When we think of the reasons for which a person believes something it is natural to think of some set of *propositions* which the person believes (or, perhaps, knows). However, as I understand them, propositions are not entities that can be causally related to other entities. How, then, can the set of reasons upon which a belief is based consist of a set of events, or states? I want to distinguish two different kinds of reasons. First, there is the kind of reasons that we are referring to when we talk about a person's *evidence*, and it is here that talk of believed (or, known) *propositions* is appropriate. Second, there are what I shall call *causal* reasons for a belief.[5] Causal reasons are, among other things, events or states of the person who has the belief. In (B) the term 'reasons' is intended to designate causal reasons, and not evidential reasons. This does not mean that a person's evidential reasons are unimportant in the context of the theory of justified belief that I am developing. Some of a person's beliefs (which are states of that person) are often among the causal reasons upon which another belief (say, the belief that h) is based; the propositions believed may very well be among the evidential reasons that this person has, and whether the belief that h is justified may depend upon the evidential connection between these propositions and h. Let us distinguish, then between two different kinds of basing. When it is appropriate to say that a person's belief is based upon some set of evidential propositions, then I shall say that the belief is *evidentially based upon* the set of propositions in question. When the conditions specified in (B) are satisfied, then I shall say that the belief in question is *based (simpliciter)* on the set of reasons R.

We have noted that a person's beliefs will often be among the reasons upon which a given belief is based. But I want to use the term 'reasons' in a way that is more inclusive than this. I want to *allow* that the set of reasons for which we believe something can (and, I believe, usually will) consist partly of *non*-belief states that we are in. I also want to allow that this can be so even if we have no beliefs about those non-belief states. I shall not attempt to give an exhaustive catalogue of the kinds of non-belief states that can appropriately be said to function as reasons. However, I believe that we can single out several major types of non-belief states that can function as reasons.

Suppose that I see a good friend of mine on a day when he is unhappy. I may come to believe that he is unhappy on the basis of observations of subtle bits of behavior, such as facial expressions, tone of voice, and bodily demeanor. The observed features of his behavior which are a cause of my belief that he is unhappy may, however, be so subtle that I do not have any specific beliefs about them. I may not even be able to describe the features in question if asked. Even so, I am in a certain complex state in virtue of my perceiving the subtle bits of behavior in question, and I want to say that my *being in this state* is among the reasons for which I believe my friend to be unhappy. The state in question is not itself a belief state, nor is it a state about which I need to have any beliefs in order for it to function as a reason. What sort of a state is this? For lack of a better term I shall call it a *perceptual state*.

Introducing the term 'perceptual state' in a philosophical essay is bound to generate confusion, perhaps even outrage. As I am using the term, to say that S is in perceptual state P does not entail that S is *perceiving* anything, although it is perfectly compatible with, and perhaps entailed by, some claim that S is perceiving something. Suppose that I am perceiving a red ball in bright daylight. Then, *part* of what is involved in my perceiving the red ball is that I am in a certain state, P, which might be characterized as the state of *being appeared to redly*, or perhaps as the state of *sensing redly*, or perhaps even as the state of *having a red sense-datum* (I am not particularly concerned about which of the philosophical theories concerning such states is correct, at least not in the present context).[6] For my purposes, the important thing to note is that the state P that I am in when I am perceiving a red ball is a state that I could have been in even if I were not perceiving a red ball, but were perhaps hallucinating instead. States of this sort are what I intend by the term 'perceptual state.' Naturally, perceptual states need not be associated with vision; a perceptual state may be associated with any of the 'external' senses. Moreover, if there is 'extra-sensory' perception, then some perceptual states may be associated with this kind of perception. I do not pretend, however, to understand 'extra-sensory' perception.

There is, perhaps, a somewhat fuzzy line between the class of perceptual states and the next major class of non-belief reason states that I want to identify namely, *sensation* states. I have in mind here such states as *being in pain, feeling overheated,* and other bodily sensation states that are not associated in any clear fashion with any of the 'external' senses. If I have a headache, then I am in a state of pain, but my being in this state would not normally be associated with my perception of anything. This distinction is, however, a fuzzy one. If I touch a very hot object, I will feel pain; is my being in pain in this instance a perceptual state? I cannot think of any *very* convincing reason for saying that it is not. If so, then some of the states that I am calling sensation states will also be perceptual states. In any event, it seems clear that sensation states can serve as reasons upon which a belief is based, and that they can serve this function even under circumstances where one does not have any specific beliefs about being in the states in question. For example, if a person is becoming ill, some of the symptoms of the illness may take the form of very subtle sensation states. These sensation states may be too subtle to be clearly noticed, and yet they may be sufficient to serve as a cause of the belief that one is becoming ill.

Another class of states that can serve as reasons are those that we rather loosely refer to as 'unconscious.' I do not have any theory of the unconscious to offer, nor would I want to try and characterize unconscious states. For that matter, I am not entirely sure that there *are* any such things as unconscious states. But many philosophers, psychologists, and other expert students of the mind seem quite convinced that there are such states, and that they play an active role in the determination of our conscious life, including the formation of beliefs (some beliefs may, of course, themselves be unconscious). Not wishing to leave out such an important, if obscure class of states, I want to allow that such states can serve as reason states.

The class of states that can serve as reasons upon which a belief is based includes beliefs, perceptual states, sensation states, and (perhaps) unconscious states. This list is not exclusive, and probably not exhaustive, but I believe that it captures some main varieties of reason states. No doubt my extension of the scope of the term 'reasons' to include such non-belief states will be met with protest. Some will argue that *only* beliefs can serve as reasons upon which another belief is based. I will not attempt at this point to convince those who disagree with me about this matter. For now I only want to note that the desire to restrict reasons to beliefs probably stems from the conception of reasons as *evidential* reasons. If we take reasons to be believed propositions, then if we want to talk about states of a person as reasons it would only be natural to restrict the scope of 'reasons' to the beliefs that have the propositions in question as their objects. On that conception of reasons, it would indeed be peculiar to talk about sensation states (for example) as reasons. But I am talking about causal reasons, not evidential reasons, and so this motivation for restricting reasons to beliefs carries no force.

1.2. Causal Connections

Let us now turn to a consideration of the conditions under which a person's belief that h can be said to be based upon a set of reasons. From this point on, I shall use the term 'reasons' interchangeably with the term 'reason states'; if I intend to be talking about evidential reasons, I shall make this quite explicit.

At the beginning of this section I suggested the set of conditions (B) as a very general formulation of a causal account of the basing relation. I also suggested that further elucidation of the following subcondition is required:

(2b)   there is an appropriate causal connection between S's having r_j at tn and S's believing that h at t.

Let us begin this further elucidation by noting that the expression 'S has r_j at tn' can be taken to express the fact that the reason state r_j is a state of the person S at the time tn. This is, I believe, quite straight-forward given the above discussion of reason states. The more difficult problem concerns the kinds of causal connections that are 'appropriate' for the basing relation, and I shall now deal with this problem at some length. Condition (2b) will be replaced with the following condition:

(2b′)   Either (i) S's being in reason state r_j at tn is a cause of S's believing that h at t;

         or   (ii) S's being in reason state r_j at tn is a pseudo-over-determinant of S's believing that h at t.

Each of the conditions (i) and (ii) of (2b′) specifies an 'appropriate' kind of causal connection. For this suggestion to be taken seriously, however, I must now say what I mean by '_____ is a cause of . . .' and by '_____ is a pseudo-over-determinant of . . .'.

I shall suggest a type of analysis of causal expressions that has only recently begun to attract any serious attention, namely, the counterfactual analysis of causation. The intuitive idea behind this approach is fairly simple. To say that the event c is a cause of the event e is to say that the occurrence of event e depended in some way on the occurrence of event c. According to the counterfactual analysis of causation, the nature of this dependence may be understood by considering various counterfactual truths. For example, if I turn on a light by flipping a switch, we would want to say that the flipping of the switch was a cause[7] of the light's going one, and in a normal setting the dependency involved is captured (at least partly) by the true counterfactual conditional 'If the switch had not been flipped, then the light would not have gone on.' The notion of causal dependence among events is to be explicated in terms of the notion of counterfactual dependence, and the notion of causation is, in turn, explicated with the aid of the notion of causal dependence. As might be expected, however, given the history of philosophical speculation about causation, a precise formulation of these relations is difficult to achieve.

In formulating the analysis I shall, obviously, use counterfactual expressions: I shall also assume that some version of the 'possible-worlds approach' to the theory of counterfactuals is correct, although I do not assume that the success or failure of the counterfactual analysis of causation ultimately hangs on the success or failure of that approach to counterfactuals.

For the purposes of this paper, I shall take the three-place relation expressed by

(c1)   World w_1 is closer to world w than is world w_2

as unanalyzed, or 'primitive.' This notion is at the heart of the possible-worlds approach to counterfactuals, and ultimately one must come to grips with the problem of specifying the criteria in accordance with which judgments about closeness are to be rendered. According to David Lewis, for example, a world w_1 is closer to a world w than is the world w_2 if w_1 resembles w in respect of *overall comparative similarity* more than w_2 resemble w.[8] But this particular suggestion faces difficult problems, and viable competitors are available.[9] Even if we take (c1) as unanalyzed, however, we can state truth conditions for counterfactual expressions which are intuitively natural and appealing. For example, I shall be concerned in this paper with counterfactual expressions of the form 'If the event c had not occurred, then the event e would not have occurred.' Following Lewis,[10] let us say:

(ct)   The proposition that if the event c had not occurred then the event *e* would not have occurred is true at a world *w* iff:

either (1)   there are no possible worlds in which the event *c* does not occur;

or   (2)   there is some world in which the event *c* does not occur and in which the event *e* does not occur which is closer to *w* than is any world in which the event *c* does not occur but in which the event *e* does occur.

(ct) is formulated in such a way that the world *w*, as well as the other worlds considered, need not be identical with our actual world. From this point on, unless otherwise specified, I shall assume that the counterfactuals are being evaluated at the actual world (that is, I shall assume that *w* is the actual world).

Given the considerations of the preceding paragraph, we can define the relation of counterfactual dependence among events:

(CfD)   Where *c* and *e* are occurrent events, *e* depends counterfactually on *c* iff: if *c* had not occurred, then *e* would not have occurred.[11]

It is tempting to think that if an event *e* is counterfactually dependent upon an event *c*, then *e* is *causally* dependent upon *c*. While this is often the case, there are exceptions that must be accounted for. The most obvious problem is that there is nothing in (CfD) that tells that *c* and *e* cannot be the *same* event. Moreover, it seems quite trivially clear that if *c* and *e* are identical, then *e* depends counterfactually on *c*. So, if we were to take counterfactual dependence simpliciter to be sufficient for causal dependence, we would get the unhappy result that every occurrent event is causally dependent upon itself. There is a generally agreed upon requirement that if one event is to be a cause of another, then the two events must be *distinct*. The same requirement holds for causal dependence. Taking this into account, and assuming some criterion for distinctness of events,[12] we can define causal dependence in the following straightforward way:

(CD)   Where *c* and *e* are occurrent events, *e* depends *causally* on *c* iff:

(1)   *c* and *e* are distinct events; and

(2)   if *c* had not occurred, then *e* would not have occurred.

Let us turn now from the notion of causal dependence to the notion of causation.

If *e* is causally dependent upon *c*, then we may say that *c* is a cause of *e;* however, from the fact that *c* is a cause of *e* we may not conclude that *e* is causally dependent upon *c*. Often, when one event is a cause of another, this is so because there is a *causal chain* of events linking them. Suppose *c* and *e* are the first and last members of a chain of events, $c, d_1, d_2, \ldots, d_n, e$ such that c is a cause of d_1, d_1 is a cause of $d_2 \ldots$, and d_n is a cause of e. Then, we would want to say that c is (also) a cause of e (the relation is transitive), but e may not be causally dependent upon c, since e might have occurred even if c had not occurred. Consequently, causation between events cannot simply be defined as causal dependence among those events. To get causation, we need the notion of a causal chain. This is easily constructed as follows:

(CC)　Where $c, d_1, d_2, \ldots, d_n, e$ is a sequence of occurrent events (but not necessarily a temporal sequence, and where c and e may be the only members), this sequence is a *causal chain* iff:

(1)　　d_1 depends causally on c; and

(2)　　d_2 depends causally on d_1; and

(3)　　d_n depends causally on d_{n-1}; and

(4)　　e depends causally on d_n;

Given this notion of a causal chain, we can put forth the following preliminary definition of causation;

(C)　　Where c and e are specific events that occurred, c is a cause of e iff: there is a causal chain of occurrent events from c to e.

I have called (C) a 'preliminary' definition of causation because it is inadequate as it stands. There are two main problems facing this definition. The first problem has to do with the fact that (C) fails to guarantee the direction of causation. There are examples which show that, for some pairs of distinct events, c and e, if c is a cause of e by (C), then e will also be a cause of c by (C). In another paper[13] I have discussed this problem at length and have suggested a solution. The matter is much too complex to be dealt with here, so I will simply assume the notion of *causal priority*, and will incorporate into (C) the requirement that c be causally prior to e.[14] The other main problem confronting (C) has to do with the fact that some events are causally *overdetermined*; since the problem is of particular importance for my account of the basing relation, I must discuss it in some detail.

I want to distinguish between cases of *genuine* overdetermination and cases of *pseudo* overdetermination (the latter, you will recall, is one of the types of causal connection referred to in (2b') above). In both types of cases we have an event e, and two (or more)[15] events, c and d, all of which occurred and which are related in such a way that the occurrence of either c or d alone would have been sufficient for the occurrence of a causal chain to e. We have a case of genuine overdetermination if both c and d have equal claim to being a cause of e, and we have a case of pseudo overdetermination if only one of the two can properly be called a cause of e. In cases of pseudo overdetermination, the event which is *not* a cause of e is the (or *a*) pseudo overdeterminant of e. Cases of genuine overdetermination are counter-examples to the definition of causation suggested in (C), while cases of pseudo overdetermination are not. However, the relation '_____ is a pseudo overdeterminant of . . . ' is a fundamental one for my theory of the basing relation. Hence, for different reasons respectively, it is important that I carefully define each of these kinds of overdetermination.

Let us first consider a simple example of genuine overdetermination; I will select an example that also serves to illustrate the basing relation. Suppose I am watching a news service ticker tape on my cable television, and at the very same time I am listening to a radio announcer reading the same ticker tape on my radio. The ticker and the announcer both tell me, at precisely the same time, that the Dow Jones average has just fallen below 700. I come to believe that the Dow Jones average has just fallen below 700. Let this belief state be e. Let the complex visual perceptual state involved in my reading the ticker tape on the television set be the event c, and let the complex auditory perceptual state involved in my hearing the ticker tape read by the announcer be the event d. In this case, it would seem, each of the events c and d has equal claim to being a cause of e. If either of them had occurred without the other occurring, e would have occurred, and neither of them is interfered with, or pre-empted, in any way. What shall we say the causal *facts* are in such a case? It seems to me that there are two primary alternatives here. On the one hand, we can say that *neither* of the events c or d is a cause of e; and on the other hand, we can say that they both are causes of e. Of these two alternatives, the second is the stronger from my intuitive point of view. Hence, that is the view that I shall develop. I believe, however, that the first alternative can also be developed using the counterfactual approach.

But if I want to say, in this example, that c was a cause of e and that d was also a cause of e, then we have a counterexample to the definition (C). Those conditions require that there be a *causal chain* from cause to effect; hence, I would have to say that there is a causal chain from c to e and another from d to e. But, even though there is a *chain* of events linking c with e and a *chain* of events linking d with e, neither of these chains is a *causal* chain. For simplicity, let us suppose that the chain from c to e and the chain from d to e have only one member in common, namely e (this is probably false, but that should not affect the point being made). Then, let the predecessor of e in the chain from c to e be called 'c',' and let the predecessor of e in the chain from d to e be called 'd'.' In order for the chain from c to e (for example) to be a causal chain, the counterfactual 'If c' had not occurred, then e would not have occurred' must (by (CC)) be true. However, this counterfactual is false; had c' not occurred, then e would have occurred anyway, for the chain of events from d to e would have been completed. An analogous argument will show that the chain from d to e is not a causal chain. Consequently, cases of genuine overdetermination fail to satisfy the conditions (C), under the assumption that each of the overdetermining events is a cause.

To deal with this problem, I propose the following definition of the genuine overdetermination relation:

(GO)   Where c and e are occurrent events, c is a genuine overdeterminant of e if and only if: There is some set of occurrent events $D=[d_1, d_2, \ldots, d_n]$ (possibly having only one member) such that

(1)   if c had not occurred and if any member d_i of D had occurred, but no other members of D had occurred, and if e had occurred anyway, then there would have been a causal chain of distinct actually occurrent events from d_i to e, and d_i would have been causally prior to e; and

(2)   if no member of D had occurred, and if c and e had occurred anyway, then there would have been a causal chain of distinct actually occurrent events from c to e, and c would have been causally prior to e.

In the case that we have been considering, it will be found that c and d are both genuine overdeterminants of e in accordance with (GO). Now, I propose that the definition (C) of causation be revised in the following way:

(C')   Where c and e are specific events that occurred, c is a cause of e iff:

Either (1)   there is a causal chain of distinct occurrent events from c to e, and c is causally prior to e;

or   (2) c is a genuine overdeterminant of e.

Given this definition, we get the result in the example at hand that the reason states c and d are both causes of my belief that the Dow Jones average has just fallen below 700. In addition, given the analysis of the basing relation expressed in (B), with (2b') replacing the original (2b), we get the result that my belief about the Dow Jones average is based upon each of these reason states, and upon the set consisting of the two of them. Of course, the *total* set of reasons that my belief is based upon will presumably be much more extensive than this.

Let us now consider an example of pseudo-overdetermination. I will again select an example that illustrates the basing relation, but I will precede this with an example that is, perhaps, a clearer illustration. Suppose we have two pushbuttons, B1 and B2, both of which are wired to a light bulb and to a live electrical source. If either of the buttons is pushed alone, then the light will go on. However, pushbutton B1 is equipped with an overriding device such that if B1 is pushed, then the circuit between the other pushbutton, B2, and the light is broken. Now suppose that the two switches are pushed simultaneously. Let the pushing of B1 be the event c, the pushing of B2 be the event d, and the light's going on be the event e. This is a clear example of pseudo-overdetermination. Only the event c (the pushing of B1) is a cause of e. That event also *pre-empted* any causal chain that might have occurred between the event d (the pushing of B2) and the light's going on. Hence, there was *no* chain of events between d and e; but there would have been such a chain, and it would have been a causal chain, had the event c not occurred (and, had d and e occurred anyway). Moreover, the event d is not a genuine overdeterminant of the event e, since the causal chain that would have occurred between d and e (had c not occurred) would have consisted of events that did not actually occur. For this reason, d is what I am calling a pseudo-overdeterminant.

Now suppose that a reliable friend, who is also a policeman, tells me that Lefty has murdered Smith. His telling me this is a cause of my believing that Lefty has murdered Smith, and this belief is, in turn, a cause of my believing that Lefty has a criminal personality. Let my believing that Lefty has murdered Smith be the reason state c, and let my believing that Lefty has a criminal personality be the state e. Then, c is a cause of e. At some later time, another reliable friend tells me that Lefty has just murdered Jones, and his telling me this is a cause of my believing that Lefty has murdered Jones; let this belief be d. We may suppose that I have continued to believe all along that Lefty has a criminal personality, and so we may suppose that my new belief, d, does not inaugurate a chain of events having that belief as a result. That chain of events has been preempted by the earlier cause. However, had I not had the earlier belief, and had I come to believe that Lefty has murdered Jones anyway, then there would have been a causal chain from this belief to the belief that Lefty has a criminal personality. Hence, my belief that Lefty has murdered Jones is a pseudo-overdeterminant of my belief that Lefty has a criminal personality.

In light of these examples, I propose the following definition of the pseudo-overdetermination relation:

(PO)   Where c and e are occurrent events, c is a pseudo-overdeterminant of e iff:

(1) c is not a cause of e (that is, there is no causal chain from c to e

and c is not a *genuine* overdeterminant of e); and

(2)   there is some set of occurrent events $D=[d_1, d_2, \ldots, d_n]$ (possibly having only one member) such that

    (a) each d_1 in D is a cause of e; and

    (b) if no member of D had occurred, but c and e had occurred anyway, then there would have been a causal chain from c to e, and c would have been causally prior to e.

Given this account of pseudo overdetermination, and given the account of basing expressed in (B), we get the result in the example involving Lefty that my belief that Lefty has a criminal personality is based both upon the belief that Lefty murdered Smith and upon the belief that Lefty murdered Jones. It is based upon the former belief because that belief is a cause of my belief that Lefty has a criminal personality, and it is based upon the latter because that belief is a pseudo overdeterminant of the belief in question.

This completes my account of the basing relation, including my account of the kinds of causal connections that are 'appropriate' for basing. I turn now to a consideration of some objections to this account of basing; hopefully, the discussion of these objections will also serve to illustrate the theory.

1.3. Objections and Replies

I have said that my account of the basing relation is a causal account. However, I have included the pseudo-overdetermination relation among the kinds of 'appropriate' causal connections. One might object to this on the grounds that pseudo-overdetermination is not a real causal connection, and hence it is misleading of me to say that I am giving a causal account of basing. I must admit, of course, that pseudo-overdeterminants are not causes; this follows from the definition of that relation. However, I find it necessary to include pseudo-overdetermination among the appropriate causal connections if my account of justification and knowledge is to be adequate. Consider again the example involving my belief that Lefty has a criminal personality. This belief, I have supposed, is based upon two other beliefs, one of which is a cause and the other a pseudo-overdeterminant of the belief. Suppose we add to the description of this case the following additional complications. Each of the beliefs upon which my belief that Lefty has a criminal personality is based is such that my believing this about Lefty is justified on the basis of that reason. However, suppose that the belief which is a cause of my belief that Lefty has a criminal personality is in fact false. My friend the policeman has made a mistake; Lefty did not murder Smith. But, the belief that Lefty murdered Jones, which is the pseudo-overdeterminant of my belief that Lefty has a criminal personality, is true. We would, I should think, say that I *know* that Lefty has a criminal personality. I cannot know this, however, on the basis of the false belief that Lefty murdered Smith; hence, I must know it on the basis of my true belief that Lefty murdered Jones. I am led, by these considerations, to include pseudo-overdetermination among the causal connections appropriate for the basing relation; for, in the case at hand, that is the connection that obtains between my belief that Lefty killed Jones and my belief that Lefty has a criminal personality.

Temporal considerations give rise to other likely objections to my account of the basing relation. One of these has to do with what I call the 'problem of distant reasons.' A belief is a state that can persist through time even though the reason states that were originally causes of that belief no longer obtain. If there is a long temporal interval between the time when a person was in the reason states that originated a belief and some later time when the belief is still held, then it may seem odd to say the belief is, at this later time, still based upon the defunct set of reason states which originated the belief. For example, many people now believe things that were told to them by their parents in childhood, and in some such cases the belief has persisted via an unbroken causal chain from that much earlier time. Typically, the reason states that originated the belief will not also have persisted. Moreover, in such cases a person will, typically, have acquired a new set of reasons over the years for the belief in question. But, on my account, the original childhood reasons will be among the reasons upon which the belief is now based. This is a distant reason, and I imagine that many will find it odd to call it a reason at all.

But let us ask why it would appear odd to include such a distant reason among the set of reasons upon which a current belief is based. One likely explanation has to do with an incorrect assumption about the basing relation. This assumption can be elicited by considering a possible line of argument against the result arrived at in the distant reasons situation. It might be argued that there is a close connection between

(1) S's belief that h is based upon reason state r at t,

and some or all of the following:

(2) S takes r at t to be a reason for which S believes that h;
(3) S believes at t that S's belief that h is based upon r;
(4) S would at t give, or describe, r if S were asked to provide the reasons upon which S's belief that h is based;
(5) S remembers at t that S was in r.

More precisely, it might be suggested that some or all of (2)–(5) are necessary conditions for (1); this is the assumption referred to above. Then, it might be argued that if a person had held a belief for a very long time, the chances are that the reason states that originated the belief would not satisfy any of (2)–(5). Hence, the belief could not be said to be based upon any such distant reason states. In response to this (imagined) line of argument, I would appeal to examples in which a person's belief *is* based upon a set of reasons, but in which none of (2)–(5) are satisfied. I take it, moreover, that some of the examples discussed in Section 1.1 (for example, the one wherein I come to believe of my friend that he is unhappy) are examples of this sort.

Another possible explanation of the apparent oddity of allowing distant reasons to be among those that a belief can be based upon has to do with the role that the concept of basing plays in the account of justified belief and knowledge. Whether a belief is justified, or whether a person has knowledge, is partly a function of the set of reasons upon which the belief is based; this manifests itself in our formulation of the analysis of knowledge (K). Distant reasons do not seem very likely candidates for reasons upon which a belief might be justified, nor upon which a belief might count as an instance of knowledge. I agree with this, but let us note that there is much more to justification and knowledge than is found in the basing relation. If the *only* set of reasons upon which a belief is based is a set of very distant reasons, then my account of justification and knowledge will almost certainly *not* yield the result that the belief is justified or that the belief is an instance of knowledge. And, in those cases where the analysis does yield these results they will, I believe, be found to be appropriate.

Temporal considerations lead to yet another line of argument that an opponent of my account might pursue. It might be argued that the conditions in (B) are not fully sensitive to the fact that a person's reasons can *change* over a period of time. For an example, consider another variation on the case involving Lefty. Suppose that I come to have a complex set of beliefs about Lefty, namely, that Lefty robbed the bank and murdered Smith. These beliefs are a cause of my belief that Lefty has a criminal personality. Suppose my belief that Lefty has a criminal personality persists over a period of time, and that there is an unbroken causal chain from my original reasons to the current belief. During this time, a reliable friend of mine informs me that Lefty did not in fact do the things that I once thought he had done; rather, Lefty stole a car and murdered Jones. At this later time, my belief that Lefty has a criminal personality comes to be based upon this new set of beliefs, and the causal connection involved is a form of overdetermination. Since there is, nevertheless, an unbroken causal chain from my original reasons to my current belief that Lefty has a criminal personality, we also have the result that my belief about Lefty is *still* based upon the old beliefs that Lefty robbed the bank and murdered Smith. Surely, it will be argued, this is a mistake. For, I have now come to believe that my old beliefs about Lefty are false, and I have given those beliefs up. Not only have I come to have new reasons for believing that Lefty has a criminal personality, this belief has ceased to be based upon the old reasons. Since my account is not sensitive to such changes, it is defective.

I do have to admit that if, as the example requires, there is an unbroken causal chain from the earlier beliefs to my present belief about Lefty's criminal personality, then the latter belief is based upon the former in accordance with my account. However, I do not see that this leads to any serious problems. For, my account is sensitive to the fact that many things have changed in the example under consideration. I have acquired some new beliefs about Lefty, and I have given up some old beliefs, while my belief about his criminal personality has persisted. We may certainly say that the set of reasons that I *have* has changed, and my account of basing yields the result that my belief about Lefty's criminal personality is *based* upon any *new* reasons. Moreover, my analysis of knowing only requires that there be *some* set of reasons R upon which a belief is justifiably based in order that a person have knowledge. My new reasons will suffice for this purpose; and, since I no longer *have* the old reasons, they will not sully my knowledge by condition (3) of (K).

The arguments considered thus far are arguments designed to show that the conditions suggested in (B) are not sufficient for the basing relation. Keith Lehrer suggests a different kind of example that might appear to be a counterexample to the *necessity* of these conditions.[16] This is an example in which a lawyer, who is also a gypsy, comes to believe that his client is innocent of a murder on the basis of a reading of his cards; his belief that the cards say his client is innocent is a cause of his belief that his client is innocent. These beliefs in turn cause him to reconsider the evidence against his client, which up to this point has been taken by everyone to show that his client is guilty. He finds that the evidence in fact conclusively establishes that his client is innocent of this murder, and he then claims to know that his client is innocent on the basis of this evidence. However, the case is an emotionally charged one, and the gypsy lawyer

... agrees that it is extraordinarily difficult to be convinced by the evidence because of the emotional factors surrounding the crime. The evidence is quite conclusive, as shown by his complicated chain of reasoning, but even he would find himself unable to believe his client could be innocent of that murder were it not for the fact that the cards told him that his client is innocent of the . . . murder, and it is that which nurtures and supports his conviction. . . . On the other hand, were his faith in the cards to collapse, then emotional factors which influence others would sway him too.[17]

Lehrer argues that this example is one in which the gypsy lawyer's belief is based upon a set of reasons but where these reasons do not " . . . explain why he believes as he does, his faith in the cards explains that, and the evidence in no way supports, reinforces, or conditionally or partially explains why he believes as he does."[18] Moreover, Lehrer offers this example in the context of a discussion of " . . . causal accounts of what is involved when the justification of a belief is based upon evidence,"[19] and it is his primary argument for the conclusion that " . . . all such theories must be rejected."[20] I believe, however, that there is at least one such theory that need not be rejected, namely, that which is suggested in (B).

The point of the example would seem to be this: the gypsy lawyer's belief that his client is innocent is based upon his belief that the evidence conclusively establishes the innocence of his client; indeed, this is what explains his knowledge. However, there is no causal connection of any sort between these beliefs. Thus, it is not a necessary condition for the basing relation that there be a causal connection. I suggest, however, that there is a causal connection obtaining between the gypsy lawyer's justifying reason state and his belief in his client's innocence, namely, the relation of pseudo-overdetermination.[21] Let 'Bsh' designate the lawyer's belief that his client is innocent, let 'Bsc' designate the lawyer's belief that the cards say the client is innocent; and let 'Bsq' designate the lawyer's belief that the evidence conclusively establishes that h. Then, oversimplifying somewhat, the situation might be diagrammed in the following way:

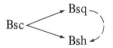

The arrow from 'Bsc' to 'Bsq' represents the fact that the gypsy lawyer's belief in what the cards say is a cause of his coming to believe that the evidence conclusively establishes his client's innocence. The causal chain would, of course, include whether events constitute his reasoning out this conclusion from the evidence in question. The arrow from 'Bsc' to 'Bsh' represents the fact that it was also the belief in what the cards say that originated the belief in the client's innocence. Finally, the dotted arrow from 'Bsq' to 'Bsh' represents the fact that S's belief that the evidence conclusively establishes his client's innocence is a pseudo-overdeterminant of his belief that his client is innocent.

To say that 'Bsq' is a pseudo-overdeterminant of 'Bsh' is to say the following things:

(a)   'Bsq' and 'Bsh' are actual states of S;

(b)   'Bsq' is not a cause of 'Bsh';

(c)   if no other reason states were causes of 'Bsh', and if 'Bsq' were still an actual state of S, then 'Bsq' would be a cause of 'Bsh'.

One might think that 'Bsq' is not a pseudo-overdeterminant of 'Bsh' because, as Lehrer has set the example up, 'Bsq' is causally dependent upon 'Bsc'; hence, if S had not believed that the cards say his client is innocent, then S would not have believed to begin with that there is a conclusive argument from the evidence to his client's innocence. But *these* (counterfactual) facts do not show that 'Bsq' is not a pseudo-overdeterminant of 'Bsh'; whether that is so depends upon whether 'Bsq' *would* be a cause of 'Bsh' if nothing else were *and if S were still in 'Bsq'*. That counterfactual may very well be true even though as a matter of fact S would not believe that q unless S believed that the cards say his client is innocent. Moreover, in the case described, it is quite *plausible* to say that S would be caused to believe that his client is innocent by his belief that the evidence is conclusive if he were to have this latter belief and nothing else were a cause of his belief in his client's innocence. On the other hand, if S's belief that the evidence is conclusive is not at least a pseudo-overdeterminant of his belief that his client is innocent, then I do not see how we can claim that this belief 'explains how he knows' that his client is innocent. I conclude, then, that the gypsy lawyer example does not, as its author suggests, give us reason to abandon a causal theory of the basing relation.

2. EPISTEMIC JUSTIFICATION

Supposing that S believes h on the basis of a set of reasons R, the question remains as to whether this belief is justified in a way that might provide the person S with knowledge. In this section, I want to suggest a highly programmatic sketch of a theory of justified belief. I shall begin by considering two examples. In the first of these examples, I shall take it as uncontroversial that the subject is justified in having the belief, and in the second example I shall take it as uncontroversial that the subject's belief is unjustified.

The first example is this. Suppose that Alfred is sitting in his study and is looking out the window. It is snowing outside. Alfred is wide awake, has normal vision, is of normal intelligence and educational background. More-over, it is daytime, the window through which Alfred is looking is clear, and there are no objects outside of the window which block Alfred's vision. Alfred is sober, undistracted, and free from hallucinatory drugs. Alfred comes to be in certain reason states, consisting, in part, of various perceptual states which are caused in him by the scene outside. He also has background beliefs about how things look when it is snowing, and he understands the relevant concepts. Of course, Alfred believes that it is now snowing on the basis of these reasons.

Here is the second example. Robert, let us suppose, has always been quite gullible. He has recently been influenced by an equally gullible friend to take up the study of astrology. With characteristic fervor, he has worked hard at this new avocation, and has in fact become quite knowledgeable about the interpretation of astrological charts. One day, having studied the charts carefully, he comes to believe that his uncle will have a serious automobile accident that day. He spends the day wrought with anxiety, and even calls his uncle to tell him of the impending danger. The next day, when no accident has occurred, Robert simply cannot understand what went 'wrong.'

We could, no doubt, multiply examples of justified and unjustified belief in many various and subtle ways. But, for my purposes here, these will suffice. What is the difference between the situation involving Alfred and the situation involving Robert? I shall not criticize the many attempts that have been made to answer this question. Rather, I should like to ask you to consider a theory of justification that begins with the observation that people are, in some respects, rather like thermometers and barometers.[22] A barometer, for ex-ample, has a structure, or composition, which makes it sensitive to changes in atmospheric pressure in its region. Such changes *cause* changes in various states of the barometer, the end result of which is a certain position of the needle on the face of the barometer. If the barometer has been carefully constructed (it is not just a toy, or a bargain-basement barometer), and if its parts are working properly and are properly lubricated, then, on a given occasion, the fact that the barometer registers a certain atmospheric pressure P is related to the proposition that the atmospheric pressure *is* P in an impor-tant way. The *probability*[23] that the atmospheric pressure is P, *given* that the barometer registers P and the barometer is well constructed and in good working order, is greater than the probability that the atmospheric pressure is other than P, given those same facts. Since these probabilistic facts obtain, we say, on a given occasion, that the barometer is a *reliable indicator* of the way the world is, at least with respect to barometic pressure.

People are, like barometers, so constituted that they are causally sensitive to certain aspects of the world around them. A barometer registers changes in atmospheric pressure by coming to be in correlative states as an effect of those changes. People register changes around them by coming to be in various perceptual states, sensation states, and belief states as a result (causal) of those changes. In saying these thing I am, of course, only stating the obvious; but, in these obvious facts we can find the ingredients, I believe, of an interesting theory of epistemic justification. We would never say, of a barometer, that its reading on a given occasion is 'justified'; however, we do say that its reading is 'accurate' or 'reliable,' and mean by this something very like what we mean when we say the same thing of a barometer.

Consider the case of Alfred, who is sitting in his study watching the snow fall outside. In coming to believe that the snow is falling, Alfred has come to be in a certain state as a result (causal) of the event of the snow's falling. This state is *analogous* to the state of the barometer which consists of the pointing of its needle to the mark '30.1' on its dial. Moreover, in constructing this case, we have supposed that Alfred is in 'good working order'; he is wide awake, sober, has good vision, and so forth. There is, in other words, some set of relevant characteristics, C, such that Alfred has these characteristics, and in virtue of his having these characteristics it can be said that he is in good working order. Just as we say of the barometer that its state of registering '30.1' on its dial is, given its condition, a reliable indicator of the atmospheric pressure, we can also say, of Alfred, that his believing that it is snowing outside, given the condition that he is in, is a reliable indicator that it is snowing outside.

In the case of the barometer, I suggested that certain probabilistic facts obtain, and because these facts obtain we can say that the barometer is, on the occasion in question, a reliable indicator of the way the world is. I believe that we can point to analogous probabilistic facts concerning Alfred and his belief that it is snowing outside. For example, we might say: The probability that it is snowing outside, given that Alfred believes that it is snowing and given that Alfred has the set of characteristics C is greater than the probability that it is not snowing outside, given these same facts about Alfred. If these probabilistic facts do obtain, then, because they obtain we may say, of Alfred, that he is a reliable indicator on the occasion in question of the way the world is (at least with respect to the question whether it is snowing outside).

By contrast, in the case in which Robert comes to believe that his uncle will have an automobile accident, we would not want to say that Robert is a reliable indicator of the way the world is (to be). This can be explained, I believe, by reference to the probabilistic facts. There is no set of relevant characteristics C such that the probability that Robert's uncle will have an accident, given that Robert believes that he will and that Robert has characteristics C is greater than the probability that Robert's uncle will not have an accident, given those same facts about Robert.

The theory of justification that I want to defend can now be given an intuitive formulation. Where S believes that h on the basis of a set of reasons R, this belief is epistemically justified just in case there is some appropriate set of characteristics C such that S has C and such that, given that S has C, S's believing that h on the basis of R is a reliable indication that h is true. Since reliability is closely tied to certain probabilistic facts, I shall call this the *probabilistic-reliability model* of epistemic justification; and, since that is a rather cumbersome name, I shall for convenience speak of the 'P-R model' of justification.

Two particularly important problems must be noted before suggesting a more precise formulation of the P-R model of justification. First, it seems generally agreed among those philosophers who have discussed justification that if a person's belief is to be justified on the basis of some other belief, then the latter belief must itself be justified. On my view, the set of reasons, R, upon which a belief is based may, and typically will, include some other belief states of the person in question. Thus, in formulating my analysis of justification, I must be careful to guarantee that the generally agreed upon principle mentioned above is satisfied for any beliefs which are a member of a set of reasons upon which some further belief is justified.

Second, there is a well-known type of problem which confronts probabilistic theories of justification, namely, the type of problem that is exemplified in the 'lottery paradox.'[24] The problem is essentially this. In lottery-type situations, the fact that a proposition is highly probable (or, much more probable than its denial) relative to the basis of one's belief is clearly not sufficient for saying that the belief is epistemically justified. This is a problem for the P-R model just as it is for any other probabilistic model. But there is a solution to the problem. The solution involves the recognition that a belief can have *competitors*, from the point of view of justification.[25] If we are asking whether I am justified in believing that h, then the denial of h is *one* of the competitors of h. But, in many situations, there are *other* competitors as well, and the lottery paradox gives us a clear illustration of such a situation. I shall here take the notion of a competitor as an undefined notion.

Having noted these two things, I suggest the following as a tentative formulation of the P-R model of epistemic justification:

(PR) S's believing that h on the basis of R is epistemically justified iff: There is some relevant set of characteristics C such that

(1) S has C; and

(2)   For every competitor q of h, the probability that h is true, given that S has C and that S believes that h on the basis of R is greater than the probability that q is true, given that S has C and that S believes that h on the basis of R; and

(3)   For every belief state Bsp_i ($i = 1,2, \ldots , n$) of S which is a member of R and which is such that $h \neq Bsp_i$, there is some relevant set of characteristics C_i and some set of reasons states R_i such that

    (i) S believes that p_i on the basis of R_i; and

    (ii) S has C_i; and

    (iii) For every competitor q_i of p_i, the probability that p_i is true, given that S has C_i and that S believes that p_i on the basis of R_i is greater than the probability that q_i is true, given that S has C_i and that S believes that p_i on the basis of R_i.

By requiring that the probability of h must outstrip the probability of any of its competitors we can, I believe, avoid the problems presented by the lottery paradox. And, by including condition (3) in the analysis we can, I believe, guarantee that the generally agreed upon principle mentioned above is satisfied.[26]

As I said at the outset, the remarks in this section are only intended as a highly programmatic sketch of a theory of epistemic justification. Naturally, this proposal needs to be illustrated in the many kinds of situations where epistemic justification is an issue, and points of detail need to be clearly specified. I cannot, unfortunately, undertake those tasks in this already too lengthy paper.[27]

NOTES

[1] The phrase 'reasons for which' is used by Gilbert Harman in his book *Thought* (Princeton University Press, 1973). I believe that Harman intends this phrase to apply to those things that other epistemologists have referred to as the basis of a person's belief. One philosopher who emphasizes the notion is Brian Skyrms, in his essay 'The Explication of "X knows that p",' *The Journal of Philosophy*, **64** 12 (June 22, 1967), 373–389; reprinted in Michael D. Roth and Leon Galis (eds.), *Knowing: Essays in the Analysis of Knowledge*, (Random House, 1970).

[2] In 1963, Edmund L. Gettier argued that justified true belief is not sufficient for knowledge in his paper 'Is Justified True Belief Knowledge?', *Analysis*, **23** (1963),

121–123; reprinted in Roth and Galis, *op. cit*. This brief paper has spawned hundreds of articles and books on the subject. A fairly balanced picture of these developments can be found in two anthologies: the one by Roth and Galis (see note 1 above); and George S. Pappas and Marshall Swain (eds.), *Essays on Knowledge and Justification*, (Cornell University Press, 1978).

[3] See 'Knowledge, Causality, and Justification,' *The Journal of Philosophy*, **69**, 11 (1972), 291–300, repr. in Pappas and Swain, *op. cit*.; 'Some Revisions of "Knowledge, Causality, and Justification",' in Pappas and Swain, *op. cit*.; and 'Reasons, Causes, and Knowledge,' *The Journal of Philosophy*, (1978).

[4] Throughout this paper I use the terms 'events' and 'states' more or less interchangeably. It should be noted, however, that there are important philosophical reasons for distinguishing between events and states; for example, events, but not states, may be said to *occur*, while states but not events, may be said to *obtain*.

[5] I borrow the term 'causal reasons' from Joseph Tolliver of The Ohio State University who uses the term in his doctoral dissertation material.

[6] Although I am claiming that such states are not themselves belief-states, I do not intend to deny that being in such a state entails some belief-state. Nor do I intend to assert such an entailment. I remain neutral on this (controversial) issue.

[7] To say that the flipping of the switch was *a* cause of the light's going on is not to say that it was *the* cause, nor the principal cause, nor any such thing. There would, presumably, be many other causes as well, such as the moving of the person's hand, the flow of electricity, etc.

[8] See David Lewis, *Counterfactuals*, (Harvard University Press, 1973). Lewis provides a counterfactual analysis of causation in 'Causation,' *The Journal of Philosophy*, **69** (1973), 556–567.

[9] For some of the problems, and a competitor, see John L. Pollock, 'The "Possible Worlds" Analysis of Counterfactuals,' *Philosophical Studies*, **29** (1976), 469–476. The best and most detailed discussion of these problems that I know of is Pollock's book, *Subjunctive Reasoning* (Reidel, 1976).

[10] Lewis provides a more general set of truth conditions: "The proposition that if A were true, then C would be true is true at a world w iff: Either (1) there are no possible A-worlds or (2) some A-world where C holds is closer to w than is any A-world where C does not hold." See *Counterfactuals, op. cit*.

[11] If we did not specify that c and e are occurrent events (that is, that they occur in the actual world), then the definition of counterfactual dependence would be more complicated: Where c and e are events, e depends counterfactually on c iff: (1) if c were to occur then e would occur and (2) if c were not to occur, then e would not occur. Since c and e are occurrent events, counterfactual (1) of this more complicated definition is 'automatically' true, and hence, in our definition (CfD) we need only use counterfactual (2).

[12] I have discussed this problem at some length in two papers: 'A Counterfactual Analysis of Event Causation,' *Philosophical Studies* (1978), and 'Causation and the Distinctness of Events,' Forthcoming in *Time and Cause*, edited by Peter van Inwagen.

[13] See 'A Counterfactual Analysis of Event Causation,' *op. cit*.

[14] If we were to leave the notion of causal priority unanalysed, then the definition of causation suggested here would be circular and distinctly uninteresting. An analysis of this notion which is non-circular can be found in 'A Counterfactual Analysis of Causation,' *op. cit*.

[15] An event can be overdetermined by more than two other events. To speak properly, we should speak of 'n-adic' overdetermination, where n is the number of overdeterminants. In the ensuing discussion, I shall concentrate on cases in which one event is overdetermined by only two other events; however, the definitions of genuine and pseudo-overdetermination to be given below will be formulated in such a way that they cover n-adic overdetermination for any n.

[16] See Keith Lehrer, *Knowledge* (Oxford University Press, 1974), pp. 124–125.

[17] *Ibid.*, p. 125.

[18] *Ibid.*, p. 125.

[19] *Ibid.*, p. 123.

[20] *Ibid.*, p. 123.

[21] I take it that Lehrer intends to rule out even this kind of causal connection when he says that the gypsy lawyer's evidential belief " ... in no way ... conditionally ... explains why he believes as he does" (p. 123)

[22] In *Belief, Truth, and Knowledge* (Cambridge University Press, 1973), David Armstrong suggests what he calls the 'Thermometer' model of noninferential knowledge. Consider this remark: "When a true belief unsupported by reasons stands to the situation truly believed to exist as a thermometer-reading in a good thermometer stands to the actual temperature, then we have noninferential knowledge" (p. 166) The view that I am developing in this section is related, at least on an intuitive level, to this view suggested by Armstrong. However, my view differs from his in at least two major respects. First, Armstrong is constructing a reliability view of *knowledge*; the account that I am suggesting is an account of epistemic justification. Second, the account of reliability that Armstrong suggests is surely too strong, for he requires that the subject's being in the state of believing that p be *nomically sufficient* for the truth of p. My account is considerably weaker than this.

[23] I shall assume that the probability expressions to be used in this section are such that they admit of some interpretation, but I shall not assume any specific interpretation to be the correct one (nor, for that matter, shall I assume that one kind of interpretation is adequate for all such probability expressions).

[24] The lottery paradox was discovered by Henry E. Kyburg, Jr., and a formulation of it can be found in his book *Probability and the Logic of Rational Belief* (Wesleyan University Press, 1961), page 197.

[25] I suggested this approach to the lottery paradox in 'The Logic of Epistemic Consistency,' in M. Swain (ed.) *Induction, Acceptance, and Rational Belief* (Reidel, 1970). In *Knowledge* (*op. cit.*), pp. 192–198, Keith Lehrer provides what may be an adequate definition of competition, and incorporates the notion into his account of epistemic justification.

[26] The following problem must be dealt with, however. Suppose S believes that h on the basis of the belief that q and believes that q, in turn, on the basis of the belief that r. The generally agreed upon principle in question requires that the belief that r be epistemically justified if the belief that h is to be justified. However, as it stands my definition of basing does not clearly guarantee that the belief that h is based upon the belief that r. Hence, it is not clear that the requirement formulated in (3) of (PR) guarantees the satisfaction of our epistemic principle. To guarantee this, I would (but will not here) reformulate the definition of basing recursively.

[27] An earlier version of this paper was presented at a conference on knowledge and

justification held at The Ohio State University in April, 1978. I am grateful to John Barker, Bryce Bate, Keith Lehrer, George Pappas, John Pollock, Larry Powers, Phillip Quinn, Ernest Sosa, and Joseph Tolliver for extremely helpful advice.

GEORGE S. PAPPAS

BASING RELATIONS

Much of what a person knows at any time is based on evidence the person has, or perhaps has had. More generally, most of a person's knowledge at any time is based on reasons that the person has or has had. But what is it for knowledge to be based on evidence or reasons? A complete answer to this question requires a full theory of inferential knowledge, something I will not try to provide here. Instead, I will examine three notions of *basing*, each of which, under some interpretation, seems necessary for knowing on the basis of evidence or reasons.

1. INFERENTIAL BASING

Evidence, I assume, is propositional. That is, the evidence a person, S, may have for believing a proposition, h, consists of some group of propositions, e, each of which, we may suppose, is believed by S. Whether each of the members of e, or some crucial sub-group of the members of e, must be true if S is to know that h on the basis of e, is here left open. Similarly left open is the issue of whether, in order to know that h on the basis of e, S must be justified in believing each of the members of e, or each of the members of some sub-group of e.

When a person knows a proposition h on the basis of evidence e it seems plausible to hold that h and e stand in some inferential relation to one another. By this I mean that either e entails h, or e inductively supports h or, perhaps, h is epistemically derivable from e.[1] Here we take the notion of inductive support very broadly: it is to include those cases in which h explains e, or some members of e, as well as cases in in which h is explained by e, in addition to enumerative and analogical inductive inference. When evidence a person has is related in one or more of the above senses to the proposition one then believes, then we will say that the believed proposition is *inferentially based* on the evidence. That is,

(1)   A person, S's, belief that h is inferentially based on evidence e that S has if and only if h is deductively or inductively supported by e, or h is epistemically derivable from e.

And, it seems quite reasonable to hold that,

51

George S. Pappas (ed.), Justification and Knowledge, 51–63.
Copyright © 1979 by D. Reidel Publishing Company.

(2)   A person S knows that h on the basis of evidence e *only if*: h is
         inferentially based on e.

Notice that (1) and (2) allow that if h is deriveable in some sense from
some small portion of the total evidence, e, then h is still inferentially based
on e.

Statement (2) strikes me as plausible and relatively free of controversy.
However, suppose we were to ask about knowing on tbe basis of reasons,
rather than on the basis of evidence? In that case, given that reasons might
include state of a person,[2] we cannot say that the proposition known by
a person S is inferentially based on the total set of reasons. However, a
similar basing relation seems to hold. Suppose we have a case in which S
knows that h on the basis of reasons r, where no member of r is a proposition.
In that case, most of S's reasons will presumably be beliefs that S then has;
in Swain's terminology, they will be belief-states of S.[3] Other reasons of S's
might include other states of him, such as perceptual states. If we imagine
that

(a)   Propositions $p_1, p_2, \ldots p_n$ make up the propositional content of
         those belief-states, $b_1, b_2, \ldots b_n$, respectively, that are among S's
         reasons for h.

and that,

(b)   For each of S's reasons, $r_o, r_p, \ldots r_z$, that are not belief-states of
         S there are some appropriate propositions, $q_1, q_2, \ldots q_n$, which
         correctly describe, respectively, $r_o, \ldots r_z$.[4]

then the following seems right:

(3)   A person S knows that h on the basis of reasons r which S has or
         has had *only if*: h is inferentially based on the conjunction of
         propositions, $p_1, p_2, \ldots p_n$, and $q_1, q_2, \ldots q_n$.

It is possible that some or all of the proposition of the sort noted in (3)
would turn out in a given case to be evidence that a person has for believing
something. However, that is not implied by (3).

We may think of inferential basing as a partial specification of what it is
for knowledge to be based on evidence or reasons. But surely there is more
to knowledge based on evidence or reasons than this. For a person might have
all sorts of evidence for a proposition which he nonetheless does not believe.
In that case the person would lack knowledge of that proposition even
though, we may presume, some inferential basing relation obtained between
his evidence and proposition in question. A believed proposition's being
inferentially based on evidence one has is at best a necessary condition for
knowing on the basis of one's evidence.

2. BELIEF BASING

A person's beliefs are sometimes based on evidence or reasons that the person has. It has even been claimed that in some cases having one's beliefs based on one's evidence or reasons is essential to knowledge. For instance, Lehrer has claimed that, " . . . if a person has evidence adequate to completely justify his belief, he may still fail to be completely justified in believing what he does because his belief is not *based on* that evidence."[5] In this context, Lehrer is discussing knowledge based on evidence, and he is assuming that one knows on the basis of evidence only if the evidence completely justifies one's belief. With respect to knowledge based on reasons, Swain has claimed that, "Whether a person S has knowledge that h depends upon the reasons for which S believes that h. The reasons for which a person believes something constitute that upon which the person's belief is based."[6] To see if Lehrer and Swain are correct, we need to clarify the notion of a belief being based on evidence or reasons.

Imagine that S is a perspicacious individual, and that he consciously decides to accept h in virtue of the fact that he has evidence e and he accepts e. Or, perhaps S consciously infers h from e, and accepts h as a result of this inference. These are fairly clear notions of basing one's belief on evidence, and each is instantiated in some situations: people sometimes base their beliefs on evidence they have in these ways. Moreover, we can grant that in some cases one has knowledge on the basis of one's evidence only if one bases one's belief on the evidence in the ways just noted. But the general claim is dubious. That is, the claim that

> (4)   A person S knows that h on the basis of evidence e which S has *only if*: S bases his belief that h on e,

is dubious if interpreted along the lines suggested above. For example, S may decide to believe some mathematical proposition h on the strength of some authority, but not thereby come to know that h. Then later he may correctly work through a proof of h, and thereby come to know that h on the basis of some evidence, e'. However, he does not base his belief on e'; rather, he has consciously based his belief on the authority's testimony which, we may suppose, makes up his initial evidence for the belief that h. Furthermore, requiring that S consciously infer from his evidence would rule out much of what we normally reckon as knowledge based on evidence. People do not typically consciously base beliefs on evidence by inferring from the evidence and believing as a result of the inference. The conscious inference construal of belief-basing is too strong, since it renders (4) false.

Should we say, then, that *S* bases his belief on evidence he then has in the sense that he unconsciously infers *h* from his evidence?[7] Again, beliefs may at times be based on evidence in this manner, but (4) is false if belief-basing is uniformly construed as unconscious inference from evidence. To see this we need only consider the sort of case discussed above, viz., one in which *S* does consciously accept *h* as a result of an inference he makes from his evidence, where he knows that *h* on the basis of the evidence.

Belief-basing that is always consciously deciding or inferring is too strong; so is belief-basing that is always unconscious inference from evidence. Perhaps the combination of these approaches will work, especially since we can agree that each construal of belief-basing already discussed has some plausibility for some cases. Thus, we could try,

(5)   A person *S* bases his belief that *h* on evidence *e* which he has if and only if: *S* consciously decides to accept *h* as a result of having *e*, or *S* consciously infers *h* from *e* and accepts *h* as a result of this inference, or *S* unconsciously infers *h* from *e*.

Understood in the light of (5), is (4) true?

I think we can agree that (4) is reasonable when construed along the lines of (5) just in case there are good reasons for positing unconscious inferences in all those cases where conscious decision and inference from evidence play no clear role. And, according to Harman,[8] there are such reasons. He maintains that positing such inferences helps to solve problems arising from Gettier and Gettier-like examples. Hence, since avoidance or resolution of such problems is an important matter, the positing of unconscious inferences of the relevant sort is justified by its beneficial effects.

I think this argument fails, however. We can agree that positing unconscious inferences helps, within the context of Harman's account of factual knowledge, to avoid Gettier problems and related problems. But there are alternative accounts of factual knowledge which are at least as plausible on all other grounds as Harman's, but which do not require positing unconscious inferences.[9] Thus, there is no clear need for Harman's posits, and we have not justified (4) by construing it in terms of (5).

Lehrer once proposed a different characterization of belief-basing. He said,

What I mean by saying that a person's belief is *not* based on certain evidence is that he would not appeal to that evidence to justify his belief. For example, a detective who rejects the truthful testimony of a reliable eye-witness to a crime, but accepts the lying testimony of an ignorant meddler, when both tell him that Brentano committed the crime, would fail to be completely justified in this.[10]

Presumably, Lehrer means that the person would not appeal to the truthful testimony of the eye-witness, but would appeal to the testimony of the meddler. This suggests that a necessary condition for a belief being based on evidence is expressible as follows:

> (6) S bases his belief that h on e *only if*: S would appeal to e if he were to attempt to justify his belief that h.

Coupled with (4), Lehrer's proposal yields,

> (7) S knows that h on the basis of evidence e which he has *only if*: S would appeal to e if he were to attempt to justify his belief that h.

There are, however, two kinds of problems facing (7). First, a person S might treat different people differently, and only appeal to e in the attempt to justify his belief that h to a certain group of people. To others, perhaps, he would appeal to different considerations if, e.g., these other people included children.[11] Yet we do not want to say that he does not know that h on the basis of e for that reason. More importantly, perhaps, is the fact that S himself might not appeal to e in the attempt to justify his belief that h, no matter what other people are involved. For imagine that although S does know that h on the basis of e, he mistakenly believes that he knows that h non-inferentially or immediately. He would not appeal to his evidence in such a case but, say, to the fact that he then perceives or experiences something, or seems to remember some event, or some such. Hence, (7) is dubious.

Perhaps this account of belief-basing can be appropriately modified to avoid the above objections. For example, one might specify an appropriate audience to whom a person would direct his attempted justification. Also, we could indicate just which inclination or desires the agent should have when he attempts to justify his belief. Presumably we would say that an agent whose sole, or at least primary, aim was to inform someone else of the strength of his evidence would appeal to his actual evidence in his attempt to justify his belief to another person. Thus, schematically, we could consider something like this:

> (8)   A person S bases his belief that h on evidence e which he has *only if*: were S to have g as his sole or primary goal relative to audience a, and were S to attempt to justify to a his belief that h, then S would appeal to evidence e.

Coupled with (4), statement (8) yields a variation on (7) which avoids the problem leveled against (7) having to do with the audience. However, it does not avoid the problem raised by the situation in which S knows that h on the basis of some evidence which he has, but he strongly believes that he knows that h immediately or non-inferentially. Thus, resort to (8), though more plausible than (6), does not help to support (4).

Thus far I have spoken of belief-basing as though such basing were an *action* of the person, as suggested by the phrase ' . . . bases his belief . . . on e.' It might be thought, however, that belief-basing is not to be construed as an action, properly speaking, but rather more generally as some relation between the person's belief and his evidence, or his having that evidence. We would express this with a passive construction, such as 'S's belief that h is based on evidence e which S has' or something similar. Two natural ways of understanding such a notion would be as causal or counterfactual dependences of some sort. Of course, such relations will not hold between the agent's belief and his evidence. We need some other way to express such dependences.

If a person has evidence e in support of his belief that h, then, I assume, h is inferentially based on e, the person believes that e, and he is justified in believing that e. We can now explicate belief-basing either as,

(9)   S's belief that h is based on evidence e which S has *if and only if*: S's belief that e is a cause of his belief that h.

or as,

(10)   S's belief that h is based on evidence e which S has *if and only if*: S would not have the belief that h if he were not to have the belief that e.

If we now replace (4), which utilizes the action notion of belief-basing, with,

(11)   A person S knows that h on the basis of evidence e which S has *only if*: S's belief that h is based on e.

we can then ask whether (11) is true if construed along the lines of either (9) or (10).

An example used earlier suffices to show that so construed (11) is dubious. S may know that h on the basis of the evidence he accumulates in working through a proof of h. Still, he may also have come to believe that h as a result of the testimony of some other person and, we may assume, this testimonial evidence is no part of the evidence he gains in doing the proof. Hence, his beliefs concerning the evidence gained in working the proof are not a cause of his belief that h; he already had the belief that h before he started the proof. Moreover, he would have had his belief that h even if he had not gained evidence apropos h by doing the proof. Thus, we should reject these two construals of (11).

There is a way of defending (11) against this example. Notice that it is reasonable to think that if S had not gained his belief that h from the testimony of someone else, then his belief that e would have been a cause of his belief that h. The belief that e is not an actual cause of the belief that h, but the former would have been a cause of the latter if something else had not been. Perhaps then we should expand (9) into:

(9.1)   A person S's belief that h is based on evidence e which S has *if and only if*: either, (1) S's belief that e is a cause of his belief that h, or, (2) if some event or state, x, is the cause of S's belief that h, where x is not identical to or a part of S's believing that e, then if x had not occurred or obtained then S's belief that e would have been a cause of his belief that h.[13]

If (11) is understood along the lines of (9.1), then the mathematical example does not succeed. Moreover, we have not reached (9.1) by means of a simple *ad hoc* adjustment of (9). For it is intuitively plausible to allow that a belief that h is based on another belief, that e, just in case the latter is an actual cause of the former, or it would have been but for the fortuitous occurrence of something else.

I think that utilization of (9.1) makes (11) quite plausible. But there is a rather bizarre example which helps to undermine this initial plausibility. Imagine that a person S is a volunteer in a strange psychology experiment. We suppose that S lives at some future time when a great deal more is known about exact relationships between brain events and psychological states and events. Specifically, at this future time so much is known about such relationships that specific psychological states are inducible artificially by electrical stimulation of the right sorts to relevant places of the brain. Thus, one sort of electrical stimulation will induce a person to have the thought that $2 + 2 = 4$, while another electrical stimulation which is ever so slightly differently placed than the first induces the belief that Bluenose will win the Preakness. S is a volunteer in a situation in which he is wired into suitable machines — the wires connect to electrodes placed on his head — and he is asked to go about some familiar and simple task while the technicians from time to time artificially cause him to have a variety of beliefs he would otherwise not have had. Presumably, some of these induced beliefs will prove quite irritating to S, since they will startle and interfere with whatever task he has been set.

Now suppose that the technicians decide to amuse themselves by inducing beliefs in S which have to do with elements of his task. S's task is to figure out the correct place for specific objects, and he is given different clues to help him in this endeavor. As he pieces the clues together, his evidence mounts in favor of the proposition that the correct place for a certain object is, say, in the corner. At some point in this evidence-gathering procedure, S comes to believe that the corner is the correct place for that object; and, at some late point in the evidence-gathering process, S comes to know that the corner is the correct place for that object. Moreover, this is knowledge he has on the basis of the evidence he has accumulated.

Unknown to S, the technicians have caused him to have the belief that the corner is the correct place for that object. He thinks that they have not induced beliefs in him for some time, since on all other occasions they have induced beliefs at odd moments and the beliefs have had nothing at all to do with his task. S believes justifiably that his belief that the object belongs in the corner ($= h$) is a result of his evidence-gathering; more specifically, of his beliefs concerning his evidence. S, that is, has evidence which he justifiably takes to be good evidence for his belief, and he justifiably takes himself to believe that h as a (causal) result of his beliefs concerning the evidence. But S is mistaken about the latter; the technicians have caused his belief that h.

One further refinement rounds out the example. We suppose that there are different technicians participating in the work, each of whom has a 'belief-inducer button' which he or she can push. Their respective machines are wired together in such a way that if one fails, the next one in the series induces the chosen belief. If the latter fails, then the third induces the belief; and so on. Each technician pushes his belief-inducer button at the same time as the others, and S is caused to have the belief that h by the machine of the first technician. However, had this machine not induced his belief that h, his beliefs concerning his evidence would not have done so either. The next machine in the series would have induced the belief instead. Hence, with belief-basing construed as in (9.1), statement (11) is false. Moreover, had we modified (10) along the lines of (9.1), the resulting interpretation of (11) would also have fallen to this example.

There are several lines open if one wants to contest this example,[14] but the most likely response would be that in the situation described S lacks knowledge that h. After all, one might say, there is no connection between his believing the evidence and his belief that h, so how could it be that S knows that h on the basis of the evidence he has?[15]

The reply to this objection is that there is a connection between S's beliefs about his evidence and his belief that h; it is just not the sort of connection specified in (9) or (9.1). S takes himself to believe that h as a result of his beliefs concerning his evidence. Moreover, he is fully justified in taking him-self to believe that h for that reason since he is fully justified in believing that the technicians are and have been leaving him alone. Further, he is justified in believing his evidence, and the evidence he has is good evidence for h.

We could say that in the example presented the wanted connection is that

S takes his belief that *h* to be based on his evidence in the sense of (9), and he is fully justified in taking his belief that *h* to be so based. And this, I think, is enough to insure, given the other factors already specified, that *S* knows that *h*.

If this example has merit, notice that it will also work against analogs of (9) and (9.1) that are stated in terms of reasons rather than believed evidence. *S* need only justifiably believe of himself that he believes that *h* as a causal result of having whatever reasons he then has. His actual reasons need not be a cause for his belief, nor even a potential cause of the sort described in (9.1).

If we take the notion of a reason broadly enough so that it includes understanding a proposition, then we might want to say tht a person's belief that *h* is causally based on a reason the person has. Thus, consider the example just given of the experiment. Although the belief that *h* is induced by the machines, we might say that the appropriate electrical stimulation is not *the* (sole) cause of *S*'s belief that *h*. For, *S* has to be in a position to understand the proposition in question. And, if we think of *S* prior to acquiring the belief that *h* as being in a state of understanding *h*, then we might say that this understanding-state of *S* is *a* cause of his belief that *h*, even when the belief that *h* is induced by the machine. Construing this understanding-state as a reason would then allow us to say that in all cases of knowing on the basis of reasons, at least one reason is *a* cause of one's belief, and in that sense one's belief is based on one's reasons. However, I take it that this is not an epistemically interesting notion of belief-basing since it is too broad a notion, applying to all belief formation.

We have thus far not found any notion of belief-basing which is adequate to render (4) or (11) true. Nor have we found any notion of belief-basing stated in terms of reasons which fares any better in this regard. So, since I know of no other appropriate notions of belief-basing, I tentatively conclude that knowing on the basis of evidence or reasons does not require having one's belief based on the evidence or reasons, despite the fact that intuitively and initially just the opposite would seem more nearly correct.

3. JUSTIFICATION BASING

Often a person's justified belief is justified on the basis of evidence or reasons the person has. Such justification-basing, as I shall call it, it seemingly distinct from both inferential-basing and belief-basing. And, it seems clear that knowing on the basis of evidence or reasons requires some justification-basing relation. That is, there would seem to be some sense of 'justified on the basis of evidence' (or reasons), such that

(12) S knows that h on the basis of evidence e which he has (or reasons r) *only if*: S's justification for belief that h is based on e (or r).

Under which construal, or construals, of justification-basing is (12) true?

To help answer this question, we can consider two proposals. The first is this:

(13) S's justification for belief that h is based on evidence e *if and only if*: (a) h is inferentially based on e; and, (b) S believes that e; and, (c) S is justified in believing that e.[16]

And the second, similar to a view once proposed by Pollock,[17] is as follows:

(14) S's justification for believing that h is based on evidence e *if and only if*: (a) h is inferentially based on e; and, (b) S knows that h is inferentially based on e; and, (c) S knows that e is good evidence for h; and, (d) S justifiably believes that e.

Clauses (b) and (c) of (14) make it much stronger than (13). Statement (14), we might say, requires that S be a perspicacious epistemic agent, since he must be aware of his evidence and be aware of a crucial connection between his evidence and the proposition he believes, viz., h. In fact, we can put even stronger requirements on S's perspicacity by insisting that he know that e, and perhaps that he reason from e to h in some conscious fashion. But these conditions are clearly too strong. Statement (13), in contrast, places no special demand on S's perspicacity, since he need not be aware of any connection between his evidence and h.

I think that many accounts of what it is to be justified on the basis of evidence one has can be scaled according to the degree of perspicacity they require of the subject. But neither of the end points of the scale, which I will here take as expressed by (13) and (14), is adequate.

When interpreted along the lines of (14), the claim made in (12) is false. Moreover, (14) is inadequate as an account of justification-basing independently of (12). For it is easy to think of cases of persons such as small children who have knowledge and justified beliefs based on evidence they have, but who also fail to meet clauses (b) and (c) of (14). The account given by (13), though sufficient to render (12) true when the latter is restricted to justification based on evidence, is too weak. Consider a case in which S has evidence e which he does in fact believe with ample justification, where he also believes that h and h is inferentially based on e, but where S consciously based his belief that h not on e or his belief that e, but on something else, say his astrological charts, Here S decides to believe that h because his astrological charts have a certain character but, we may imagine, he has no warrant whatever for thinking that his charts are evidence for h and indeed they are not. Here we would deny that S's belief that h is justified on the basis of e since, I surmise, we would agree that S is not in fact justified in his belief that h. Yet, all three conditions of (13) are satisfied.

Given these considerations, it becomes natural to think that we should agreement (13) with some account of belief-basing. That is, we should observe that,

(15) S's justification for belief that h is based on evidence e *only if*:
         S's belief that h is based on evidence e.

But, although tempting, (15) is to be rejected. For, given (12), (15) ensures that S knows that h on the basis of evidence e only if S's belief that h is based on e. However, in Section 2, it was argued that the latter claim, viz., (4), is dubious. Furthermore, the considerations adduced earlier concerning (4) can be utilized to undermine (15) independently of the latter's insertion into (13).

We want there to be some connection between S's having evidence e and his justification for believing h. Given that we have rejected (15) and rejected, *inter alia*, strong perspicacity demands, it might seem that there is nowhere else to seek the appropriate connection. However, there is one way to proceed here which is suggested by our earlier psychological experiment example. There we rejected a causal version of belief-basing by means of an example in which S took himself to believe that h on the (causal) basis of believing his evidence and his so doing was justified. Suppose, now, we add to (13) two clauses corresponding to these matters, so that what results are:

(13d) S takes himself to believe that h as a (causal) result of believing
         that e;

(13e) S is justified in taking himself to believe that h as a (causal) result
         of believing that e.

These two clauses add a weak perspicacity requirement to (13), requirements which still leave (13) considerably weaker than (14). Even so, it might be argued, (13) is still too strong, since there will be cases of a person's belief being justified on the basis of evidence he or she then has but where clause (d) is not satisfied. Once again the example of small children would be sufficient to show that so construed (13) is dubious.

To help meet this objection we need to say something about taking. In one sense a taking is an occurrent believing; it is in this sense that the small children example is forceful against (13) by falsifying (13d). A person might also be said to take himself to believe that h is a result of believing that e in the sense that were he to consider why he believes that h, then he would occurrently believe that he believes that *h* as a result of believing that *e*. With taking understood in these two senses, I am included to think that the small children problem is largely met. There is, though, another problem facing (13), having to do with immediate or non-inferential justification.

Suppose we construe a person's belief that *h* as immediately, non-inferentially justified just in case the belief that *h* is justified and it would be justified even if it were not justified on the basis of evidence. Even so, all five conditions of (13) might be met by a non-inferentially justified belief. Thus, imagine that a person believes that he then feels a pain. If he is attentive to his current mental going-on and not impaired with respect to making judgments about them, and he then believes that he then feels a pain, then it is reasonable to hold that he is justified in this belief even though he is not justified on the basis of any evidence. But imagine that *S* is wired into a cerebroscope which is reading his brain events, that there are well established correlations holding between occurrences of specific brain events and occurrences of pain, that *S* knows about these correlations and knows that he is wired into a normally functioning machine. In such a case, *S* has evidence concerned with the machine readings in support of his belief that *h*, his evidence inductively supports *h*, and *S* is justified in believing his evidence. Moreover, *S* might believe that his belief concerning his evidence is a partial cause of his belief that *h* and be justified in believing this if, for instance, he had good reason to think that in most cases his beliefs were causal products of his total evidence. Still, *S*'s belief that *h* is immediate, non-inferentially justified since it would be justified even if it were not justified on the basis of all of this evidence derived from the machine readings and *S*'s background knowledge. The conditions noted in (13), even if individually necessary, are not jointly sufficient for justification based on evidence.

I think the foregoing problem can be handled by adding one more clause to (13), namely,

(13f)   *S* would not be justified in believing *h* if he were not justified in believing *e*.

Not only is (13), with clauses (a) through (f), a plausible account of justification-basing, but, I believe, with it statement (12) is true.[18]

SUMMARY

Philosophers who have spoken of knowing based on evidence or reasons have often had in mind different notions of basings. Three notions of basing have been distinguished, but of these only two seem required if one is to know on the basis of one's evidence or reasons. Contrary to what one would have expected initially, we have found that there is no notion of belief-basing such that one knows on the basis of evidence or reasons only if one's belief is based on that evidence or reasons.[19]

NOTES

[1] On epistemic derivability, see M. Swain, 'Epistemic Defeasibility,' *American Philosophical Quarterly,* 11, (1974); reprinted in G. Pappas & M. Swain, eds., *Essays on Knowledge and Justification*, (Ithaca: Cornell University Press, 1978).

[2] See M. Swain, 'Reasons, Causes and Knowledge,' *Journal of Philosophy,* 65 (May, 1978), 230.

[3] *Ibid.*

[4] The word 'appropriate' is a fudge word with which I will not try to deal.

[5] K. Lehrer, 'Knowledge, Truth and Evidence,' in M. Roth & L. Galis, eds., *Knowing*, (New York: Random House), 1970, p. 56.

[6] Swain, 'Reasons, Causes and Knowledge,' *op. cit.*, pp. 229–230. Compare G. Harman, *Thought*, (Princeton: Princeton University Press), 1973, Chapter 2.

[7] See Harman, *op. cit.*

[8] *Ibid.*, Chapter 5.

[9] For instance Swain's, provided in 'Epistemic Defeasibility,' *op. cit.*

[10] Lehrer, 'Knowledge, Truth and Evidence' in Roth & Galis, *op. cit.*, p. 56. Compare Lehrer, *Knowledge*, (London: Oxford University Press) 1974, pp. 156–157.

[11] Elsewhere, Lehrer notes this point; see *Knowledge*, pp. 156–157.

[12] Lehrer raises a similar objection in a related context. See *Knowledge*, p. 157.

[13] Statement (9.1) expresses something close to what Marshall Swain calls 'causal pseudo-overdetermination;' see his 'Reasons, Causes and Knowledge,' *op. cit.*, or his 'Justification and the Basis of Belief' in this volume. I assume a similar but more complex amendment can be made in(10), but a consideration of (9.1) will suffice for our purposes.

[14] Another line would be to appeal to D. Davidson's theory of anomalous monism, and to his claim that there are no psycho-physical laws. See his paper, 'Mental Events' in J. Swanson & L. Foster, eds., *Experience and Theory*, (Amherst: University of Massachusetts Press), 1970. For criticism of Davidson's view see W. Lycan & G. Pappas, *Materialism*, (forthcoming).

[15] This is the objection presented most forcefully at the conference.

[16] See Fred Dretske, *Seeing and Knowing*, (New York: Humanities), 1969, for a defense of an account similar to (13). For criticism, see B. Aune's review in *Philosophical Review*, 80, (July, 1971).

[17] See J. Pollock, 'The Structure of Epistemic Justification,' *American Philosophical Quarterly*, Monograph Series, # 4, (1970), pp. 64–66. Compare Pollock's account of implicit reasons in *Knowledge and Justification*, (Princeton: Princeton University Press), 1974.

[18] I here omit the issue of justification based on reasons.

[19] I am indebted to Marshall Swain and the late James Cornman for helpful advice and criticism. I am responsible for all of the mistake that remain, however.

KEITH LEHRER

THE GETTIER PROBLEM AND THE ANALYSIS
OF KNOWLEDGE

The problem that Edmund Gettier formulated is, I believe, still unsolved.[1] It has been explored and developed to such an extent that it is worthwhile stating just what the problem is. It is, in my opinion, the problem of showing that a falliblistic theory of epistemic justification is possible. For, the problem arises in certain cases in which a person is justified, whether he knows it or not, in believing or accepting some false proposition which transmits justification to some true proposition. Thus, for a Cartesian who held that epistemic justification must proceed from what is certain by certain steps to arrive at what is known, the problem would not arise. For a philosopher who avers, as I do, that epistemic justification is fallible, the problem is to articulate a theory of falliable epistemic justification which allows us to distinguish between those cases in which justification, though fallible, yields knowledge, and those in which some false proposition deprives one of obtaining knowledge from justification. I shall present an analysis of knowledge and theory of justification incorporating a fourth condition to solve the problem Gettier raised.

1. THE ANALYSIS OF KNOWLEDGE

To formulate my solution to the Gettier problem, I shall introduce some familiar notions which I shall use in a special way. On the analysis of knowledge I wish to defend, S knows that h if and only if (i) h, (ii) S accepts h, (iii) h is evident for S, and (iv) there is no false proposition f such that if f were doubtful for S, then h would not be evident for S. The terms of this definition are, in the first three conditions, taken from Chisholm, but I intend to use them in my own way.[2]

2. ACCEPTANCE AND BELIEF

Let us first consider acceptance. A person may accept something he believes, but he may also accept something he does not believe, and he may refuse to accept something he does believe. To accept a proposition in this context means to assent to it when one's only purpose is to assent to what is true and

George S. Pappas (ed.), Justification and Knowledge, 65–78.
Copyright © 1979 by D. Reidel Publishing Company.

to refuse to assent to what is false. What a person believes is not entirely up to him. One is endowed with certain beliefs, and one may conclude that some of what one believes one should not accept as a truth seeker. One person may find, for example, that he believes that someone is tenderly concerned about his welfare, but, looking at the evidence, conclude that this is probably not true. He wishes it to be so with such fervor that he cannot help but believe it nonetheless. Similarly, there may be something that is so distasteful for a second person to believe that he cannot do so, even though the person becomes aware that it is evidently true. In the quest for truth, the first person might refuse to assent to what he believes, and the second might assent to what he does not believe. In this way, acceptance may differ from belief.

This distinction is of some importance in judging whether a person knows, for philosophers have erroneously held a person who believes something from irrational motives lacks knowledge. This is a mistake. A person may believe something for the wrong reasons, perhaps he cannot help but do so, and, nevertheless, know that it is true because he assents to it for the right reasons. A person may believe something because the stars or the tarot deck tell him it is so, but in the quest for truth, he may assent to it on proper grounds. The man, then, accepts the proposition as well as believing it to be true, and the reasons for which he accepts it may lead us to conclude that the third and fourth conditions of knowledge are satisfied.

This distinction between belief and acceptance also vitiates those causal theories of knowledge that maintain that whether a person knows something to be true depends on the causal relation between a person believing something and the fact that is is so. Belief may arise in particular and sundry ways, but no matter how a person comes to believe something, and no matter how his belief is sustained, he may know that what he believes is true if he accepts the proposition in question on proper grounds.

Drawing upon an analogy suggested by Dennett, one might think of relation between belief and acceptance in a way similar to the way one thinks of the relation between desire and choice.[3] A person finds himself with a natural endowment of desires and beliefs at any given moment which he may not be able to alter immediately. But one may refuse to accept what one cannot help but believe just as one may refuse to choose what one cannot help but desire. To borrow from Descartes, it is as though we find ourselves with a basket of apples, some of which we picked and others of which were given to us, and we face the problem of sorting through the collection to decide which ones are good to eat and which are not. We sort through our collection of desires and beliefs to decide which desires should be acted on and which ones not, and we sort through our beliefs to decide which ones should receive our assent and which ones not.

3. THE EVIDENT

With these remarks concerning acceptance, let us turn to the question of what is epistemically justified or evident for a person. Whether a proposition is evident for a person depends, I maintain, on how well the proposition fares in conflict with other propositions. Thus, I propose that h is evident for S if and only if, for any proposition c that competes with h for S, either h beats c for S or c is neutralized with respect to h for S. To elucidate this definition, we shall have to explicate what it means to say that a proposition competes with, beats, or neutralizes another. I shall take as primitive for this discussion a comparative notion of epistemic reasonableness. Thus, I shall say that one epistemic state is more reasonable than another, for example, that accepting a proposition is more reasonable than accepting another. This is Chisholm's strategy. However, I do this only for convenience. Epistemic reasonableness is epistemic expected utility, and the latter may be explicated in terms of probability and utility.

4. COMPETITION

To elucidate the definiens of the definition given above, let us first turn to the notion of a competitor. A proposition need not contradict another to conflict with it. The proposition that I am now undergoing intensive hallucination does not contradict the proposition that I am now seeing a table because one may see objects when oen is hallucinating. But the proposition that I am hallucinating in this way competes with the proposition that I am now seeing a table in that the former deprives that latter of epistemic status. If I am now hallucinating, then it is not as reasonable for me to accept that I see a table as it would be if I were not hallucinating. Thus, a competitor of a proposition is one that diminishes the epistemic worth or reasonableness of accepting the proposition. I am certain that I am not now hallucinating, and I am also certain that I see a table before me. Suppose, on the contrary, that I were certain that I *was* now hallucinating. In that case it would be less reasonable for me to accept that I now see a table. It would be by no means certain that I do.

These reflections suggest the following definition of competition: c competes with h if and only if it would be less reasonable for S to accept h if *c* were certain for *S* than if the denial of *c* were certain for *S*. We may here define certainty as Chisholm does and say that *k* is certain for *S* if and only if it is more reasonable for *S* to accept *k* than not to, and there is no proposition that it is more reasonable for *S* to accept than *k*. The certain is the maximally reasonable.[4]

5. BEATING AND NEUTRALIZING

We must say what it is for a proposition to be beaten or neutralized. As definitions, I propose that if *c* competes with *h* for *S*, then *h* beats *c* if and only if it is more reasonable for *S* to accept *h* than to accept *c*, and *c* is neutralized with respect to *h* for *S* if and only if there is some proposition *n* such that the conjunction of *n* and *c* does not compete with *h* for *S* and it is as reasonable for *S* to accept the conjunction as it is for him to accept just *c*.

Let me illustrate the implications of these definitions. For a proposition to be evident for a person, the proposition must meet two kinds of skeptical challenge. The first is one that comes from a skeptic who advances a hypothesis that contradicts what a person claims to know. If a skeptic claims that I am not now seeing but am asleep and dreaming, I shall reply to him that it is more reasonable for me to accept the proposition that I now see a table than to accept the proposition that he avers to be true. That reply would require defense before the skeptic would be satisfied, but the reply is, as stated, perfectly true. This means that a competitor that the skeptic suggests is beaten by the proposition I claim to know.

A more subtle skeptical challenge might have to be neutralized rather than beaten. For a subtle skeptic might remark, when I claim to know that I now see a table, that people sometimes dream such things. That people sometimes dream such things competes with the proposition that I now see a table, and it is by no means obvious that it is more reasonable for me to accept the latter than the former. This skeptic has challenged my claim to know without contradicting the proposition that I now see a table. He has attempted to defeat my claim to know, not by contradicting the proposition that I now see a table, but by diminishing the claim by innuendo, by reminding me of something that I know to be true which seems to diminish the reasonableness of my claim. What he says is perfectly true, and it does compete with what I aver. How should I reply?

This sort of information cannot be beaten, but it may be neutralized. For, the innuendo is that I am now dreaming. If I am not now dreaming, then the fact that people sometimes dream that they see tables loses its competitive force. The conjunction of the propositions that people sometimes dream they see tables and that I am not now dreaming does not compete with the proposition that I now see a table. Moreover, it is as reasonable for me to accept the conjunction as it is for me to accept the skeptic's remark alone. So the remark of the skeptic, though not beaten, is neutralized. Many skeptical challenges must be dealt with by neutralization.

A remark here is necessary about my claim that it is as reasonable for me to accept the conjunction as it is for me to accept just the skeptic's claim that people sometimes dream. The skeptic might reply that his claim is more reasonable because it is less likely to be false than the conjunction of his claim and mine. For a conjunction like this one is less probable than a conjunct within it. My answer is that the probability of error is not the only relevant consideration, and the assumption that it is so gives unnecessary succor to the skeptic. For, as truth seekers, we are interested not only in avoiding error, we are also interested in getting hold of truth. The greater the content of a proposition, the more truth we obtain when it is true. Thus, expected epistemic utility or reasonableness of accepting a proposition is a function of our interest in content and our interest in avoiding error. These two objectives must be balanced one against the other. We want to avoid error in the story we tell, but we want to tell the whole story. A conjunction can be no more reasonable to accept than the least reasonable conjunct, but it may be just as reasonable as the least reasonable conjunct. Since it is so improbable that I am now dreaming, the epistemic utility of accepting that I am not together with the skeptical remark outweighs epistemic utility of accepting just the latter. The conjunction is more informative, surely, and the added risk of error is worth taking.

It might appear that the appeal to content would allow a skeptic to concoct an unbeatable competitor for any hypothesis or a dogmatist to fabricate an artificial neutralizer. For, suppose that a skeptic has a competitor c for h which is beaten by h. The skeptic could conjoin to c a proposition p, which, though irrelevant to h, is virtually immune from error and highly informative. Then the conjunction of c and p would compete with h and more effectively so, one might think, because the conjunction is so much more informative than the c alone. Similarly, a dogmatist trying to find some proposition n to neutralize a competitor c might conjoin some irrelevant information to a neutralizing proposition attempting to bolster the reasonableness of it. The addition of irrelevant information by either the skeptic or the dogmatist is a sort of smokescreen intended to obscure the relevant weakness of a competitor or neutralizer. However, such a ruse will be ineffective. For, as we noted above, a conjunction can be no more reasonable than the least reasonable conjunct of it just as a chain can be no stronger than the weakest link of it. The light of reason clears the smokescreen when we note that the conjunction of c and p concocted by the skeptic can be no more reasonable than c alone. Hence, if h beats c, then h will also beat the conjunction of c and p in spite of the informativeness of p. Similarly, if the intended neutralizer n fabricated by the dogmatist contains a proposition r that is relevant to the original competitor c but less reasonable than c, and another irrelevant but informative proposition q that is more reasonable than c, the proposition n will be no more reasonable than r, and, therefore, less reasonable than c. A smokescreen of irrelevant information is epistemically impotent.

It is perhaps worth noting that some of the foregoing ideas are relevant to historical epistemological disputes. Thomas Reid claimed that perceptual claims such as that I see that there is a table are certain, indeed, as certain as the more cautions claim that I *think* I see that there is a table.[5] The latter is less likely to be erroneous than the former. So how can the former be as certain as the latter? If we suppose that informativeness is an epistemic virtue, then we may defend Reid by saying that the perceptual claim, that I see that there is a table, though more likely to be in error than the claim that I think that I see that there is a table, is also more informative, and hence equally reasonable in epistemic terms. The greater content balances the greater risk of error, and the result is maximal reasonableness. This claim may be controverted, but it does show how we may defend claims that propositions are certain or evident even though there is some risk of error in accepting them.

6. THE GETTIER PROBLEM: A FOURTH CONDITION

With this discussion of the notion of evidence before us, let us turn to the Gettier problem. The fourth condition I propose is as follows:

(iv)   There is no f such that f is false and such that if f were doubtful for S, then h would not be evident for S.[6]

I use the expression 'doubtful' in a technical sense. It is that f is doubtful for S if and only if it is more reasonable for S to decline f than to accept f. To say that S declines f means that he does not accept f but leaves open the question of whether he accepts the denial of f.

A number of philosophers suggest the following sort of condition, though sometimes in other terms, which I think is defective.

(ive)   There is no f such that f is false and such that if the falsity of f were evident for S, then h would not be evident for S.[7]

One way of explaining the advantage of the condition I propose is to show how it remedies a defect in (ive). There are two problems with (ive) that are paramount. The first concerns misleading evidence, and the second concerns extraneous information.

7. MISLEADING EVIDENCE

For an example of misleading evidence, consider the case of Tom Grabit that Paxson and I proposed.[8] The example is one in which I see Tom Grabit, a student in a very small class of six members, take a book off the shelf in a library, conceal it beneath his coat, and walk out of the library. I know that Tom Grabit took a book out of the library. Now suppose that, quite unknown to me, Mr. Grabit, Tom's father, is just now remarking that Tom Grabit is not in Tucson today (where I am) and that his identical twin John is in Tucson, indeed, at the library. With only this much of the story told, some might doubt whether I really do know that Tom Grabit took a book out of the library. However, Mr. Grabit is entirely demented, talking only to an imaginary person in a room in the mental hospital. There is no brother John, and Mr. Grabit has no information whatever concerning the whereabouts of Tom. Since Mr. Grabit's remarks were heard by no one, they are not testimony in the public domain. Moreover, we may imagine that if anyone were to ask Mr. Grabit where Tom is today he would stare blankly in catatonic silence. The mere coincidental remark of Mr. Grabit about Tom surely fails to show that I do not know that I saw Tom Grabit take a book out of the library.

Let us consider how conditions (iv) and (ive) deal with this case. Let m be the proposition that Tom Grabit was not in Tucson today and that his identical twin brother was in town at the library. Mr. Grabit said that m. Each condition asks us to evaluate the statement

    (c)   It is not evident for me that Tom Grabit took a book from the library,

given a counterfactual assumption. Condition (ive) asks up to consider the assumption equivalent to

    (ae)   It is evident for me that Mr. Grabit said that m.

While conditions (iv) asks us to consider the condition

    (a)   It is doubtful for me that Mr. Grabit did not say that m,

where the latter means that declining the proposition that Mr. Grabit did not say that m is more reasonable than accepting that Mr. Grabit did not say that m.

Assumption (a) is one that would already have been fulfilled in the original case. When I see Tom Grabit take the book from the library, I do not know anything about Mr. Grabit, not even that such a person lives. In this circumstance, declining propositions about Mr. Grabit is surely more reasonable than accepting such propositions. I have no information that would make it reasonable for me to accept any proposition about what Mr. Grabit might or might not say. Thus, assuming that it is evident for me that Tom Grabit took the book, which it is, assumption (a) introduces no epistemic alternation. Therefore, condition (iv) is satisfied. My analysis is, therefore, consistent with the correct conclusion that I know that Tom took a book from the library.

But the situation is different with respect to (ae) and condition (ive). For if it were to become evident to me that Mr. Grabit said that Tom was not in Tucson and that his identical twin John was in Tucson at the library, then it would no longer be evident for me that it was Tom who took the book from the library. For, I have no other information about Mr. Grabit. It is as though some completely dependable person told me that Mr. Grabit said what he did and then the informant left without giving any other information about Mr. Grabit. I have no reason to think Mr. Grabit is lying or ignorant or that his remarks are in any way deceptive. In short, I have no way of neutralizing the proposition that Mr. Grabit said that m which competes with the proposition that Tom Grabit took the book from the library. If we attempt to neutralize it with the proposition that Mr. Grabit is lying or misinformed, we fail. It is by no means evident that this is so and, by assumption, it is evident that Mr. Grabit said that m. Thus (ive) is not satisfied in this case, and the analysis containing it yields the incorrect result that I do not know that Tom took the book.

8. EXTRANEOUS INFORMATION

Let us now consider the case of extraneous information. Suppose I am sitting in my office and begin to put away some implements in my office. I put my pen in the middle drawer in my desk, knowing that I do this, and then put the manuscript I was working on in the top drawer of the filing cabinet, knowing that I do this. I would claim to know that my pen is in the middle drawer of my desk and the manuscript is in the top drawer of my filing cabinet. Now imagine that, quite unknown to me, a workman came in to repair my desk, leaving a hole in the back of the drawer so that, unknown to me, the pen slipped into the opening and fell out of the drawer. I do not know that the pen is in the middle drawer of my desk because it is not there.

I do know that my manuscript is in the top drawer of my filing cabinet, having placed it there.

Condition (ive) yields the incorrect result that I do not know that the manuscript is in the top drawer of my filing cabinet, while condition (iv) yields the correct result that I do know this. Consider the conjunctive proposition, k, that my fountain pen is in the middle drawer of my desk and my manuscript is in the top drawer of the filing cabinet. That conjunction is false because the proposition about the pen is false. Consider the following two assumptions to evaluate (ive) and (iv) respectively:

(ae)   It is evident for me that it is false that k.

(a)   It is doubtful for me that k.

The question is whether we would conclude from these assumptions that

(c)   It is not evident for me that my manuscript is in the top drawer of my filing cabinet.

Now (ae) amounts to the assumption that it is evident for me that either the pen is not in the middle drawer of the desk or the manuscript is not in the top drawer of the filing cabinet. That proposition competes with the proposition that my manuscript is in the top drawer of my filing cabinet. Can it be neutralized? One way to neutralize it would be with the proposition that my pen is not in the middle drawer of my desk. But I have no way, from the evidence I possess, of deciding whether I am wrong about the whereabouts of the pen or the manuscript. Consequently, I cannot reason from my evidence that my manuscript is in the top drawer of my filing cabinet.

Now consider assumption (a). Here we are required to assume that declining k is more reasonable than accepting k. We are not required to assume that it is *evident* that k is false. Since the proposition that k is false is not evident on this assumption, I may reason that the proposition that my manuscript is in the top drawer of the filing cabinet because I put it there. The assumption that declining k is more reasonable than accepting k does not render it evident or even reasonable to suppose that k is false. Hence, the denial of k, which competes with the proposition that my manuscript is is the top drawer of the filing cabinet, is easy enough to neutralize. The proposition that I put my manuscript in the top drawer of the filing cabinet will neutralize the denial of k. The conjunction of that proposition and the denial of k is surely as reasonable to accept as the denial of k alone.

Perhaps a less technical way of representing the difference between (ive) and (iv) would be helpful. To that end, imagine that some completely reliable person tells me after examining the two drawers in question that conjunction k is false. That would make it evident for me that I was wrong about either the location of the pen or manuscript. It would not, then, be evident for me that the manuscript is in the top drawer of the filing cabinet. This result corresponds to condition (ive). Imagine now that the man who tells me this often enjoys fooling me on such matters and I cannot ever tell when he is deceiving me. Declining the conjunction is more reasonable than accepting it, but it might remain evident for me that the manuscript is in the top drawer of the filing cabinet. I put it there, after all. This result corresponds to condition (iv).

9. GETTIER COUNTEREXAMPLES

Having argued that condition (iv) allows us to say that we know when we do know, does it rule out typical Gettier counterexamples? Take the case in which I have strong evidence that Nogot, who is in my class, owns a Ford, no evidence that anyone else does, but Havit, who is also in my class, owns a Ford, quite unknown to me, and Nogot does not. I do not know that someone in my class owns a Ford. Condition (iv) asks us to consider the assumption that declining the proposition that Mr. Nogot owns a Ford is more reasonable than accepting that Mr. Nogot owns a Ford. This has the effect of blocking my reasoning from the evidence for Nogot owning a Ford to the conclusion that someone in my class owns a Ford. We have evidence that seems to make it evident that Mr. Nogot owns a Ford. We have his testimony, seen him drive the car, examined documents, and so forth. But in spite of that we must assume that it is more reasonable to decline the proposition that Nogot owns a Ford than to accept that proposition. This can only mean that evidence is in some way deceptive. Otherwise it would be evident for me that Nogot owns a Ford.

The proposition that evidence we have that Nogot owns a Ford is deceptive competes with the proposition that someone in the room owns a Ford. Moreover, it cannot be neutralized. That Nogot owns a Ford anyway is not as reasonable for me to accept given our assumption as the proposition that my evidence about Nogot owning a Ford is deceptive. Thus, the proposition that Nogot owns a Ford, when taken in conjunction with the proposition that my evidence about Nogot owning a Ford is deceptive, is not as reasonable for me to accept as the simple proposition about the evidence being deceptive. In short, given our assumption, it is very reasonable for me to accept that my evidence is deceptive. Because it is so reasonable to accept that, potential neutralizers of that proposition fail. Condition (iv) is not satisfied and this explains why I do not know that someone in my class owns a Ford.

A slight modification of this counterexample reveals the superiority of condition (iv) to other methods for dealing with the Gettier problem. Other solutions depend on the assumption that the proposition that someone in my class owns a Ford is *inferred* from the proposition that Nogot owns a Ford or that I *believe* that Nogot owns a Ford.[9] These solutions require that justification not be based essentially on any false belief or lemma of inference. However, we can modify the example so that no false lemma or belief is involved. Suppose that in the previous example I am asked whether I know that there is a Ford owner in my class. I claim that I do know this. It is then suggested to me that I claim to know this because I believe that Nogot owns a Ford, or because I inferred my conclusion from that premise. But I demur. I point out that, though I do have excellent evidence that Nogot owns a Ford, I have not been asked whether I know that *he* owns a Ford, and so there is no need for me to take a stand on that issue. For, I note, even though my primary evidence for claiming to know that there is a Ford owner in my class is the evidence I have concerning Nogot, there are many other members of the class, and, if by some odd quirk it should turn out that Nogot does not own a Ford, someone else in the class might own one. Thus, even if the proposition that Nogot owns a Ford should happen to be false, I might still be correct in claiming that someone in my class owns a Ford. So I choose to decline the proposition that Nogot owns a Ford, in order to guard against the remote chance of being in error there. I need not commit myself on that proposition in order to claim that *someone* in my class owns a Ford. My inference proceeds directly from my evidence, which consists of propositions I know to be true. This is, in fact, the reply that Gettier gave to Harman when the latter claimed that the problem can be solved by requiring that the inference to a conclusion not involve a false lemma.[10]

The method for dealing with the original Nogot example based on condition (iv) works equally well for the modified example. The proposition that Nogot owns a Ford is false whether or not it is believed or is a lemma of inference. Since it is false, we must ask whether the proposition that someone in my class owns a Ford remains evident for me on the assumption that it is doubtful for me that Nogot owns a Ford. If that is doubtful, then, again, my evidence must be deceptive, because the evidence I have for that proposition would, if not deceptive, render it evident and not at all doubtful. Then, as before, the proposition that my evidence is doubtful cannot be beaten or neutralized. Again, (iv) is not satisfied.

It is worth noting in passing that condition (iv) is not so strong that it yields the result that a person lacks knowledge when there is a good inferential chain as well as a defective inferential chain to a conclusion. Thus, if the situation concerning Nogot is as before, I have good evidence he owns a Ford, though he does not, but I also *know* that Havit, who is also in my class, owns a Ford, it will turn out that I know that someone in my class owns a Ford. We shall have to consider the consequences of declining on the proposition that both Nogot and Havit own Fords, for that proposition is false. But that does not block me from reasoning from the evidence that I have that Havit owns a Ford to the conclusion that he owns a Ford and, therefore, to the conclusion that someone in my class owns a Ford. On the assumption that it is doubtful that they both own Fords, I must concede that the evidence that they *both* own Fords is deceptive, but I need not concede that the evidence that I have that Havit owns a Ford is deceptive.

While considering modifications of the original Nogot example, I should also like to make it clear that a very simple modification of that example suffices to defeat attempts to deal with the Gettier problem in causal terms, for example, by requiring the fact that makes a proposition a person believes true be a cause of his believing it. For, it may well have occurred to some readers of the original Nogot example to wonder why Nogot should have gone to so much trouble to deceive me into believing that he owned a Ford when he did not. The answer, we may suppose, is that Nogot knows that Havit owns a Ford, and Nogot has a compulsion to try to trick people into believing true propositions by getting them to believe some false propositions. Thus, the fact that someone in my class owned a Ford caused Nogot to cause me to believe that someone in my class owned a Ford. So the fact that someone in my class owned a Ford is, indirectly, the cause of my believing that someone in my class owns a Ford. But this is still not anything I know. Moreover, the deception need not involve a human agent but might arise from some peculiarity in the natural cause of events, like a name fading in a peculiar way on a document.

There are two other cases might profitably be considered here. One is the Chisholm example in which a man who usually knows a sheep when he sees one, looks out into a field, sees a rock which looks very much like a sheep, and, consequently, takes the rock to be a sheep.[11] Let us suppose that the rock looks so much like a sheep that it is evident for him that there is a sheep in the field. Moreover, let us suppose that there is, in fact, a sheep in the field, though he does not notice this sheep. It is false that what appears to him to be a sheep is a sheep. So, by condition (iv) we consider the assumption that it is doubtful for him that what appears to him to be a sheep is a sheep. If that is doubtful for him, then appearances are misleading. The way the object appears is misleading in some way, and the proposition that it is misleading in some way cannot be beaten or neutralized. Therefore, on the assumption in question, it is not evident for the person that there is a sheep in the field. Hence, by (iv) the person does not know that there is.

Another, rather difficult, example from Skyrms, concerns the man who is striking a Sure-Fire match, a kind of match that has always lighted before when struck.[12] However, we are supposed to imagine that the person who has witnessed the perfect regularity with which Sure-Fire matches have lighted when struck has no causal hypothesis about the relation between striking and lighting. He proceeds according to the Newtonian directive of hypotheses *non fingo*. He infers from the past correlation that the present match he is about to strike will light, but without any causal assumption. The match does light, but in fact it is a defective match which only lights because some Q-radiation raises the temperature of the match. Why does he not know the present match will light if struck?

Again, this case can be dealt with in the manner of the modified Nogot case. Our condition does not require tht a person believe or infer anything from a false proposition for the falsity of that proposition to be relevant to whether the person knows. In this case, the false proposition is that the present match is in as good a condition for lighting when struck under similar circumstances as the previously observed matches. This proposition is false. Thus we must consider the consequences of assuming that it is doubtful. If it is doubtful that the match is in as good a condition for lighting when struck under similar circumstances as the previously observed Sure-Fire matches, then the evidence of the previous lighting of the other Sure-Fire matches fails to make it evident that the present match will light. Again the reasonableness of declining the proposition blocks the chain of inference from the evidence to the conclusion that the match will light. If it is more reasonable to decline than accept the proposition that this match is in as good a condition for lighting when struck under similar circumstances as the previously observed Sure-Fire matches, then it is very reasonable to accept that the evidence from previous matches may be misleading. There is no way that this proposition can be neutralized, and it competes with the proposition that the present match will light if struck. The proposition is, therefore, not evident for the man. Condition (iv) is not satisfied, and he does not know the proposition is true.

In summary, the fourth condition I have proposed requires that for a person to know something it must remain evident for him when any false proposition is assumed to be doubtful for him. This does not require that he assume that it is evident for him that the proposition is false. Moreover, the condition does not depend on the person believing or inferring anything from the false propositions that deprive him of knowledge. The false propositions, when assumed to be doubtful, block the transmission of justification from false propositions to true ones. In that way our analysis provides a falliblistic theory of epistemic justification.

NOTES

[1] Gettier, Edmund L., 'Is Justified True Belief Knowledge?' *Analysis,* **23**, 6 (1963), 121–123. Articles on the problem are collected in Roth, Michael D., and Leon Galis, eds., *Knowing: Essays in the Analysis of Knowledge*, New York: Random House, 1970. Also see the bibliography in Pappas, George S., and Swain, Marshall, eds., *Essays on Knowledge and Justification*, Ithaca: Cornell, 1978, 370–374.

[2] Chisholm, Roderick M., *Theory of Knowledge*, Englewood Cliffs,: Prentice-Hall, 1977. Note that in the foregoing definitions time references are not made explicit, but all definitions and conditions are assumed to be relativized to some specific time.

[3] Daniel Dennett formulated this idea at a Chapel Hill symposium, 1977.

[4] Chisholm, *op. cit.*, 10.

[5] Reid, Thomas, *Essays on the Intellectual Powers of Man*, 1785, Essay II, Chapter 20.

[6] The subjunctive conditional 'if f were doubtful for S, then h would not be evident for S' imbedded in (iv) may be eliminated in terms of current possible worlds analyses of such conditionals provided that consideration of possible worlds is restricted to those in which f is doubtful for S in a way that is the least unfavorable to h being evident for S.

[7] Cf. Hilpinen, Risto, 'Knowledge and Justification,' *Ajatus* **33**, 1 (1971), 7–39, and Klein, Peter D., 'A Proposed Definition of Propositional Knowledge,' *Journal of Philosophy,* **68**, 16 (1971), 471–482.

[8] Lehrer, Keith and Paxson, Thomas, Jr., 'Knowledge: Undefeated Justified True Belief,' *Journal of Philosophy,* **66**, 8 (1969), 225–237.

[9] A solution depending on inference is proposed in Harman, Gilbert, *Thought*, Princeton: Princeton University Press, 1973, and one depending on belief in Lehrer, Keith, *Knowledge*, New York: Oxford University Press, 1974.

[10] Gettier was replying to Harman at a symposium of the American Philosophical Association, Eastern Division, 1970.

[11] Chisholm, *op. cit.*, 105.

[12] Skyrms, Brian, 'The Explication of 'X knows that p'',' *Journal of Philosophy,* **64** 12 (1967), 373–389.

ERNEST SOSA

EPISTEMIC PRESUPPOSITION

What follows introduces and explains a concept of epistemic presupposition with the following features:

I.   It helps elucidate some obscure concepts essential to recent theories of knowledge and justification.

II.   It facilitates a solution to the Gettier problem.

III.   It enables a disposition of several other vexing puzzles concerning knowledge and justification.

The first three sections to follow correspond to I to III above. These three sections are intended to show the clarificatory and systematic value of the concept of epistemic presupposition, and to motivate the reader to enter the fourth and final section, Section IV. This last section provides a more detailed and precise explication of epistemic presupposition, which then serves as the core of a proposed general account of propositional knowledge.

We may plausibly view every bit of knowledge as resting on a tree of knowledge, a tree-like justificational structure that terminates and involves no essential falsehood. It may perhaps be thought that this commits one to foundationalism. And in a sense it does, but only to 'formal' foundationalism, which must be distinguished from 'substantive' foundationalism, since even radical coherentism turns out to be a kind of formal foundationalism. For the coherentist trees of justification wither down to little more than stumps, but they do not disappear. (In any case, this distinction between formal and substantive foundationalism requires more attention than it has received.)

In Sections I to III, there will be some informal references to trees of knowledge or justification. A precise explanation of the nature of these structures will be provided in Section IV. By way of informal preliminary characterization, however, let me say that these so-called trees simply trace back the justifiers of a justified belief, and the justifiers of their justifiers when these are themselves justified beliefs, and so on, back to terminating nodes none of which can involve epistemic justification: e.g., no terminating node can be a fact that some belief of the subject's is justified.

George S. Pappas (ed.), Justification and Knowledge, 79–92.
Copyright © 1979 by D. Reidel Publishing Company.

I

Several recent theories of knowledge and justification make essential use of concepts or assumptions that require further elucidation. Harman uses a notion of 'undermining evidence one does not possess,' Goldman uses a notion of 'relevant alternatives,' and I use a notion of 'being in a position to know.'

Harman's notion of 'undermining evidence' is approximately that of evidence one does not possess whose existence precludes a certain belief of one's own from being a case of knowledge.[1] Goldman's notion of a 'relevant alternative' is approximately that of a possible situation in which one would have sensory experience like that which one has in actuality but in which the causal origin of one's experience does not include a fact belief in which it prompts and justifies. But among such possible situations only *some* are 'relevant'.[2] My notion of 'being in a position to know' is approximately that of being in a position such that one has only to believe correctly and with adequate justification in order to know.[3] Each of these notions may well be of use in helping to close the gap between justified true belief and knowledge. But surely no one would deny that each admits of further elucidation, and indeed requires it.

Each of the three obscure notions can be defined or closely approximated by means of the concept of epistemic presupposition. Thus with respect to S and his justified belief that p buttressed by a certain tree of justification T, 'undermining evidence' is any fact F whose negation is epistemically presupposed according to the tree, i.e., any fact F such that some node of the tree gives a set G as S's basis for believing a proposition Q, where in believing Q on the basis of G, S presupposes not-F.

A 'relevant alternative' is approximately an alternative such that in justifiably believing that p on a basis G, one epistemically presupposes R, a proposition that would rule out one way in which that alternative might be actual, where in fact R is *false*.

One is 'in a position to know' with respect to the proposition that p iff there is a possible tree of knowledge for one and the proposition that p, i.e., a tree of justification that involves one in no false justified belief or epistemic presupposition.

These notions will be given fuller explication in Section III below, but first let us turn to the Gettier problem.

II

From some justified belief of his, S draws an intermediate conclusion C, which though justified is false, and from *C* he draws a final conclusion *H* which is true as well as being justified. Surely *S*'s belief of *H* is not knowledge. And if the only source of his justification for accepting *H* is his grounding of his belief of *H* on his justified belief of *C*, our account will explain why justified true belief of *H* does not amount of knowledge on the part of *S*. It does not thus amount of knowledge simply because all trees of justification for *S* and *H* will be defective, including as they all do a node that attributes a false belief to *S*, namely, the intermediate conclusion *C*.

Thus, if I have a justified false belief that Tom here is neurotic and deduce that someone here is neurotic, and unknown to me I myself am neurotic, then I have justified true belief that someone here is neurotic. But if the only source of my justification for my belief that someone here is neurotic is my inferring it from my justified belief that Tom here is neurotic, then our account will explain why my justified true belief that someone here is neurotic does not amount to knowledge. That belief of mine is not knowledge simply because all trees of justification for me and the proposition that someone here is neurotic are defective, including as they all do a node that attributes to me a false belief, namely, my belief that Tom here is neurotic.

It may be argued, however, that I could have bypassed the intermediate conclusion that Tom here is neurotic, thus avoiding false beliefs in arriving at a justified true belief that someone here is neurotic. And how *then* could our account explain why that justified true belief does *not* amount to knowledge?

For instance, I might have reasoned that given my evidence that Tom here is neurotic I *would* be justified in believing on that basis that Tom here is neurotic, but that since the proposition that someone here is neurotic is logically weaker it would be *safer* to believe. My neurotic need for security might then have led me to believe that someone here is neurotic while suspending judgment on whether Tom here is neurotic.

It seems clear, however, that in basing my belief that someone here is neurotic on my justified belief that constitute excellent evident that Tom here is neurotic I *presuppose* that Tom here is neurotic. For (i) those beliefs would *prima facie* ground for me that Tom here is neurotic, while (ii) my belief that someone here is neurotic would *not* (by itself) *prima facie* gound that Tom here is neurotic, and (iii) those beliefs together with my belief that Tom here is *not* neurotic would *not prima facie* ground for me that someone here is neurotic.

Once again, therefore, if my only evidence for believing that someone here is neurotic is the evidence I have for believing that Tom here is neurotic, it seems clear that every tree of justification for me and the proposition that someone here is neurotic would involve me in a false justified belief or in a false presupposition. Hence there is then no tree of knowledge for me and that proposition. And hence my belief in that proposition is no knowledge.

A Gettier case is always a case in which a justified belief that p falls short of knowledge because in some sense the subject's belief involves him with a falsehood. The Gettier problem is to specify the sense in which one's belief involves one with a falsehood. I submit that the sense in which that is so may be put more precisely by saying that every tree of justification for the subject and the proposition that p involves that subject in a false justified belief or in a false epistemic prsupposition. That is to say, every such tree *either* contains a node to the effect that S is justified in believing Q, for some false Q, or gives a set G as S's basis for believing a proposition Q such that, in believing Q on the basis of G, S presupposes a falsehood.

III

There are other troublesome cases in which a justified true belief falls short of knowledge, however, besides those in which one deduces a truth from a justified false belief. Thus there are such cases where the justified true belief is perceptually prompted and not deduced. And there are other interesting examples in addition, to which any acceptable account of propositional knowledge must be adequate. In discussing the examples to follow I will not spell out how the account of knowledge based on trees of knowledge would bear on them. Instead, let us make some simplifying assumptions that will greatly facilitate our discussion.

Each of our examples will be one in which the subject's belief of a proposition Q is based on a set G which grounds that belief for him. Let us assume that S's belief of Q is justified only because it is grounded by the set G, i.e., that S has no alternative justification for that belief. Thus, if, in believing Q on the basis of G, S presupposes a falsehood, that will be sufficient (in the context of our assumption) to show that by our account his belief of Q is no knowledge.

1.   Causal Indicators

Consider S's believing that there is a fire in the distance on a basis G that includes his observation of some smoke there, smoke that does *not* derive from the fire that is there by coincidence. S fails to know of the fire because in believing that there is a fire in the distance on the basis of G, he presupposes the falsehood that the observed smoke comes from a fire there. (That is to say, (i) G would *prima facie* ground for S that the observed smoke comes from a fire there, (ii) S's believing that there is a fire there would not alone *prima facie* ground for S that the observed smoke comes from a fire there, and (iii) the union of G and S's believing that the observed smoke does *not* come from a fire there would *not prima facie* ground for S that there is a fire there.) Thus, our account explains why S fails to know of the fire in the distance.

Many other such causal-indicator examples in the literature can be handled as is the smoke-fire example above. It may perhaps be thought, however, that while our account can deal plausibly with such cases of justified true belief that falls short of knowledge, it is in fact too strong in yielding a 'no knowledge' verdict for certain cases of actual knowledge. I will not attempt to canvass every argument to that effect that can be gleaned from the extensive literature on our topic. Let us consider only one especially difficult case.

2. Pseudo Underminers

One particularly troublesome argument derives from Harman, who points out that the claim:

(L)   If this is not a ticket that will win a trillion-ticket lottery, then not-H

is true (without regard to the content of H) with respect to one of the trillion tickets. Suppose that entirely by coincidence the claim *is* made about what happens to be the winning ticket.

Adding L to my evidence for something that I am justified in believing may well defeat my justification for that belief. And yet the fact L is, of course, not a real underminer of my justification for that belief, but only a psudo underminer. That does seem right, but surely it requires an explanation of the difference between real and pseudo undermining. Our account of epistemic presupposition helps provide the explanation.

Let us consider how our account would deal with the pseudo underminer L. ('$G \rightarrow P$' will symbolize 'G would *prima facie* ground P for S'.)

Suppose that S believes H on the basis of a set of facts G, such that G grounds H for S. And consider now not-L (i.e., that this is not a ticket that will win a trillion-ticket lottery and H). It might seem plausible that

(i) $G \rightarrow$ not-L, and

(ii)   not-$[G \cup \{S$'s believing $L\} \rightarrow H]$.

Thus it might seem that S presupposes the falsehood not-L in basing his belief of H on G. But since no restrictions have been placed on G or H, it would follow that one could not know a truth by virtue of the fact that one's belief of it is based on a basis, no matter what the basis, inasmuch as in thus basing one's belief on a basis one would inevitably presuppose the falsehood not-L.

Our account is not really subject to this difficulty, however, since its requirements for epistemic presupposition go beyond (i) and (ii) above and include *also*:

(iii)   not-$[\{S$'s believing $H\} \rightarrow$ not-$L]$.

(That is to say, if not-L is to be an epistemic presupposition that one makes in believing H on the basis of G, then in a sense H must not be epistemically prior to not-L).

But it is easy to verify that the present example violates this requirement. Therefore, we can conclude that in basing his belief of H on basis G, S does *not* after all epistemically presuppose the false not-L. Therefore L is only a pseudo-underminer of S's justification for H.

3. Relevant Alternatives

Out for a drive in the country, I see a barn nearby standing out from its surroundings in sharp focus, and thus perceptually acquire a fully justified belief that it is a barn. In both directions along my road there are numerous barn facsimiles, however, mere shells presenting to the road a facade that would draw an attribution of barnhood no less justified than my own when by luck I happen to take notice of the one real barn in the area. Surely my justified true belief that I see a barn is no knowledge. But just how do we explain why?

It may be suggested that what explains why my justified true belief falls short of knowledge is the fact that I might have been in a perceptual state just like that which now prompts my belief that I see a barn, with no barn there but only a barn facsimile. This suggestion won't do as it stands, however, for *whenever* anyone is justified in believing that he sees something of a certain sort, he might have been in perceptual state just like that which then prompts his belief that he sees something of that sort, with nothing of that sort actually there, as is shown by such familiar alternatives as those in which one is dreaming, hallucinating, or under the control of an evil demon. It may be argued that these alternatives are in some sense 'irrelevant,' whereas the alternative in which one's perceptual state is brought about by the sight of a nearby barn facsimile is 'relevant.' That does seem right, but surely it requires an explanation of the difference between relevant and irrelevant alternatives. Our account of epistemic presupposition helps provide the explanation.

Let us now consider how our account would deal with the case of the barn facsimiles. Surely (*G*) what grounds for *S* that it is a real barn he sees (*H*) would *prima facie* justify for him that if his object of sight is barnlike to the eye then it is a real barn, and in the particular example of a drive in the country his grounds would prima facie justify that conditional for him only because they would prima facie justify for him (*P*) that in that general vicinity nothing appears from the road barnlike to the eye from that distance and perspective unless it is a barn.

So we have a situation in which

(i) $G \rightarrow P$ (That is to say, *G* would *prima facie* justify *P* for *S*.)

(ii)   not-$[G \cup \{S$'s believing not-$P\} \rightarrow H]$.

(iii)   not-$[\{S$'s believing $H\} \rightarrow P]$.

Hence, in believing that it is a real barn he sees *S* epistemically presupposes the falsehood that in that general vicinity nothing appears from the road barnlike to the eye from that distance and perspective unless it is a barn. And this explains why the alternative in which his perceptual state is prompted by a nearby facsimile is relevant, and explains also why it is that despite his justified true belief he does not know that it is a real barn he sees.

4. Being in a Position to Know

Some time ago I found it plausible to recognize a type of situation where correct, fully warranted belief falls short of knowledge owing to no neglect or faulty reasoning or false belief. Despite commendable thoroughness and impeccable reasoning unspoiled by falsehood, one may still fail to be 'in a psoition to know,' because of faults in one's relevant cognitive equipment.

A good example of defective cognitive equipment is provided by deaf and blind Mr. Magoo, who survives and indeed flourishes only by incredible luck. Consider now his expectations as he breezes through a normal day narrowly avoiding disaster at every turn. If Magoo's expectations do not represent knowledge on his part, just how are they to do distinguished from ours, which presumably do amount to knowledge of our surroundings? After all, Magoo's expectations are based on a long and varied background of successful experience, or so we may assume by supposing his defects to be congenital. Shall we say that because of his defects, Magoo is simply 'not in a position to know'? That does seem right, but surely it requires an explanation of just what it is to be 'in a position to know.' Our account of epistemic presupposition helps provide the explanation.

In view of our obvious universal limitations, in gathering information about our surroundings we are generally cognizant of the fact that we inevitably overlook or are unable to grasp unaided much evidence that is relevant to the stream of beliefs in a normal day. But in froming our beliefs and assumptions on the basis of the evidence that we do grasp, we must surely assume that this evidence is not skewed but is rather representative of the total relevant evidence; and it will not do, of course, simply to assume this in the face of contrary data; in other words, we must not only just assume that the evidence we do have is representative, but must indeed be justified in making that assumption.

What grounds for us a hypothesis (H) about our surroundings (call such grounds G) would therefore presumably *prima facie* justify for us (P) that anyone more widely informed on the question whether H is the case, who also had a justified belief on that question, would also believe H unless he presupposed a falsehood. That is to say, anyone with relevant facts who formed a justified opinion on whether or not H is true on that broader basis would also believe H unless he presupposed a falsehood.

Once again we have a situation in which

(i) $G \rightarrow P$

(ii)   not-$[G \cup \{S\text{'s believing not-}P\} \rightarrow H]$.

(iii)   not-$[\{S\text{'s believing } H\} \rightarrow P]$.

Hence in expecting something (H) about his surroundings on a basis G, Magoo epistemically presupposes (P) that anyone with a grasp of a richer variety of relevant facts who formed an opinion on whether or not H is true on that broader basis would also believe H unless he presupposed a falsehood. And this presupposition of Magoo's is *false*, for anyone with good hearing and eyesight who was also cognizant of Magoo's data would justifiably disbelieve rather than believe H.

Unless we have been badly misled, the concept of epistemic presupposition can be used to throw light on a variety of much discussed puzzles and paradoxes concerning propositional knowledge. I hope that the reader will have been thus persuaded to join me in an attempt to clarify that concept and to use it in developing a more precise general account of propositional knowledge. For that is the purpose of our final section below.

IV

This section provides a more precise and detailed explication of epistemic presupposition, and embeds it in a general account of propositional knowledge.

Let A, B, and G be sets of propositions, let P and Q be propositions, and let S be a subject of thought and experience. (For convenience, time references will be left implicit.)

1. Let us take as primitive the notion of a set of propositions A being such that it *would prima facie justify* a further proposition P for a subject S, i.e., being such that if all the members of A were true that would *prima facie* justify S in believing P.

This notion taken here as primitive is of course reminiscent of W. D. Ross's concepts of *prima facie* obligation and right-making characteristics. Thus if $A = \{S$ promised to $\phi\}$ then A would *prima facie* justify ϕ'ing for S, since A is then such that if all its members were true that would *prima facie* justify S in ϕ'ing.

When a set A is such that it would *prima facie* justify a proposition P for a subject S, the joint truth of the members of A would entail that S's believing P would have a warrant-inducing property. For example, A might specify that S's believing P has a certain appropriate basis through perception, memory, or inference.

Note that often a set A that would *prima facie* justify a proposition P for a subject S is such that among its members there are propositions that attribute justification to other beliefs of S. (Consider the beach case given just after definition 5 below.)

2. A *prima facie justifies* P for S iff (i) A would *prima facie* justify P for S, and (ii) A has only true members.

3. B *overrides* A as a *prima facie* justifier of P for S iff (i) A *prima facie* justifies P for S, (ii) B has only true members, and (iii) the union of A and B does not *prima facie* justify P for S.

4. A *justifies* P for S iff (i) A *prima facie* justifies P for S, and (ii) there is no B such that B overrides A as a *prima facie* justifier of P for S.

(4'.) P is *justified* for S iff there is an A such that A justifies P for S.

(4''.) S is *justified in believing* P iff (i) S believes P, and (ii) P is justified for S.

5. A set of propositions G *would prima facie ground* a further proposition P for a subject S iff there is a set A such that
   (a) A would *prima facie* justify P for S, and
   (b) A is composed of
   (i)   the proposition that S's belief of P is (causally) based on (the members of) G, and

(ii)   for some or all of the beliefs attributed to S by members of G, proposition to the effect that S is justified in having such beliefs.

Thus consider the set of propositions $G1 = \{S$'s believing that there are footprints on the beach, S's believing that if there are footprints on the beach, someone has been walking on the beach$\}$. $G1$ would *prima facie* ground the proposition $P1$ (that someone has been walking on the beach) for S, since there *is* a set $A1$ such that

(a) $A1$ would *prima facie* justify $P1$ for S, and

(b) $A1$ is composed of

(i)   the proposition that S's belief of P is (causally) based on (the members of) $G1$, and

(ii)   for each of the beliefs attributed to S by a member of $G1$, the proposition that S is justified in having that belief.

The word 'causally' appears in parentheses because it is controversial whether or not a belief that is justified in virtue of a relation that it bears to certain other beliefs must bear to those other beliefs the relation of being caused or causally sustained by them. Since that is a controversial issue, I wish to make my accounts of epistemic presupposition and of knowledge independent of it. Thus I would ask you to understand the basing relation in such a way that causation is not necessarily involved. Indeed, let us avoid commitment to any particular basing relation. If you accept the view that a belief can be justified in virtue of its mere co-existence in a single mind with various other beliefs whether or not it is causally related to those other beliefs, then you can understand *co-existence in a single mind* as an appropriate basing relation.

Nevertheless, the fact that I do include the word 'causally' *at all* reflects my opinion that appropriate warrant-inducing relations of a belief to other beliefs and experiences *are* in fact causal. It seems esepecially counterintuitive to me that one should be able to know that p in believing that p despite the fact that one's only reasons for believing that p are absurdly poor and irrelevant, and thus insufficient to give one knowledge. Thus if my reason for believing-that-p is that the cards indicate that p, then even if I am aware that e is true and that it is true that e is good evidence for believing-that-p, if this plays no part whatever in my actual reasoning, it remains the case that my reason — my *only* reason — for believing-that-p is absurdly poor, and in that case it would seem that I have no knowledge that p. What is more, that seems to be so despite the co-existence of my belief that p with other beliefs such that if I correctly appreciated their force by believing that p on their causal basis, *then* I *would* perhaps know that p.

Admittedly, the contrary intuition does not seem *totally* lacking in plausibility. On the contrary, there is in it enough plausibility to suggest a sense of knowledge for which it is appropriate. For instance, we could say that in believing that p S has *virtual* knowledge that p iff he in fact has justified beliefs such that if he were to believe that p on the causal basis of those justified beliefs, then he would be justified in believing that p.

Let me reiterate, however, that no matter how we resolve the foregoing issue, the accounts of epistemic presupposition and of knowledge under development here will not be affected in any essential respect. For these accounts can accommodate any of the conflicting intuitions by appropriate specification of the basing relation, on the nature of which we can here remain open minded.

The following definition is not essential for our present sequence, but it will be useful later.

(5'.) A set of propositions G *grounds* a further proposition P for a subject S iff there is a set A such that
 (a) A justifies P for S, and
 (b) A is composed of
 (i)   the proposition that S's belief of P is (causally) based on (the members of) G, and
 (ii)   for some or all of the beliefs attributed to S by members of G, propositions to the effect that S is justified in having such beliefs.

Let '$G \rightarrow P$' symbolize 'G would *prima facie* ground P for S.'

6. P is an *epistemic presupposition* made by S in believing Q on the basis of (the members of) G iff
 (i) $G \rightarrow P$
 (ii) $G \cup \{S$'s believing not-$P\} \nrightarrow Q$
 (iii) $\{S$'s believing $Q\} \nrightarrow P$
Thus when one believes something Q on the basis of certain grounds G, one epistemically presupposes P if and only if: *first*, P is not 'epistemically posterior' to Q (clause iii); *second*, adding belief of *not-P* to one's grounds G would defeat those grounds as good grounds for Q (clause ii); and *third*, grounds G, in isolation, would *prima facie* ground P for one (clause i).

Let 'JQ' symbolize 'S is justified in believing Q.'

7. A *fully justifies* P for S iff there is a sequence of subsets of A, $C1, \ldots, Cn$, such that (i) $C1$ justifies P for S, (ii) for all i, if JQ is a member of Ci, then

C_{i+1} justifies Q for S, and (iii) no member of the last subset, Cn, is to the effect that S is to any degree justified in believing a proposition Q.

S's full justification for P can thus always be expressed by a tree such as the following, the ranks of which (RI, RII, and RIII) correspond to the sequence of subsets in our definition of full justification.

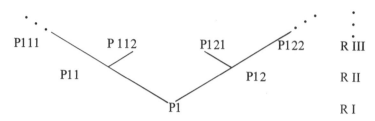

The following requirements on a tree of justification for S and P flow from the fact that trees are intended to correspond to the fully justifying sets defined above, and from the fact that the ranks of trees are to correspond to the subsets $C1, \ldots, Cn$ of the definition.

(Let us call a node x a 'direct successor' of node y relative to tree T iff there are x' and y' such that (i) x' stands for x on T and y' stands for y on T, (ii) x' and y' are connected by a straight branch on T, (iii) y' is closer than x' to the representative of the root node on T, and (iv) there is no z' such that z' is a representative on T for some proposition, and x', y', and z' are connected by a straight branch on T, and y' is closer than z' to the representative of the root node on T, and z' is closer than x' to the representative of the root node on T.)

T1.   The set of all nodes that directly succeed a given node JQ must justify the object of that node, Q, for S.

T2.   No terminal node can attribute any justification to any belief on the part of S.

T3.   The root node, $P1$, must be the proposition JP, that S is justified in believing P.

T4.   Each branch must terminate.

8. A tree of justification T for S and P is non-defective and is a *tree of knowledge* for S and P iff (i) no node of T is to the effect that S is justified in believing Q, for any false Q, and (ii) no node of T gives a set G as S's basis for believing a proposition Q such that some falsehood is an epistemic presupposition made by S in believing Q on the basis of G.

Briefly, then, a tree of justification for S and P is a tree of knowledge for S and P iff it involves S in no false justified belief or false epistemic presupposition. Finally,

9. *S knows* that p iff
    (i) S correctly believes that p, and
    (ii)   there is a tree of knowledge for S and the proposition that p.

It is this account of knowledge that underlies the earlier sections, I to III. On its basis, several obscure concepts essential to recent theories of knowledge have been explicated (I), a solution to the Gettier problem has been proposed (II), and several other vexing puzzles concerning knowledge and justification have been faced (III).[4,5]

NOTES

[Either the relevant portion or the entirety of each of the items cited in these notes is reprinted in G. S. Pappas and M. Swain (eds.), *Essays on Knowledge and Justification* (Ithaca: Cornell University Press, 1978).]

[1] Gilbert Harman, *Thought* (Princeton: Princeton University Press, 1973).
[2] Alvin Goldman, 'Discrimination and Perceptual Knowledge,' *The Journal of Philosophy* 73 (1976) 771–791.
[3] Ernest Sosa, 'How Do You Know?' *The American Philosophical Quarterly* 11 (1974) 113–122.
[4] In addition to the virtues mentioned, unfortunately, the approach defended here also faces what seems, at least *prima facie*, to constitute a serious problem. Consider the proposition
    (W)   that this is not a ticket that wins a million-ticket lottery,
where, by incredible coincidence, this happens to be the one ticket that does win a million-ticket lottery. Suppose now that S makes a true epistemic presupposition P in believing H on the basis of G (for some $S, P, H,$ and G). It now seems dangerously likely that S would *ipso facto* also make a false epistemic presupposition, namely (W & P). For it may well seem plausible that:
    (i) $G \rightarrow (W \& P)$,
    (ii)   not-$[G \cup S$'s believing not-$(W \& P) \rightarrow H]$,
    (iii)   not-$[\{S$'s believing $H\} \rightarrow (W \& P)]$,
on the assumption that P is an epistemic presupposition that S makes in believing H on the basis of G.

I reject the move from ($G \rightarrow P$) to $G \rightarrow (W \& P)$, however, even on the assumption that $\phi \rightarrow W$ (or that W is intrinsically justified). It seems straightforwardly true that if S is justified in believing P on the basis of G, and if he is intrinsically justified in believing W, then he will be justified in believing ($W \& P$) not on the simple basis G but rather on the basis $\{S$'s believing $P,$ S's believing $W\}$ or at most on the basis G U $\{S$'s believing $W\}$. So on closer thought the problem appears to be spurious.

5 My fellow participants in the Ohio State Conference on Knowledge and Justification of 1978, and especially Keith Lehrer, gave me helpful comments and criticisms. The members of my epistemology seminar of 1977–78 were also helpful critics. My thanks to all the following for discussion, written comments, objections, or suggestions: Diana Ackerman, Roderick Chisholm, Mark Engelmann, Thomas Paxson, John Pollock, Allen Renear, Deborah Shope, Robert Scaduto-Horn, Marshall Swain, and James Van Cleve.

JOHN L. POLLOCK

A PLETHORA OF EPISTEMOLOGICAL THEORIES

I

A perennial question of epistemology is, 'Does knowledge have foundations?' This question is almost as difficult to formulate precisely as it is to answer. Epistemological theories form a complex array, and as we will see, many of them are not happily classifiable as either foundations theories or non-foundations theories. The purpose of this paper will be to exhibit some of the structure of this array of epistemological theories, and to say something about which of these theories might be true.

Let us begin with a critical examination of the foundations/non-foundations distinction. According to foundations theories, knowledge has foundations. These foundations consist of a set of *epistemologically basic propositions* which are supposed to provide the basis upon which we know or are justified in believing other propositions. It is supposed that we, in some sense, have 'direct knowledge' of epistemologically basic propositions. Belief in such propositions is reputed to be incorrigible, or self-justifying, or directly evident, etc. It is further supposed that our justification for believing other propositions must derive ultimately from our justified belief in epistemologically basic propositions.

This crude characterization suggests that an adequate characterization of foundations theories will consist of two things: (1) a characterization of what it is to be an epistemologically basic proposition; and (2) a characterization of the sense in which non-epistemologically basic propositions are supported by epistemologically basic propositions. Given these two notions, a foundations theory endorses the following principle:

(F)   Necessarily, a person S is justified in believing a proposition P iff ($\exists \Gamma$) (Γ is the set of epistemologically basic propositions believed by S & Γ supports P for S.)

The epistemologically basic propositions are supposed to be the propositions with which one starts in building knowledge. One can be justified in believing an epistemologically basic proposition without having to appeal to any other beliefs for support. This suggests that we define:

(EB) P is an *epistemologically basic proposition* relative to a person S

93

George S. Pappas (ed.), Justification and Knowledge, 93–113.
Copyright © 1979 by D. Reidel Publishing Company.

iff it is logically possible for S to justifiably believe P without having any reason for believing P.

This is a bit vague without an account of what it is to have a reason for believing a proposition, but we can leave that for specific epistemological theories to fill out in their own ways.

It might seem reasonable to define a foundations theory to be any epistemological theory which endorses principle (F), defining 'epistemologically basic' as in (EB). However, such a characterization would be inadequate. Consider a coherence theory which alleges that any belief is automatically justified unless you have a reason for rejecting it (an 'incoherence' in your system of beliefs). Definition (EB) would result in all propositions being epistemologically basic, and the theory would endorse (F) by construing epistemic support as consisting of S's system of beliefs not providing a reason for S to reject P. Clearly, we do not want to count such a coherence theory as a foundations theory despite its advocacy of (F). It is essential to a foundations theory that the epistemologically basic propositions constitute a special class of 'privileged' propositions which have a status not shared by all propositions. I suggest that we tentatively define a *classical foundations theory* to be any epistemological theory which, adopting definition (EB), endorses principle (F) and alleges that not all propositions are epistemologically basic.

Different classical foundations theories arise from different accounts of epistemologically basic propositions and different accounts of the manner in which epistemologically basic propositions epistemically support other propositions. With regard to epistemologically basic propositions we must know two things: (1) which propositions are epistemologically basic; and (2) what their epistemic status is (e.g., are they incorrigible?). The logically weakest status which epistemologically basic propositions could have seems to be that of being prima facie justified:

(3) P is *prima facie justified* for S iff □ (if S believes P and has no reason for rejecting his belief in P, then S is justified in believing P).

The justification attaching to *prima facie* justified propositions is defeasible. In the absence of any other relevant beliefs, if one believes a *prima facie* justified proposition then one is automatically justified in that belief; but it is possible to have good reasons for thinking either that such a proposition is false or that under the circumstances one is an unreliable judge of whether it is true, and given such reasons one would not be justified in believing the proposition.[1]

A stronger status which epistemologically basic propositions might have is that of being incorrigibly justified:

(4) P is *incorrigibly justified* for S iff $\Box$(if S believes P then S is justified in believing P).[2]

The justification attaching to incorrigibly justified propositions is not defeasible.

Prima facie justification and incorrigible justification have to do only with the justificatory status of a proposition. It has frequently been claimed that believing an epistemologically basic proposition ensures not just its justification but also its truth. Such propositions are said to be 'incorrigible'. We might initially try defining:

(5) P is incorrigible for S iff $\Box$(if S believes P then P is true).

However, this would make all necessarily true propositions incorrigible. Our concern here is with the notion of belief guaranteeing truth *and hence* justification. This suggests defining:

(6) P is *incorrigible* for S iff P is incorrigibly justified for S and $\Box$(if S believes P then P is true).

This gives us three different epistemic statuses which might be attributed to epistemologically basic propositions. However, I argued in [16] that a proposition cannot be incorrigibly justified without being incorrigible. The argument is as follows. Suppose P is an epistemologically basic proposition which is not incorrigible. For example, P might be 'I am appeared to redly'. As it is not incorrigible for S that he is appeared to redly, S could believe that and be mistaken. But then it is presumably possible for S to have reasons for thinking that he is mistaken in believing that he is appeared to redly.[3] To continue to believe the epistemologically basic proposition in the face of such reasons would be to believe it unjustifiably, and hence it is not incorrigibly justified.

This leaves us with just two possible statuses which epistemologically basic propositions might have: *prima facie* justification, and incorrigibility. Other statuses have sometimes been proposed,[4] but with very few exceptions they are all either stronger than incorrigibility (and so entail it) or else incompatible with foundationalism.

As far as I can see, classical foundations theories must require that epistemologically basic propositions are at least *prima facie* justified, and there is no obvious intermediate status between *prima facie* justification and incorrigibility. Most classical foundations theories have opted for incorrigibility, and many of the arguments against classical foundations theories have focused on incorrigibility, but it must be recognized that that is more than is minimally required for classical foundations theories. As such, one cannot refute all classical foundations theories in one fell swoop by proving that there are no

incorrigible epistemologically basic propositions. This is an important observations because some non-foundationalists have thought they could do just
that.[5]

Turning to epistemic support, there is a great deal of latitude regarding
what foundations theories must say. There is an old and (I hope no longer
respectable) philosophical tradition which would require that in order for a
set of epistemologically basic propositions to support a proposition P, it must
logically entail P. I presume that we can take this tradition to have been discredited by the recent history of epistemology. A more plausible account of
epistemic support would proceed in terms of reasons, where it is recognized
that a good reason need not be a logically conclusive reason. I would propose
the following way of proceeding.[6] Reasons are propositions or sets of propositions. Taking $\Pi\Gamma$ to be the conjunction of a finite set Γ of propositions, we
define:

(7) Γ is a *logical reason* for S to believe P iff $\Diamond(S$ justifiably believes
         P & S's reason for believing P is Γ & S has no independent reason
         for believing $[\Pi\Gamma \supset P]$).

Logical reasons need not be logically conclusive. Those that are not are defeasible, which leads to the notions of a defeater and a *prima facie* reason:

(8) Q is a *defeater* for Γ as a logical reason for S to believe P iff $\Diamond(\Pi\Gamma$
         & P & Q) and Γ is a logical reason for S to believe P and $\Gamma\cup\{Q\}$
         is not a logical reason for S to believe P.

(9) Γ is a *prima facie reason* for S to believe P iff $(\exists Q)$ (Q is a de-
         feater for Γ as a logical reason for S to believe P).

Prima facie reasons are logical reasons that are defeasible. On this account,
epistemic support arises from stringing together undefeated logical reasons.
Epistemologically basic propositions provide logical reasons for believing some
non-basic propositions, the latter provide reasons for believing some more
non-basic propositions, and so on. It is important to observe that philosophers
can agree on this general structure of reasons while holding very different
views on what specific reasons there are of these different sorts. Presumably
anyone untroubled by logical necessity will agree that there are some logically
conclusive reasons, and if he believes in some form or other of induction he
should agree that that provides an example of a *prima facie* reason.

The details of the definition of epistemic support which arises from this
approach are highly complex, and for the most part not germane to the present discussion. However, it is worth our while to make one simple observation here. If logical reasons were not defeasible, we could define epistemic
support very simply in terms of 'pyramids of reasons'. First we define:

(10)   Γ *directly supports* P for S iff Γ is a logical reason for S to believe P and Γ is S's reason for believing P.

Then a *pyramid of reasons* for P is a structure of propositions looking like this:

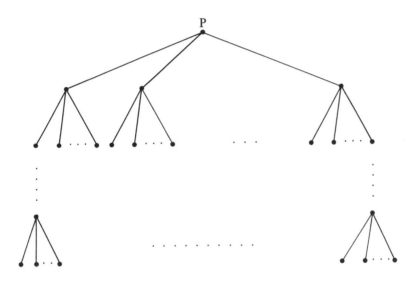

where each node is a proposition, each proposition is directly supported by the ones directly beneath it, and the lowermost propositions are epistemologically basic.[7] If we did not have to worry about defeasibility, we could conclude that a set Γ of epistemologically basic propositions supports P iff there exists a pyramid of reasons for P the lowermost members of which are members of Γ. However, given that logical reasons can be defeasible, the existence of such a pyramid is not sufficient for epistemic support, because Γ might also support defeaters for some of the logical reasons involved in the pyramid. Countenancing *prima facie* reasons forces epistemic support to have a much more complicated structure. In order to determine whether Γ supports P, we start by constructing such pyramids, but pyramids constructed at one stage may get disqualified at a later stage by the construction of pyramids supporting defeaters, and might be reinstated at a still later stage by obtaining defeaters for the pyramids supporting the defeaters, and so on. Due to its extreme complexity, it is not worth our while to try to make this construction precise at this time. However, this discussion illustrates that the admission of defeasible reasons gives epistemic justification something of a coherence structure reminiscent of that associated with non-foundations theories rather than the kind of linear structure traditionally associated with foundations theories. In principle, everything is relevant to everything else. The difference between foundations theories and non-foundations theories on this score is much less than has often been supposed.

The analysis of epistemic support in terms of logical reasons is the one I favor, but there are other possibilities. For example, Chisholm at one point urged that our basic epistemological principles are synthetic *a priori* rather than logically necessary. But whatever the source of our epistemic reasons, moves similar to the above must be made in analyzing epistemic support in terms of reasons.

II

I have discussed the framework of classical foundations theories in some detail, indicating a richness of alternatives and a sophistication of structure which has generally been overlooked by critics of foundations theories. The two principal sources of this richness lie (1) in the fact that epistemologically basic propositions need not be incorrigible, and (2) in the fact that the justificatory structure of a theory which admits *prima facie* reasons comes much closer to a coherence theory than has generally been recognized. These two observations have the result that a number of general arguments which have been employed in the attempt to refute foundations theories really only apply to the most conservative and least plausible of those theories.

Nevertheless, as I have defined the notion, all classical foundations theories are false. The difficulty lies with principle (F). According to principle (F), all epistemic support derives ultimately from what epistemologically basic propositions one believes. Unfortunately, one rarely believes any epistemologically basic propositions at all. Consider, for example, perception. Bearing in mind that epistemologically basic propositions must be at least *prima facie* justified, there are only two kinds of propositions which are plausible candidates for being the epistemologically basic propositions out of which perceptual knowledge arises.[8] These are, on the one hand, propositions describing the content of our perceptual experience ('I am appeared to redly', 'I am experiencing a red sense datum', 'I see a red percept', or however one wishes to formulate them), and on the other hand propositions of the form 'I see that P' (e.g., 'I see that there is something red before me'). Propositions that are not similarly 'about my perception' cannot be epistemologically basic for the foundations theorist. For example, consider the proposition that *there is* something red before me. This cannot be epistemologically basic for the following reason. Suppose I believe there to be something red before me but do not take myself to *see* it (e.g., I am in a darkened room) and I have no other reason for believing it to be there. Surely my belief would be unjustified despite my having no reason for thinking that there *wasn't* something red before me. This is not yet sufficient to show that the proposition is not *prima facie* justified, because it might be urged that my lack of reasons for thinking there is something red before me gives me a reason for rejecting my belief that there is. However, if it is granted *in this case* that an absence of reasons constitutes a reason for rejecting my belief, then it seems this must be granted in general, with the consequence that *all* propositions are *prima facie* justified and epistemologically basic — a conclusion incompatible with classical foundationalism. Thus we must either reject foundationalism by taking all propositions to be epistemologically basic, or we must acknowledge that propositions like 'There is something red before me' are not epistemologically basic. The latter acknowledgement is equally fatal to classical foundationalism, because in a normal case of perception, the *only* belief one is apt to have is the belief that there is something red before him. Only with considerable sophistication does one come to have any beliefs at all about perception itself. One's beliefs are not about oneself but about the world around oneself.

It might be responded here that although one does not have occurrent beliefs about perception, one has dispositional beliefs about perception; e.g., one has the dispositional belief that he is appeared to in a certain way. The notion of a dispositional belief is notoriously difficult to make clear, but having a dispositional belief in P must at least require that one has the disposition to occurrently believe P under some circumstances or other. And, as the Gestalt psychologists observed, perceivers have to *learn* to become aware of the way they are appeared to. Artists work hard to develop such an awareness. They have no natural disposition to have occurrent beliefs which reliably characterize the way in which they are appeared to.

I think it must be concluded that the justification one has for the beliefs at which one arrives through perception cannot derive from *belief* in epistemologically basic propositions. I argued in [16] that there are epistemologically basic propositions in the sense of our definition, but that what the foregoing considerations indicate is that they need not confer epistemic support on other propositions by being *believed*. Other options are available. For example, the theory I called *direct realism* replaces (F) with the principle:

(DR) $\Box(\forall S)\ (\forall P)$ [S is justified in believing P iff $(\exists \Gamma)$ (Γ is the set of *true* epistemologically basic propositions relative to S & Γ supports P)] .[9]

Perhaps we defined 'foundationalism' too narrowly, ruling out theories like direct realism when we should not have done so. Should direct realism be regarded as a foundations theory? I defended a theory of this sort in [16], and I thought of myself as defending a foundations theory. But upon reflection, I now think that that had more to do with the genesis of the theory than with its content. I arrived at the theory by starting with a classical foundations theory and modifying it to meet the objection that we do not ordinarily believe epistemologically basic propositions. One could have arrived at the theory in quite a different manner. For example, Quine's 'discus theory of knowledge' is ordinarily regarded as a non-foundations theory, but upon reflection it too can be seen to be a version of direct realism. According to Quine, "total science is like a field of force whose boundary conditions are experience. A conflict with experience at the periphery occasions readjustments in the interior of the field."[10] We adjust our beliefs in accordance with what happens at the 'experiential periphery' of the field, but apparently Quine does not believe that this process proceeds in terms of beliefs about experience.[11]

It would be at least contentious to classify direct realism as a foundations theory, although it cannot be denied that it is intimately connected with foundations theories. However, whether direct realism should or should not be regarded as a foundations theory is really just a matter of how we are going to define our philosophical terminology, and nothing ultimately turns upon it. What *is* of considerable importance is that the rather indeterminate status of direct realism illustrates that the boundary between foundations theories and non-foundations theories is not nearly so neat as it has generally been supposed to be. We can generate a whole class of theories by replacing principle (F) with the generic principle:

(F⁺) $\square(\forall S)$ $(\forall P)$ (S is justified in believing P iff $(\exists \Gamma)$ [Γ is the set of epistemologically basic propositions relative to S which have the property B & Γ supports P]).

Different epistemological theories are generated by different properties B. B could be the property of being believed by S, the property of being true, some mixture of truth and belief, or some other quite different property.

Some theories generated in the above manner will be classical foundations theories. Others, like direct realism, will be closely related to classical foundations theories. But we can also generate theories very different from classical foundations theories. For example, if we take B to be the property of being believed by S, require epistemologically basic propositions to be *prima facie* justified, but include *all* propositions in the class of epistemologically basic propositions, we have a coherence theory.

Epistemological theories make up a rather rough continuum. At one extreme we have classical foundations theories which give a *very* privileged status to a certain narrow class of propositions – the epistemologically basic propositions. At the opposite extreme we have *pure coherence theories* which regard all propositions as being on an epistemological par with one another and give no privileged status to any. Between these two extremes we have a rather ragged collection of theories which give some sort of privileged status to some propositions, but a lesser status than that conferred by classical foundations theories. By rejecting classical foundations theories we have effectively lopped off one end of the continuum. Let us turn our attention to the other end of the continuum. That is the domicile of the coherence theory.

III

The essential feature of a coherence theory is that every proposition has the same *a priori* epistemic status as every other proposition. Insofar as we can demand reasons for believing one proposition, we can demand reasons for believing any proposition; and insofar as we can be justified in believing one proposition without having a reason for doing so, we can be justified in believing any proposition without having a reason for doing so.

There are two kinds of coherence theories. On the one hand, there are coherence theories which take all propositions to be *prima facie* justified. According to these theories, if one believes a proposition P, one is automatically justified in doing so unless one has a reason for rejecting the belief. According to theories of this sort, reasons functions primarily in a negative way, leading us to reject beliefs but not being required for the justified acquisition of belief. Let us call these *negative coherence theories*. The other kind of coherence theory (a *positive coherence theory*) demands positive support for all beliefs.

Positive coherence theories demand that the believer actually have (here and now) reasons for holding each of his beliefs. It is not sufficient merely that he could find reasons for his beliefs if challenged. The latter requirement generates a negative coherence theory which construes the believer's apparent inability to find a positive reason for believing P to be a reason for him to reject his belief in P. A positive coherence theory must require the believer to already have all of his reasons before he can be justified in holding his beliefs.

Different positive coherence theories are generated by giving different accounts of reasons and different accounts of what it is to 'already have' a reason.

A positive coherence theory has two choices regarding reasons. On the one hand it can embrace essentially the same kinds of reasons as are embraced by classical foundations theories. On this view, P is a reason for S to believe Q by virtue of some relation which holds specifically between P and Q. A positive coherence theory of this sort will be called *linear*. On the other hand, a positive coherence theory can take a holistic view of reasons according to which in order for S to have a reason for believing P, there must be a relation between P and the set of *all* of the propositions S believes (hence the term 'coherence'). A positive coherence theory of this sort will be called *holistic*. [12]

There are two familiar arguments which have been employed repeatedly against coherence theories. These are the *isolation argument* and the *regress argument*. [13] The isolation argument objects that coherence theories cut justification off from the world. According to coherence theories, justification is ultimately a matter of relations between the propositions one believes, and has nothing to do with the way the world is. But our objective in seeking knowledge is to find out the way the world is. Thus coherence theories are inadequate.

Although I am guilty of having employed the isolation argument myself, it now strikes me as a very bad argument. It would be telling against a coherence theory of *truth*, but not against a coherence theory of *justification*, and it is the latter with which we are concerned here. The isolation argument is not telling against a coherence theory of justification, because according to such a theory justification is not a matter of coherence with the set of *all* propositions, but only with the set of propositions which one *believes*. What one believes is causally influenced by the way the world is, so the world is not being unjustly ignored. If it is felt that this provides an inadequate connection to the world, note that it is the same connection as that embodied in many foundations theories. A foundations theory which eschews incorrigibility makes justified belief entirely a matter of what beliefs one has, the only connection with the world being the way in which one's epistemologically basic beliefs are causally influenced by the way the world is. Thus, despite my earlier predilections, I can now see no merit in the isolation argument. [14]

It is harder to evaluate the regress argument. This is the objection that coherence theories lead to an infinite regress of reasons and such a regress cannot provide justification. This objection is telling against some coherence theories and not against others. It has no apparent strength against negative coherence theories, because they do not require reasons for beliefs. It only really bears upon some of the least plausible of the positive coherence theories. A linear positive coherence theory which identifies *already having P as a reason for believing Q* with *having explicitly inferred Q from P* would run afoul of the regress argument, because it would require one to have performed infinitely many explicit inferences before one could be justified in believing anything, and that is presumably impossible. However, weaker understandings of what it is to already have P as a reason for believing Q make the regress argument problematic, and holistic positive coherence theories would seem to avoid the regress argument altogether. It appears that those foundations theorists who have attempted to give general arguments which simultaneously dispose of all coherence theories are guilty of the same sins as those coherence theorists who have tried to do the same for all foundations theories. They have given arguments which bear only upon the least plausible coherence theories and have supposed those to refute all coherence theories.

Nevertheless, although the customary arguments do not accomplish this, it seems that we can rule out all linear positive coherence theories. According to such a theory, for each justified belief I must have a reason. Suppose I believe on the basis of perception that there is something red before me. My reason for this might be in part that I am appeared to redly. But according to a linear positive coherence theory, I would also have to have a reason for believing that I am appeared to redly. It is hard to imagine what would count as a reason for believing this. Grasping at straws, it might be suggested that my reason is that I *believe* I am appeared to redly and my beliefs about the way I am appeared to are generally reliable. I have no doubt that an ingenious coherence theorist could find some such proposition which might reasonably be considered a reason for believing that I am appeared to redly. The difficulty is that the search for such a reason requires considerable philosophical reflection. It cannot reasonably be claimed that most people even have such self-reflective beliefs, much less that they constitute the reasons people have for believing that they are appeared to redly. Thus linear positive coherence theories can be uniformly rejected.

There is also a reason for being suspicious of holistic positive coherence theories, although it is less compelling than the objection to linear positive coherence theories. The objection is this: There is a distinction between being justified in believing P and believing P unjustifiably when you have adequate justification available to you but have not made the right connections. For example, a man might have but systematically ignore adequate evidence for believing that his wife is unfaithful to him. However, when his mother, whom he knows to be totally unreliable in such matters and biased against his wife, tells him that his wife is unfaithful to him, he believes it on that basis. Then he is not justified in believing that his wife is unfaithful to him despite the fact that he has adequate evidence available to him to justify that belief. We might say that the proposition is *warranted* for him but he is not justiffied in believing it. To say that P is warranted for S is to say, roughly, that S has good reasons whether he believes P for those reasons or not.[15] Conversely, to say that S is justified in believing P is to say not only that P is warranted for S, but also that S's believing P somehow 'derives from' the way in which it is warranted. A non-coherence theory which takes justification to accrue from the functioning of reasons can explain the distinction between justified and unjustified belief in a warranted proposition by appealing to the psychological notion of 'believing on the basis of'. Being justified in believing P would consist of your believing P *for* good reasons, and your reasons for believing those reasins being good reasons, etc.

Holistic positive coherence theories are probably best construed as theories of warrant. They are about the objective relation between propositions which lead to their being warranted. Nevertheless, despite their not being directly about justified belief, if they are to be adequate they must not make it impossible for us to distinguish between justified belief and unjustified belief in a warranted proposition. I suspect that holistic positive coherence theories do precisely that. According to such a theory, P is warranted for you if P 'coheres' with the set B of all of your beliefs. Being justified in believing a warranted proposition P would have to consist of your belief somehow 'arising out of' the fact that P coheres with B. This is a partly causal notion. In order for justified belief to be possible within such a holistic theory, the coherence relation (whatever it is) must be such that P's cohering with B *can* cause one (in an appropriate way) to believe P. It must be 'appropriately causally efficacious' in the formation of belief. There are two possibilities here. First, the causal chain leading from coherence to belief in P could proceed via my coming to believe that P coheres with B. But this would require that whenever I justifiably believe P on the basis of its cohering with B, I have the belief that it coheres and believe P on the basis of that belief. There appear to be no plausible coherence relations which have this character. For example, Harman ([8] and [9]) and Lehrer [10] have both proposed accounts of coherence in terms of inference to the best explanation. More recently, Lehrer ([11] and [12]) has proposed an account in terms of P standing in certain probability relations to the members of B. In either case it is clear that we do not ordinarily believe that P coheres with B when we justifiably believe P. Thus the causal chain leading from coherence to belief cannot ordinarily proceed via our coming to believe that P coheres with B. Consequently, it must be possible for the kind of causal chain which can lead to justified belief in P to be 'non-doxastic' in the sense that does not contain the belief that P coheres with B as one essential link. But then the coherence relation must be such that P's cohering with B *can* cause belief in a non-doxastic way. Once more, if the coherence relation involves something like inference to the best explanation, or probability relations, how could coherence conceivably cause one to believe P except via one's first coming to believe that P coheres with B? It seems quite unlikely that there could be any coherence relation which could simultaneously constitute holistic warrant and be appropriately causally efficacious in the formation of belief so that it could be used to distinguish between justified and unjustified belief in warranted propositions. This argument is not conclusive, because we cannot examine all possible putative coherence relations, but it provides a strong reason for being suspicious of holistic coherence theories as a group, and it seems to provide a conclusive reason for rejecting all of the concrete examples of such theories with which I am familiar.

The preceding arguments appear to at least suggest the rejection of all positive coherence theories. If any coherence theory is to be defensible, it must be a negative coherence theory. Recall that negative coherence theories allege that all beliefs are automatically justified unless one has a reason for rejecting them. It may appear that the argument we have just used against holistic positive coherence theories can be turned against negative coherence theories as well, but let us hold that question in abeyance temporarily.

IV

Negative coherence theories, as a group, strike me as being quite plausible. It is often not realized how close they can come to classical foundations theories. Given any classical foundations theory, we can construct a negative coherence theory by saying that a person S is justified in believing a proposition P iff he does believe P and he has no reason to think that his belief in P could not be justified in accordance with the foundations theory if he were sufficiently reflective about those states of himself which are reported by the propositions considered epistemologically basic by the foundations theory. This coherence theory would be one way of avoiding the difficulty which led to the rejection of classical foundations theories.

I shall now turn to the defense of a particular negative coherence theory. In [16] I defended a version of direct realism according to which epistemologically basic propositions are incorrigible and epistemic support for other propositions arises out of a structure of logical reasons. According to that theory, what supports what is a matter of logical necessity. I still find the arguments I gave there convincing, but there is a counter-argument which also seems compelling and which leads to a negative coherence theory:

> Suppose P is a logical reason for S to believe Q, but S believes that P is not a good reason to believe Q, and so despite his believing P, S does not believe Q. Suppose further that R is not a good reason for S to believe $\sim Q$, but S believe it is and believes $\sim Q$ on that basis. Surely, given S's beliefs about reasons, it would be irrational for him to believe Q or to refrain form believing $\sim Q$. But then, S could not justifiably believe Q on the basis of P, and he does justifiably believe $\sim Q$ on the basis of R, which contradicts our suppositions about logical reasons.[16]

In this way, depending upon precisely how we define the notion of a logical reason, we seem compelled to conclude either that nothing is a logical reason for anything, or that everything is a logical reason for everything else.

Similarly, suppose P is an incorrigible epistemologically basic proposition, and S believes P. But suppose that S does not believe P to be incorrigible, and instead believes, contrary to logical possibility, that he has good reason for thinking that P is false. On this basis he comes to reject P. Under the circumstances, it would be irrational for him not to reject P. His continued belief in P would be unjstified, and so P is not incorrigibly justified and hence not incorrigible after all.

Similar arguments appear to establish that epistemic statuses or relations can never be dictated by logical considerations. In deciding what to believe, we have only our own beliefs to which we can appeal. If our beliefs mutually support our believing P, then it would be irrational for us not to believe P and hence belief in P is justified. There is no way that one can break out of the circle of his own beliefs. Furthermore, as each person has only his own beliefs to go on, it would be irrational for him to arbitrarily reject any of his beliefs unless he believes he should. In other words, if S believes P, S is justified in believing P unless his other beliefs support the rejection of P. If S holds certain epistemological views, his overall set of beliefs may support the rejection of P whenever he does not have a reason of a certain sort for believing P, but this is just to say that *given those epistemological views*, the absence of a reason becomes a reason for rejecting P. As a person need not hold those epistemological views, no logical necessity attaches to the principle that one should not believe P unless one has a reason for believing P.

The foregoing considerations lead us to a certain kind of negative coherence theory, and apparently to the rejection of direct realism and any other form of *epistemological objectivism* which attempts to found epistemic relations on logic or any other intersubjective basis.[17] Let us see if we can make this coherence theory more precise.

The fundamental allegation of the theory is that all propositions are *prima facie* justified. No matter what proposition P may be, if S believes P then S is automatically justified in believing P unless he has some reason for thinking he should not believe P. Let us say that S's *doxastic system* is the set of all propositions which S believes. If B is S's doxastic system, and $P \in B$, then S is justified in believing P iff B does not support the rejection of P.

To complete this account, we must know under what circumstances a doxastic system supports the rejection of one of its members. In effect, what is required here is an account of the crucial notion of coherence. We might once more consider accounts in terms of explanatory coherence or in terms of probability relations. However, the arguments which led us to the present coherence theory also compel us to reject any such account of coherence. A relation between S's doxastic system B and one of its members P can only give S a reason to reject his belief in P if he regards it as giving him such a reason. B cannot support the rejection of P simply by standing in some objective relation to P if S either does not believe that B stands in that relation to P or does not regard B's standing in that relation to P as constituting a reason for rejecting P. In either of the latter cases, it would be irrational for S to reject his belief in P, and so that belief is justified despite the objective relation to B.

It might seem that Lehrer's account in [11] in terms of subjective probability escapes this objection, because, after all, subjective probability is just a matter of what S believes. Ignoring certain sophistications, Lehrer's account is the following:

(L) S is justified in believing P iff prob(P) > prob($\sim P$) and for any Q, if prob(P/Q) < prob(P) then prob(P) > prob(Q).

prob(Q) is the subjective probability of Q, i.e., a measure of how strongly S believes Q, and the conditional probability is defined in the usual manner as:

(11) $\text{prob}(P/Q) = \dfrac{\text{prob}(P\&Q)}{\text{prob}(Q)}$

But suppose the analysans of (L) were false, e.g., suppose that for some Q, prob(P/Q) < prob(P) and prob(P) ⩽ prob(Q), but S just did not regard that as relevant to whether he should believe P. Then, as above, it would be irrational for him to reject P. If principle (L) is convincing, this is only because we have certain beliefs about the circumstances under which we should continue to believe a proposition which we now believe.[18] If we did not have those beliefs, then the application of principle (L) could not make it rational for us to reject P. The same moral applies to any other principle which would result in S's doxastic system supporting the rejection of P on the basis of some relation between P and the doxastic system which S might fail to regard as relevant to whether he should believe P.

Apparently, if S believes P, there is just one kind of circumstance in which S should reject that belief, namely, when he *believes* that he should. If S believes that he should not believe P, then it would be irrational for him to continue to do so; and if S does not believe that he should not believe P, then it would be irrational for him to reject P:

(C)   If B is S's doxastic system and $P \in B$, S is justified in believing P iff B does not also contain the proposition that S should not believe P.

Principles like Lehrer's (L) or the putative logical reasons of direct realism are only relevant to the determination of what S is justified in believing insofar as S has beliefs and inclinations which make those reasons or probability relations causally efficacious in S's coming to believe propositions of the form 'I should not believe P'. Logical relations, probabilistic relations, synthetic *a priori* relations, etc., can only be relevant to justification insofar as they have the contingent power to influence S's beliefs about what he should believe.

Principle (C) constitutes a very simple negative coherence theory. I believe, in fact, that it is a true theory. It is illuminating to inquire a bit further into the status which epistemic principles must have according to (C). People are, in fact, guided in their beliefs by what we call 'reasons'. If a person believes both P and $(P \supset Q)$, he will ordinarily regard that as relevant to whether he should believe Q, and in fact, he will normally either come to believe Q and that he should believe Q, or come to reject one of the initial beliefs. Similar remarks apply to the more specialized reasons which epistemologists have proposed in accounts of perception, induction, memory, etc. For example, in [16] I alleged that a person's being appeared to redly gives him a *prima facie* reason for believing that there is something red before him. Principle (C) rejects this *prima facie* reason as carrying automatic (*prima facie*) justification with it, but principle (C) countenances something of the spirit of my foundationalist allegation by allowing that a person will normally acquire beliefs about there being red things before him on the basis of the way he is appeared to and believe that he should or should not hold those beliefs under the same circumstances as a theory embodying that *prima facie* reason would tell him that he should or should not hold them. Thus the functioning of principle (C) will lead to a normal individual's being justified in such perceptual beliefs under precisely the same circumstances as a direct realist theory which endorses this *prima facie* reason, but the justification will derive from a different source and there is no logical necessity to conference of justification by this putative *prima facie* reason.

Having started out by defending direct realism, I seem to have done a complete about-face, instead defending a coherence theory and the rejection of direct realism and any other version of epistemological objectivism. Despite all of this, I still believe that direct realism is true. I also believe that my coherence theory is true, and I believe that they are compatible. The source of the compatibility lies in an equivocation on the term 'justified'.

In defending principle (C), I argued as follows:

(12)   Suppose S believes both P and Q, and Q is so related to P that Q would ordinarily be regarded as a good reason for believing $\sim P$. If S did not regard Q as a good reason for believing $\sim P$, then it would be irrational for him to reject P on that basis. Thus his continued belief in P would be justified.

A similar argument is frequently encountered in ethics. Consider an individual who sincerely believes that it is morally permissible to drown baby girls. If he is the head of an impoverished family, he might reason that only by drowning his new baby girl can he continue to support his family. Thus, he concludes that that is what he should do, and he does it. We, who are morally enlightened, may find his reasoning repugnant, and protest that he should not have drowned his child. But at the same time, it could be said in his defense that given his sincere moral beliefs, it would have been irrational for him to have done otherwise. Under the circumstances, it would actually have indicated a lack of moral fibre had he not drowned his child. In other words, he did precisely what he should have done given his beliefs.

This sort of dialogue has traditionally been taken to show that there are two senses of 'should' in ethics — a subjective sense and an objective sense. In the objective sense, our man should not have drowned his child; but in the subjective sense, given his objectively mistaken beliefs, he did what he should have done.[19] The same distinction is invoked in explaining the difference between judgments regarding what a person should have done given the actual (possibly unforseen) consequences of his actions and judgments regarding what he should have done given his beliefs about the consequences of his actions.

The same distinction, or an analogous one, is at work in epistemology.

What is at issue is what a person should believe. But, just as in ethics, we can distinguish between what a person should believe given what are in fact good reasons for believing things, and what a person should believe given his possibly mistaken beliefs about reasons. The former is the objective sense of 'should believe' and the latter is the subjective sense. Given this distinction, it seems clear that the arguments involved in the defense of principle (C) relate to the subjective sense of 'should believe', whereas direct realism and its brethren are concerned with the objective sense of 'should believe'.

One might doubt that there really are these two senses of 'should believe', but I don't think it is too hard to see that there must be. There is clearly a sense in which the coherence-theoretic arguments are compelling. But surely there is also a sense in which we can reasonably protest against an aberrant reasoner that what he takes to be a good reason for one of his beliefs just is not a good reason. Or if a person's overall set of epistemological beliefs and inclinations is so abnormal that there is no way we could rationally lead him to agree that a certain set of data is a good reason for believing an inductive generalization P, we can still protest, with perfect justice, that he's just all screwed up. The set of data really is a good reason for beleving P, whether he sees that it is or not.

The distinction between objective and subjective senses of 'should' makes just as much sense in epistemology as in ethics, and it generates a corresponding distinction between an objective and a subjective sense of epistemic justification. Accordingly, we can generate different epistemological theories by reading 'justified in believing' in different ways in otherwise identical theories. This gives us another dimension to the classification of epistemological theories. By far the most natural way (and I think the only compelling way) to read principle (C) is as a principle about subjective justification. Note, however, that there is really room for two equivocations in our formulation of (C), because both 'justified' and 'should believe' occur in it. I propose that (C) should be disambiguated as follows:

(C*)   If B is S's doxastic system and $P{\in}B$, S is subjectively justified in believing P iff B does not also contain the proposition that S *obj*ectively should not believe P.

(C*) is the principle I want to affirm in saying that there is a true coherence theory. (C*) is compatible with direct realism or any other epistemologically objective theory about objective justification. The theories are about two different subject matters. Thus there is no problem in endorsing theories of both kinds.

I have now developed a negative coherence theory which is about subjective justification. Have we any other options regarding the subject matter of a negative coherence theory? We might take such theories to be about either warrant or objectively justified belief. As theories of warrant they are unacceptable. A proposition is warranted for a person S if, roughly, S would be justified in believing it if he correctly worked out all of its objective relations to his epistemic situation. A negative coherence theory about warrant would allege that a proposition is warranted for S if S simply believes it and has *not* worked out considerations which may be available to him which would defeat the warrant. That is just the opposite of the way the concept of warrant works.

That negative coherence theories cannot be plausible theories of objectively justified belief follows from the fact that, like holistic positive coherence theories, they would make it impossible for us to distinguish between justified belief and unjustified belief in a warranted proposition. As they would make all belief *prima facie* justified, they would imply that one is objectively justified in believing any proposition for the belief of which he is unaware of defeaters, no matter how he came to believe that proposition. Thus, the principle (C*) constitutes what I suspect is the only reasonable negative coherence theory.

V

The ultimate conclusion of this paper is twofold. First, I have attempted to give some indication of the wide range of epistemological theories potentially available to us. The major conclusion here is that the field is not exhausted by foundations and coherence theories. A number of theories lie somewhere in between foundations and coherence theories. Second, I have attempted to narrow the range of possibilities by arguing that classical foundations theories and coherence theories are all false when construed as theories about warrant or objectively justified belief. I have attempted to explain the appeal of coherence theories by arguing that there is a coherence theory which is true when construed as a theory of subjectively justified belief and that some of the more persuasive arguments advanced in favor of coherence theories really only support this theory. That leaves us with theories intermediate between foundations theories and coherence theories as the only plausible theories of warrant and objective justification.

NOTES

[1] In [15] and [16] I defined *prima facie* justification differently as requiring that $\square$(if S believes P and has no reason for believing $\sim P$ then S is justified in believing P). It now

seems evident to me that no proposition could have this stronger status without being incorrigible, for reasons analogous to those given in the text for concluding that incorrigibly justified propositions must be incorrigible.

[2] This definition is from my [13] and [16]. It is the same as Alston's notion of a *self-warranted* proposition in [1] and [2].

[3] I am not claiming in general that if it is possible to mistakenly believe a proposition then it must be possible to have reasons for thinking one is mistaken in believing it. I am endorsing this principle only in connection with propositions of the sort foundationalists have traditionally regarded as epistemologically basic.

[4] See Alston [1].

[5] For example, see Lehrer [11], and Alston's response in [3].

[6] These definitions are taken, with modifications, from my [14] and [16].

[7] See Sosa [18] for a discussion of these pyramids and their role in knowledge.

[8] This argument is adapted from a similar argument in [16] which, however, proceeded in terms of the stronger notion of *prima facie* justification to which I alluded in Note 1.

[9] This requires us to either affirm that a person's reason for believing a proposition may be a proposition which he does not believe or to revise our definition of 'support'. The first alternative was adopted in [16].

[10] [17], p. 47.

[11] Of course, Quine holds different views about the relation of epistemic support than I do, but given those views his theory endorses (DR).

[12] Examples of holistic positive coherence theories are provided by Bonjour [4], Harman [8] and [9], and Lehrer [10], [11], and [12].

[13] I somewhat naively employed both of these arguments in [15] and [16].

[14] See Bonjour [14] for a nice discussion of this point.

[15] It might be supposed that this is the same as the distinction between subjective and objective justification in Section IV, objective justification being identified with warrant. That this is a different distinction can be seen as follows. Knowledge requires not just warrant but justified belief. But subjective justification is not sufficient for knowledge — you must have objective justifications. Thus the subjective/objective distinction is a distinction within justified belief, and hence is not the same as the distinction between warrant and justified belief.

[16] It might be responded that S believes $\sim Q$ on the basis, not of R, but of $\ulcorner R$ & R is a good reason to believe $\sim Q\urcorner$, and this latter conjunction *is* a good reason to believe $\sim Q$. However, no such retrenchment is required in the case of *good* reasons: if T were a good reason for believing $\sim Q$, S could simply believe $\sim Q$ on that basis, without appealing instead to the conjunction $\ulcorner T$ & T is a good reason to believe $\sim Q\urcorner$. If it were insisted that we must always appeal to such conjunctions, we would have an infinite regress. But given that S can believe $\sim Q$ directly on the basis of a good reason, without going through such a conjunction, then surely S can also believe $\sim Q$ directly on the basis of a specious reason as well. There are no grounds for insisting that S's reason for believing $\sim Q$ must be the conjunction $\ulcorner R$ & R is a good reason to believe $\sim Q\urcorner$.

[17] This is reminiscent of Lehrer's argument in [11] and [12].

[18] In effect, I am using the argument Lehrer [12] employs against Chisholm [6], and turning it against Lehrer himself.

[19] My subjective sense of 'should' is what Brandt [5] calls 'the putative sense of "should" '.

BIBLIOGRAPHY

[1]   Alston, William P., 'Varieties of privileged access', *American Philosophical Quarterly* **8** (1971), 223–241.
[2]   Alston, William P., 'Self-warrant: a neglected form of privileged access', *American Philosophical Quarterly* **13** (1976), 252–272.
[3]   Alston, William P., 'Has foundationalism been refuted?', *Philosophical Studies* **29** (1976), 287–305.
[4]   Bonjour, Laurence, 'The coherence theory of empirical knowledge', *Philosophical Studies* **30** (1976), 281–312.
[5]   Brandt, Richard, *Ethical Theory*, Prentice-Hall, 1959.
[6]   Chisholm, Roderick, *Perceiving*, Cornell, 1957.
[7]   Chisholm, Roderick, *Theory of Knowledge*, second edition, Prentice-Hall, 1977.
[8]   Harman, Gilbert, 'Induction', in *Induction, Acceptance, and Rational Belief*, ed. Marshall Swain, Reidel, 1970, 83–99.
[9]   Harman, Gilbert, *Thought*, Princeton, 1973.
[10] Lehrer, Keith, 'Justification, explanation, and induction', in *Induction, Acceptance, and Rational Belief*, ed. Marshall Swain, Reidel, 1970, 100–133.
[11] Lehrer, Keith, *Knowledge*, Oxford, 1974.
[12] Lehrer, Keith, 'The knowledge cycle', *Nous* **11** (1977), 17–26.
[13] Pollock, John L., 'Criteria and our knowledge of the material world', *Philosophical Review* **76** (1967), 28–62.
[14] Pollock, John L., 'The structure of epistemic justification', *American Philosophical Quarterly*, monograph series 4 (1970), 62–78.
[15] Pollock, John L., 'Perceptual knowledge', *Philosophical Review* **80** (1971), 287–319.
[16] Pollock, John L., *Knowledge and Justification*, Princeton, 1974.
[17] Quine, Willard van Orman, 'Two dogmas of empiricism', *From a Logical Point of View*, Harvard, 1953, 20–46.
[18] Sosa, Ernest, 'The concept of knowledge. How do you know?', *American Philosophical Quarterly* **11** (1974), 113–122.

RODERICK M. CHISHOLM

THE DIRECTLY EVIDENT

1. INTRODUCTION

In the present paper, I shall correct and refine a theory of the directly evident which I have defended in a number of recent publications. The theory, I now believe, rests upon a mistaken general presupposition.

The essence of the theory of contained in the following two definitions, which were set forth in the second edition of my book, *Theory of Knowledge*, [1]

> h is self-presenting for S at t = Df; h occurs at t; and necessarily, if h occurs at t, then h is evident for S at t.
>
> h is directly evident for S at t = Df; h is logically contingent; and there is an e such that (i) e is self-presenting for S at t and (ii) necessarily, whoever accepts e accepts h.

I had said that the expression 'self-presenting,' which is borrowed from Meinong, was used to refer

to certain thoughts, attitudes, and experiences which [are] assumed to be such that it is evident to a man that he is thinking such a thought, taking such an attitude, or having such an experience if and only if he *is* thinking such a thought, taking such an attitude or having such an experience. [2]

I then went on to say that one could affirm such principles as the following, all pertaining to self-presenting states:

'Necessarily, for any S and any t, if S believes at t that Socrates is mortal, then it is evident to S at t that he then believes that Socrates is mortal'; 'Necessarily, for any S and any t, if S thinks at t that he perceives something that is red, then it is evident to S to t that he then thinks he perceives something that is red.' Other principles of this sort would refer to such intentional phenomena as hoping, fearing, wishing, wondering; for example, 'Necessarily. for any S and any t, if S wonders at t whether the peace will continue, then it is evident to S at t that he then wonders whether the peace will continue.' Still others would refer to certain ways of sensing or being appeared to. Thus there is a possible use of 'is appeared to redly' which is such that, if we give the expression that use, then we may say: 'Necessarily, for any S and any t, if S is appeared to redly at t, then it is evident to S that he is then appeared to redly'. [3]

The theory thus seems to presuppose that the vehicles of direct evident are

115

George S. Pappas (ed.), Justification and Knowledge, 115–127.
Copyright © 1979 by D. Reidel Publishing Company.

primarily certain 'I'-propositions – my 'I'-propositions being the propositions that I would express in English by using the first person and your 'I'-propositions being the ones that *you* would express in English by using the first person. The theory, being a version of what is sometimes called 'foundationalism,' thus presupposes that the propositional knowledge that each person has is based upon that person's 'I'-propositions.

But I am now sceptical as to whether there *are* any 'I'-propositions. And so the therpy requires emendation.[4]

2. THE PROBLEM OF 'I'-PROPOSITIONS

In saying I am sceptical as to whether there are any 'I'-propositions, I do not meant to suggest that there are no 'I'-*sentences*. What I mean to suggest is, rather, that the difference between your 'I'-sentences and my 'I'-sentences does not lie in the fact that they express different first-person propositions. For I think there are no first-person propositions.

Let us recall the nature of propositions or – as I would prefer to call them – states of affairs.

Whether or not anyone is in pain, there is the proposition, *someone is in pain*, just as there are the propositions, *there are horses* and *there are round squares*. If we take the term *proposition* in what is now its most common philosophical sense, we will say that propositions are eternal objects having this nature: they are capable of being asserted or accepted or entertained.

But let us now consider the question: Is there, in this sense of 'proposition,' a proposition corresponding to the English expression 'I am in pain' – a different proposition for each person who could utter the words 'I am in pain'?

If there are such first-person propositions, then, one would think, they could all be in the form, 'The *F* is in pain,' but with a different subject-term for each person. Let us consider the consequences of this assumption.

We can say, of propositions, not only that they imply other propositions but also that some of them imply certain *properties*. The concept of a proposition implying a properly is imply enough: a proposition implies a certain property if the proposition is necessarily such that, if it is true, then something has the property. Thus the proposition, *the man in the corner is in pain*, implies such properties as being a man, being in a corner, and being in pain. And just as some propositions may be said to *imply* certain properties, some propositions may be said to *exclude* certain properties. The proposition that there are no unicorns may be said to exclude the property of being a unicorn. This means that the proposition is necessarily such that, if it is true, then nothing has the property. I believe we may say that , for every contingent proposition p and every contingent proposition q, if p logically implies q and q does not logically imply p, then either (a) p *implies* some property that q does not imply or (b) p *excludes* some property that q does not exclude.

Now if there are first-person propositions, different ones for different people, then it would seem, my 'I'-propositions would imply a certain property that only I have and yours would imply a certain property that only you have. Thus my 'I'-propositions would be expressible in the form 'There is an x such that x is F and x is in pain' — where in place of F there would be an expression connoting a property that only I have. And analogously for yours. But what would these identifying properties be?

Some philosophers — for example, Frege and Husserl — have suggested that each of us has his own idea of himself, his own *Ich-Vorstellung* or individual concept — where the individual concept of a person is his individual essence, a property that that person must have and that no other entity can possibly have. Some of the things that such philosophers have said suggest the following view: The word 'I', in the vocabulary of each person who uses it, has for its reference that person himself and has for its sense that person's *Ich-Vorstellung* or individual concept. The difference between my 'I'-propositions and yours would lie in the fact that mine imply my *Ich-Vorstellung* and not yours, and that yours imply your *Ich-Vorstellung* and not mine.[5]

Let us consider some of the implications of this view.

Could we make a list of *Ich-Vorstellungen*, a list of individual concepts, as we might make a list of colors? We could make a list of colors and then go on to say, 'This first color is the color of that thing, this second color is the color of that other thing, and this third color is the color of that third thing.' But surely we cannot make a list of *Ich-Vorstellungen* in this way and go on to say, 'Here is the *Ich-Vorstellung* that that person expresses in his "I"-sentences, here is the one that that second person expresses in *his* "I"-sentences . . . '.

It may be tempting to say: 'The property of *being me* is a property that I know myself to have and that distinguishes me from all other things.' If this statement were true, then one could go on to say: 'This property of *being me* is *essential* to me: for, if I didn't have it, I wouldn'r exist. And it is repugant to everything else; for no *other* thing could possibly have the property of being me.' And then we could go on still further and formulate an essentialistic theory of 'I'-sentences and 'I'-propositions. We could say: 'The word "I", for each person who uses it, has the speaker himself as its reference and his individual essence or haecceity as its sense. The person uses "I"-sentences to express his "I"-propositions – propositions whih imply his individual essence or haecceity. Thus my sentence, "I am in pain," expresses a proposition which implies, not only the property of being in pain, but also the property of being me, which property is my individual essence'.

If this essentialistic theory were true, then every time a person understands what he expresses by means of an 'I'-sentence, he could grasp his own individual essence or haecceity. But, one wonders, do I *ever* thus grasp my individual essence or haecceity?

Brentano says that we *never* grasp any properties that are individuating. Any property which I am able to grasp, either in 'inner' or in 'outer' perception, is a property which, at least theoretically, is capable of existing in several different things at one.[6]

One may object: 'But surely, for each thing, there is the individuating property of *being identical just with that thing*, and mine is the one I intend when I speak of property of *being me*.' The answer is this: There is no good reason to suppose that the expression 'being identical with that thing' has *any* property as its sense. I assume that we can say of properties something very much like what Spinoza said of substance: a property is 'that which is in itself and is conceived through itself: in other words, that the conception of which does not need the conception of another thing from which it must be formed'. But since some properties are compounds of other properties and therefore cannot be conceived unless their components are also conceived we might modify our Spinozistic statement so that it will say rather this: 'a property is that which is conceived either through itself or through another property, it is that the conception of which does not require the conception of anything that is not a property'. I take this to imply that, although some properties can be conceived only by reference to other properties, no property is such that it can be conceived only by reference to some individual thing.

It would seem that the expression, 'being identical with that individual thing' can always be eliminated in any non-metaphysical discourse. Thus, to say that, for each thing, there is the property of being identical just with that thing, is to say no more than that each thing is identical with itself and that no two things are identical with each other. No proposition that we know to be true implies any property which might serve as the sense of the expression 'being identical with just that thing'.

We presuppose that all properties are 'pure' in the following sense: any property which is such that it can be exemplified by only one thing can be reduced to properties which can be exemplified by more than thing. In other words, every identifying property is equivalent to a conjunction of repeatable properties — properties which are such that they can be had by any number of things. Thus the property of being the tallest man is equivalent to the conjunction of (i) the property of being a man taller than all other men and (ii) the property of being such that there is one man taller than all other men. The latter property, it should be noted, is a universal property — a property which everything has.[7]

If what I have been suggesting is correct, then we may say that the function of first-person *sentences* is not that of expressing first-person *propositions*. And analogously for sentences using other indicator words or what Russell called 'genuine proper names'. Such sentences can *not* be said to express propositions in the way in which, say, 'All men are mortal' and 'The tallest man is wise' may be said to express propositions.[8]

Whether or not there *are* any 'I'-propositions and whether or not we do have *Ich-Vorstellungen*, or individual essences, it is hardly plausible to suppose that those directly evident propositions, which constitute the basis of all our knowledge, are propositions which imply our individual essences. If this is so, then the basis of our knowledge cannot consist of 'I'-propositions. And therefore, as I have said, the account of the directly evident that I have given requires correction.

3. THE DIRECTLY EVIDENT *A POSTERIORI*

In setting forth an account of the directly evident, I will make use of the following undefined concepts: that of epistemic preferability ('*p* is more reasonable than *q* for *S* at *t*'); that of *de re* necessity ('*x* is necessarily such that it is *F*'); that of obtaining (or, alternatively, being true); and that of accepting (or believing) a proposition or state of affairs. The other theories of the directly evident that are familiar to me make use of a considerably greater number of undefined locutions. Some even offer definitions that are formulated in contrary-to-fact conditionals.

We restrict the concept of direct evidence to what is *certain*, in the following sense.

(D1)   *h* is *certain* for *S* = Df, *h* is beyond reasonable doubt for *S*, and there is no *i* such that accepting *i* is more reasonable for *S* than accepting *h*.

I leave open the question whether this general definition of certainty should be replaced by two definitions — one of empirical certainty and of non-empirical certainty. The two definitions would be:

(D2)   *h* is *empirically certain* for *S* = Df; *h* is non-necessary and is beyond reasonable doubt for S; and there is no i such that i is non-necessary and accepting i is more reasonable for S than accepting h.

(D3) h is nonempirically certain for S = Df; h is necessary and is beyond reasonable doubt for S; and there is no i such that i is necessary and accepting i is more reasonable for S than accepting h.

The definitions that immediately follow are schematic; the letter 'F' is replacable by any predicative expression.

Our first problem is characterize 'self-presentation' without appeal to 'I'-propositions. To do this, we may note certain facts about the nature of empirical certainty and its relation to some of our psychological states. Taking sadness as an example of such a state, we may note first, that if I am sad then the proposition that *someone* is sad is one that is empirically certain for me. And we may note, secondly, that if the proposition that someone is sad is one that is empirically certain for me, then I am sad. We may say of empirical certainty what Brentano said about the directly evident: one cannot be empirically certain that a given property is exemplified unless one has that property oneself.

In the first definition, we introduce 'self-presentation' as an absolute concept — a concept holding eternally of states of affairs. It is assumed that some states of affairs are necessarily such that they cannot obtain without being the object of someone's certainty.

(D4)   The state of affairs, something being F, is self-presenting = Df. The property of being F is necessarily such that, for every x and for any time t, if x is F at t, then the state of affairs, something being F, is certain for x at t.

I assume, as a general principle of epistemology, that, if a self-presenting state of affairs, something being F, *is* thus certain *for* a subject S at t, then S is in fact F at t. This assumption follows from a 'principle of unity of consciousness' set forth in Section 7 below.

(D5)   It is self-presenting for S at t that he then has the property of being F = Df. S has the property of being F at t; and the state of affairs, something being F, is self-presenting.

(D6)   The state of affairs, something being F, is self-presenting for S at t = Df. It is self-presenting for S at t that he then has the property of being F.

(D7)   Being F is a self-presenting property = Df. The state of affairs, something being F, is self-presenting.

What if we replace 'F' by 'round and square'?[9] Then, given (D4) we must say that the state of affairs, something being round and square, is self-presenting. But this state of affairs will not be self-presenting *for* anyone. And no one will have the self-presenting *property* of being round and square.

(A refinement of this account of self-presentation has been suggested by Giudo Küng.[10] Küng distinguishes that which is *self-presenting* from that which is *self-presented*. Adapting this distinction to the present account, we may illustrate it by reference to the state of affairs, someone being in pain. The state of affairs is *self-presenting* provided it is necessarily such that, if it is considered or entertained by a person who is in pain, then it is evident for that person. And the state of affairs, someone being in pain, is *self-presented* provided it is self-presenting and is in fact considered or entertained by someone who is in pain.)

We may now characterize the directly evident *a posteriori*:

(D8)   *h* is *directly evident a posteriori* for S = Df; *h* is logically contingent; and there is an *e* such that (i) *e* is self-presenting for S and (ii) necessarily, whoever accepts *e* accepts *h*.

This expression '*h* is logically contingent' is here taken to abbreviate 'It is false that *h* is necessarily such that it obtains and it is also false that *h* is necessarily such that it does not obtain'.

What would be directly evident *a posteriori* but not self-presenting? We may note that many propositions which are not self-presenting may be entailed by what is self-presenting. For example: (i) there is someone; (ii) there is someone who is not in pain; and (iii) there is someone who is such that either he is thinking about what he takes to Albuquerque or he wishes he were on Mt. Monadnock. The first of thse propositions is directly evident to anyone for whom anything is self-presenting; the second is directly evident to any person who is not in pain and who asks himself whether he is in pain; and the third is directly evident to anyone who is thinking about what he takes to be Albuquerque while at the same time wishing that he were on Mt. Monadnock.

Should we say that the conjunction of any two directly evident propositions is a proposition that is evident?[11] It will not follow that the conjunction of everything that is evident to S is something that is *known* by S. For it is possible that a proposition is evident to S even though it is not accepted by S.

With these definitions, we can speak of the certainty of contingent propositions without presupposing that any of these propositions are 'I'-propositions. They will be *true* of the person to whom they are certain in that he will have all the self-presenting properties that they imply. Thus the proposition, *someone is in pain* may be directly evident to me, and if it is, then I am in pain.

A further difference between the present account of self-presentation and that referred to at the beginning of this paper may be noted. Where the earlier account characterized self-presentation in terms merely of the *evident*, the present account characterizes it in terms of the *certain.* [12]

4. THE DIRECTLY EVIDENT FOUNDATION OF OUR KNOWLEDGE

To characterize the empirical foundation of our knowledge, we first introduce the concept of one state of affairs being such that it *tends to confirm* another.

(D9) e tends to confirm h = Df; e is necessarily such that, for every subject x, if e is beyond reasonable doubt for x and if everything that is beyond reasonable doubt for x is logically implied by e, then h has some presumption in its favor for S.

We next introduce the concept of a state of affairs being such that it is *epistemically unsuspect* for a given subject S:

(D10) e is epistemically unsuspect for S at t = Df. No conjunction of propositions that are acceptable for S at t tends to confirm not-p.

A state of affairs may thus be epistemically acceptable without being epistemically unsuspect. We may compare such a state of affairs with a free citizen who has been charged but has not yet been convicted. Certain epistemic functions, we might say, can be performed only by states of affairs that are epistemically unsuspect. (The 'rules of evidence,' whic I attempted to formulate in *Theory of Knowledge*, should thus be restricted to what is epistemically unsuspect.) And it is in terms of this concept that we may define the *evident*.

An adequate definition of the evident must enable us to say that any state of affairs that is *known* is one that is evident. It should also enable us to say, of that which is evident, that is more than merely beyond reasonable doubt and yet that it need not be certain. Given the concept of the epistemically unsuspect, we may now define the evident as follows:

(D11) e is evident for S at t = Df; e is beyond reasonable about for S at t; and e is epistemically unsuspect for S at t.

We may characterize the concept of an *evidence-base*:

(D12) e is the evidence-base at t for S = Df; e is the conjunction of all those states of affairs that are directly evident *a posteriori* for S at t.

And we may say what it is for one state of affairs to be S's epistemic basis for another state of affairs:

(D13) e is a basis of h for S at t = Df; e is directly evident for S at t; h is epistemically unsuspect for S at t; and necessarily, for any subject x, if e is directly evident for x at t, and h is epistemically unsuspect for S at t, then h is evident for x.

A state of affairs e may thus be a basis for a state of affairs h without e being itself an evidence-base. But if e is a basis of h for S, then S's evidence-base will *also* be a basis of h for S.

This concept of a basis enables us to say, finally, what it is for one state of affairs to *confer evidence upon* another:

(D14) e confers evidence upon h for S at t = Df; e is evident for S at t; and for every b, if b is a basis of e for S at t, then b is a basis of h for S at t.

We could say that e confers evidence upon h 'demonstratively' provided e confers evidence upon h and also logically implies h; and we could then say that e confers evidence upon h 'nondemonstratively' provided e confers evidence upon h and does not logically imply h. But it is important to note, that if anything thus confers evidence 'nondemonstratively' upon h, then there is also something (for example, h itself, or h in conjunction with any other evident state of affairs) which confers evidence 'demonstratively' upon h. Yet there is an important concept which we might express by saying 'S has only nondemonstrative grounds for h.' It is clear that many states of affairs are such that our 'grounds' for them can be said to be only nondemonstrative.

To say that S has demonstrative grounds for h is clear enough. This would be:

(D15) S has demonstrative grounds for h = Df; h is entailed by S's evidence base.[13]

But what are the *grounds* for h? Surely not h itself, much less h in conjunction with some other proposition. *The* grounds that one has for a proposition or state of affairs h will normally be something short of one's entire evidence base; and they will also normally be something short of any basis one has for the conjunction of h with any other independent evident state of affairs. I think we can say this:

(D16) e constitutes S's grounds for h = Df; e is a basis of h for S; and e is entailed by everything that is a basis of h for S.

If a person has grounds, in this sense, for any proposition that is not directly evident or not known *a priori*, then his grounds for that proposition will be nondemonstrative. And this is true even of such propositions as Moore's 'this is a hand' and 'there is a clock on the mantelpiece'.

5. THE DIRECTLY EVIDENT *A PRIORI*

If one's evidence base at any time consists of states of affairs that are directly evident *a posteriori* at that time, what is the status of the *a priori*?

In one of its traditional senses the word 'axiom' is used to refer to a proposition which is necessarily such that, if one understands it, then one sees that it is true. I believe that the sense of this conception is captured by the following definition

(D17)   *h* is *an axiom* = Df; *h* is necessarily such that (i) it obtains and (ii) for every *S*, if *S* accepts *h*, then *h* is certain for *S*.

An alternative to (D1) would be obtained by substituting 'entertains' for 'accepts'.

(D18)   *h* is directly evident *a priori* for *S* = Df: (i) *h* is an axiom and (ii) *S* accepts *h*.

(D19)   *h* is known *h a priori* by *S* = Df. There is an *e* such that (i) *e* is directly evident *a priori* for *S*, (ii) the state of affairs, *e implies h*, is axiomatic for *S*, and (iii) *S* accepts *h* and *e implies h*.

(D20)   *h* is directly evident for *S* = Df. Either *h* is directly evident *a posteriori* for *S*, or *h* is directly evident *a priori* for *S*.

Concerning the relation between what is self-presenting and what is *a priori* we may note: (1) since accepting (as well as entertaining) is self-presenting, then the self-presenting state which is the acceptance (or entertainment) of an exiomatic state of affairs will *confer evidence* upon that state of affairs (and therefore what is directly evident *a posteriori* may confer evidence upon what is directly evident *a priori*); and (2) one's knowledge *that* a certain state of affairs is self-presenting (in the absolute sense set forth in (D4) above of the previous section) is *a priori*.

6. DOES THE CERTAIN COINCIDE WITH THE DIRECTLY EVIDENT?

Shall we now say that the *certain* coincides with what is directly evident? It would seem that the concept of the certain is wider than that of the directly evident.[14] Suppose that *p* is directly evident and that *q* is some independent state of affairs. We know that *p* does not *entail* the disjunction, *p* or *q*. But what if the subject now *entertains* the disjunction, *p* or *q*?[15] The disjunction will not be directly evident by our definitions, but shouldn't we say that it is certain? Our definition of *a priori* knowledge above (D14) suggests the following principle:

If there is an *e* such that (i) *e* is directly evident for *S*, and (ii) the state of affairs, e implying h, is directly evident for S, then h is certain for S.

7. THE UNITY OF CONSCIOUSNESS

Let us now relate what we have said to what is sometimes called 'the unity of consciousness.' For this topic, obviously, is directly related to the question whether there are 'I'-propositions.

I suggest that the following principle is true. We might call it 'the principle of the unity of consciousness'.

> For every x, if it is empirically certain for x that something is F and if it is empirically certain for x that something is G, then (i) is F and x is G, and (ii) it is empirically certain for x that something is both F and G.[16]

In other words, one's self-presenting properties all present themselves as belonging to one and the same thing. This fact is doubtless at the basis of what Kant called 'the transcendental unity of apperception'.[17]

Instead of beginning clause (ii) in our principle, with 'it is empirically certain for x,' we might use instead, 'it is evident for x.' This is in accord with Kant's suggestion that the subject need not unite representations into a single consciousness, but should merely be such that he *could* so unite them – or, as we might say, that he should be in a position so to unite them.[18]

What we have said is in the spirit of the following remark that Russell made in his early paper, "On the Nature of Acquaintance" (1914):

We are thus forced ... to ask ourselves whether our theory of acquaintance in any way implies a direct consciousness of the bare subject. If it does, it would seem that it must be false, but I think we can show that it does not. Our theory maintains that the datum when we are aware of experiencing an object O is the fact 'something is acquained with O'. The subject appears here, not in its individual capacity, but as an 'apparent variable'; thus such a fact may be a datum in spite of incapacity for acquaintance with the subject.[19]

The unity of consciousness gives us a means by which we can identify without recourse to a middle term. If the property G is self-presenting to me and also the property H, then, *ipso facto*, I can be certain that there is something having both G and H.

The person's self-presenting properties, then, are such that he is absolutely certain that they are all had by one and the same thing. And this is the closest he comes – and can come – to apprehending himself directly. But this awareness that there is something having the properties in question is what constitutes our basis at any time, for all the other things that we may be said to know at that time.

NOTES

[1] Roderick M. Chisholm, *Theory of Knowledge*, Second Edition (Englewood Cliffs, N. J., Prentice-Hall, Inc., 1977); the definitions appear on page 22 and page 24, and are numbered D2.1 and D2.2.

[2] The quotation is from my paper, 'On the Nature of Empirical Evidence,' in George S. Pappas and Marshall Swain, ed., *Essays on Knowledge and Justification* (Ithaca and London: Cornell University Press, 1978), 253–278; the quotation appears on page 269. It should be noted that this version of the paper in question differs significantly from the previously published versions.

[3] *Ibid.*

[4] I leave open the question whether the two definitions can be *reinterpreted* in a way that does not presuppose that there are 'I'-propositions.

[5] Compare Frege, 'The Thought: A Logical Inquiry,' *Mind,* **LXV** (1956), 289–311, and Husserl, *Logical Investigations* (London: Routledge and Kegan Paul, 1970), 315–6. I defended this view in Chapter One of *Person and Object: A Metaphysical Study* (London and La Salle, Ill., Allen and Unwin, Ltd., and the Open Court Publishing Company, 1976).

[6] See *Psychology from an Empirical Standpoint* (London: Routledge and Kegan Paul, 1973), 311–5, and *Kategorienlehre* (Hamburg: Felix Meiner Verlag, 1968), 153–160.

[7] This way of reducing the property of being the tallest man to a conjunction of repeatable properties was suggested to me by Richard Potter.

[8] A more positive account of the function of such sentences is not relevant to the present paper. I intend to set forth such an account in a series of lectures, entitled *The First Person*, to be presented before the Royal Institute of Philosophy, in May, 1979).

[9] This question was suggested by Keith Lehrer.

[10] In a paper 'Understanding and Rational Justification,' submitted to the Conference on Explanation and Understanding, held in Magglingen, Switzerland, May 4–7, 1978.

[11] A definition of 'evident' will be given below.

[12] The change was made in order to circumvent certain criticisms which have been suggested by Herbert Heidelberger.

[13] I have use 'e entails h' to mean the same as: 'e is necessarily such that, if it obtains, then h obtains, and whoever accepts it accepts h'.

[14] This was pointed out to me by Herbert Heidelberger.

[15] The expression 'entails,' as it is used here, may be defined as follows: '*P* entails *q*' for '*p* is necessarily such that (a) if it obtains then *q* obtains and (b) whoever accepts it accepts *q*'.

[16] Could it be empirically certain for anyone that there is something which is believed to be the successor of 2? If it could be, that the statement of the principle should be qualified, perhaps by restricting '*F*' and '*G*' to properties that can be had only by contingent things. But I question whether such a proposition could be empirically certain. (The question was suggested by John Pollock).

[17] See the *Critique of Pure Reason* A98–130, A345–9; B131–138. But Kant uses one or the other of these two types of formulation: (i) "all representations belong to a single consciousness"; (ii) "all of the representations experienced by any given subject belong to a single consciousness." Strictly speaking, of course, what the first formulation expresses is false.

[18] "The thought that the representations given in intuition one and all belong to me, is therefore equivalent to the thought that I unite them in self-consciousness, or can at least so unite them." B134.

[19] Bertrand Russell, *Logic and Knowledge: Essays 1901–1950* (London: George Allen and Unwin Ltd., 1956), 164. Compare Franz Brentano, *Kategorienlehre* (Hamburg: Felix Meiner, 1968), 153–165.

JAMES W. CORNMAN

ON JUSTIFYING NONBASIC STATEMENTS BY BASIC-REPORTS

One of the crucial problems that faces a foundational theory of justification has been the difficulty of finding some plausible way to warrant inferences from what is foundational to other, nonfoundational statements. Without some such warrant only the very limited foundational statements are justified, and some form of epistemological skepticism seems reasonable. This latter is surely true if the foundation for each person is 'Cartesian', that is, consists only of what I call 'basic-reports' or first-person reports that concern only present psychological states of that person. This, of course, has traditionally been the foundation, whether for Descartes with a base of what is initially or noninferentially certain, or for C. I. Lewis who also seems to allow some statements that are merely initially acceptable, or for R. M. Chisholm who permits only the 'directly evident' at the foundation. It has, unfortunately, been the despair of ever finding a way to extend justification from such a narrow base that has caused many philosophers to flee to some nonfoundational theory. But, if what I have argued elsewhere is correct, there is no haven from skepticism there.[1] Our only hope – slim as it may seem – lies with some form of foundationalism.

My aim in this paper is twofold. First, I wish to re-enforce the view that, as the task of inferring nonfoundational statements from basic-reports has been pursued, skeptical doubts are justified. I shall do this by assuming that we are to place basic-reports at the foundation, and then arguing that no plausible set of principles warrants inferences from premises consisting solely of basic-reports, and analytic sentences to conclusions that consist of even the simplest observation-reports, such as:

p_1 'I am now seeing something yellow'.

In doing this, I will, in effect, be arguing that neither the 'Cartesian', nor 'Lewisean', nor 'Chisholmian' approach to the justification of empirical statements is successful. But it is my second goal to argue that a quite different way of construing what it is for an observation-report to be acceptable or probable or justified *relative* to basic-reports will succeed. I shall begin my first task by considering deductively inferring observation-report, p_1 from basic-reports (and analytic sentences), then turn to an examination of whether any of three forms of inductive inference will help, and end by rejecting the

129

George S. Pappas (ed.), Justification and Knowledge, 129–149.
Copyright © 1979 by D. Reidel Publishing Company.

'epistemic principles' which Chisholm proposes as supplements to deductive and inductive rules of inference.

1. ON BASIC-REPORTS ENTAILING NONBASIC STATEMENTS

The abundance of reasons that have been provided for rejecting the view known as 'analytical phenomenalism', can be used to justify the claim that no deductive argument will warrant inferences from basic-reports to nonbasic statements. To see this, let us pick one that would seem to be easiest to deduce that is, once again, p_1. And let us be as generous as possible regarding what we allow to be included among the premises. It is clear we can allow any basic-report, and that includes any conjunction, disjunction, or negation of any basic-reports. We can also include any analytic sentences on the grounds that deductive validity with analytic statements would show that p_1 is entailed by some basic-reports, and that is enough to justify that p_1 is certain, if the basic-reports are certain.

Our strategy is to try to uncover the basic-report that is most likely to yield p_1. We can approach this task by beginning with:

q I am now having an experience of something yellow, and I am now believing I am now seeing something yellow.

It is easy to show that q does not entail p_1 by the strategy of finding another sentence of any sort for which it is clear that its conjunction with q does not entail p_1. Then q does not entail p_1. For this purpose, we need only:

r I am in a room that has never contained anything yellow.

The problem, of course, is that because of the possibility of hallucination as well as illusory experience and perceptual relativity, no statement merely about present experience and belief guarantees veridical perception.

2. ON ANALYZING PHYSICAL-OBJECT STATEMENTS BY SUBJUNCTIVE CONDITIONALS

It is generally thought that subjunctive conditionals provide the best hope for yielding analyses of physical-object statements.[2] It might be suggested, then, that we should supplement q with the appropriate conditionals. But this would not help us. Our present concern is not the analysis of a physical-object statement by any sort of sensation-statement, but rather the derivation of at least one physical-object statement from some foundational basic-report. However, no subjunctive conditionals are basic-reports, and even if some of them were basic-reports, it seems clear that none of those would be initially acceptable, let alone initially certain. They would be, at best, inferentially acceptable or certain, and so not foundational.

Furthermore, the purpose of using subjunctive conditionals in analyses of physical-object statements is not to help provide basic-reports that entail observation-reports, but rather to provide basic-statements entailed by physical-object statements that are not observation-reports, such as 'There is something yellow here'. This sentence does not entail that someone is having an experience, and so the best hope for a phenomenalistic analysis of the sentence is a subjunctive conditional about what someone would experience if certain facts should be true of him. But p_1 would seem to entail that I am now having some visual experiences, so there is no reason to think that any conditional found in what entails p_1 need be subjunctive. So, it seems quite clear that deductive inference will not allow us to infer something nonbasic from basic-reports.

3. CONCLUSION: THE FAILURE OF DEDUCTIVE INFERENCE TO AVOID SKEPTICISM

The failure of the thesis that basic-reports entail nonbasic statements shows why what I call the 'Cartesian' species of traditional foundationalism leads to skepticism. This species requires not only a foundation of certainty, but also that, of empirical sentences, only basic-reports are initially certain, and that the extension of knowledge beyond the foundation is by deductive inference alone. This last requirement is made in order to guarantee inferential certainty of what is known. Thus, on this Cartesian view, each of us must begin only with his own basic-reports and 'conceptual' truths as initial premises and try to extend his knowledge by deductive derivation. But we have just seen that justification, and so knowledge, is not extended to nonbasic statements from basic-reports by deductive inference. None of this, however, shows that foundationalism in general leads to skepticism. In fact, it does not even show this for everyone who requires only certainty at the foundation and extension of justification only where there is inferential certainty. If, as I would urge, such a person adopts a probability sense of certainty, and if many basic-reports are initially certain, then this person can plausibly argue that whatever has a probability of one, given what is initially certain for someone at some time, is certain for him at that time. So, if some nonbasic statements have a probability of one, given certain basic-reports, and they are not initially certain, then they are inferentially certain. Similarly, if some nonbasic statement which is not initially acceptable, is probable, for a person, s, at a time, t, given basic-reports of s which are certain for s at t, then the nonbasic statement is highly credible (acceptable) for s at t. Someone who argues in either of these ways would not be what I have called a 'Cartesian' traditional foundationalist. But he might be what I call a 'Lewisean' traditional theorist, that is, one who holds that inductive as well as deductive inferences can extend both certainty and acceptability.

4. ON ENUMERATIVE INDUCTIVE INFERENCES FROM BASIC TO NONBASIC STATEMENTS

Might some sort of inductive argument with only basic-reports and analytic sentences as premises yield that some nonbasic-statement is probable? Generally, it is thought that there are two kinds of inductive argument where the premises are nonprobabilistic statements of fact and the conclusion is a probability statement. These can be called 'enumerative induction' and 'induction by analogy.' Unfortunately, it is not clear in either case just what the correct forms of these inductive inferences are. However, for our purposes, it is enough to approximate them and show where problems arise. Accordingly, I propose that we use A. Plantinga's explication of what he calls a 'direct inductive argument' as our example of the form of enumerative inductive arguments. Plantinga says,

A direct inductive argument for S is an ordered pair of arguments of which the first member is a simple inductive argument a for S, and the second is a valid deductive argument one premise of which is the conclusion of a, the other premise being drawn from S's total evidence.[3]

And Plantinga also says,

A simple inductive argument for S is an argument of the following form:
Every A such that S has determined by observation whether or not A is B is such that S has determined by observation that A is B. Therefore, probably every A is B.[4]

There are reasons why we should not take simple inductive arguments as embedded in every enumerative inductive argument. One reason, noted by Plantinga, is that it does not accomodate arguments where only some fraction of A's, such as m/n, has been determined by observation (that is, by experiencing these A's) to be B's. In such a case, the conclusion would seem to be that, probably, n/m A's are B's. Another reason is that, as described by Plantinga, a simple inductive argument will allow someone to conclude that it is probable that all A's are B's, when, for example, he has intentionally limited his observation of A's to those that other people have told him are B's, as he desires. But regardless of these and other problems, I shall use this direct inductive argument form to illustrate why enumerative induction fails to warrant inference from basic-reports to a conclusion about the probability of some nonbasic statement. I do this because I find that whatever amendments might succeed in avoiding these problems would not affect the inability of enumerative induction to warrant the inferences that concern us.

It is easy to see why enumerative induction is no help for us. Consider again observation-report, p_1. If I use a direct inductive argument to show it to be probable, I need something like the following as the conclusion of a simple inductive argument:

(1)   Probably, every (almost every) time when I have an experience of something yellow is a time when I am seeing something yellow.

Then with the basic-report: 'I am now having an experience of something yellow', I can supposedly infer that it is probable that I am now seeing something yellow $[p_1]$.[5] But in order to warrant the inference to (1) by a simple inductive argument, the following premise is needed:

(2)   Every (almost every) time when I have an experience of something yellow, such that I have determined by observation whether such a time is also a time when I am seeing something yellow, is such that I have determined by observation that it is a time when I am having an experience of something yellow, and is also a time when I am seeing something yellow.

And (2) is to be justified by a series of statements about me at present and in the past which are of the form:

(3)   The present time is a time when I am having an experience of something yellow and have determined by observation that this, which is such a time, is also a time when I am seeing something yellow.

The problem, of course, is that (3) is not a basic-report, because

(4)   I have determined by observation that the present time is a time when I am seeing something yellow,

is not a basic-report. And, as this argument for p_1 by means of (2) and (1) illustrates, any other direct inductive argument for p_1 will have the same flaw. In order to use any basic-report, whether simple like q or more complicated, to derive that p_1 is probable, the substitute for (1) must be of the form:

Probably, every (almost every) A is a B (where B = time when I am seeing something yellow).

And to justify this by means of a simple inductive argument, we need the same substituend for 'B' in any replacement for (2) and (3). But it is just that substituend which keeps (3) and (4) from being basic-reports. Consequently, no direct inductive arguments, and, more broadly, no enumerative inductive arguments which have only basic-reports and analytic sentences as premises yield the conclusion that p_1 is probable. So we can conclude that enumerative inductive arguments are no more helpful than deductive arguments.

5. ON INDUCTION BY ANALOGY FROM BASIC TO NONBASIC STATEMENTS

It is now quite easy to see that induction by analogy fails for the same reason as enumerative induction. I think it is fair to represent the form of an analogical argument as follows:

(i)   Entities $o_1, o_2, \ldots, o_n$ have properties $P_1, P_2, \ldots, P_m$.
(ii)   Entities $o_2, o_3, \ldots, o_n$ have property P_{m+1}.
Therefore
(iii)   It is probable that entity o_1 has property P_{m+1}.

The point here is that the more something is like a group of other things in certain known respects, the more probable it is that it is also like them in some additional, unknown respect. To make this argument form relevant to p_1 we should rephrase p_1 as:

The present moment [o_1] is a time when I see something yellow [P_{m+1}].

Premise (i) need cause no problem because we can let properties P_1 through P_m be those ascribed in basic-reports. But premise (ii) is clearly not a basic-report, because it ascribes the property P_{m+1} to moments of time, o_2 through o_n, and no sentence stating that a moment has property P_{m+1} is a basic-report. So no analogical inductive argument succeeds.

6. HYPOTHETICAL INDUCTION AND INFERENCE FROM BASIC TO NONBASIC STATEMENTS

With the failure of enumerative and analogical induction to help us, the only remaining variety of induction would seem to be that one known variously as 'hypothetico-deductive argument,' 'inference to the best explanation,' and 'hypothetical inductive argument'. As G. Harman puts it:

In making an inference to the best explanation one infers, from the fact that a certain hypothesis would explain the evidence, to the truth of that hypothesis. In general, there will be several hypotheses which might explain the evidence, so one must be able to reject all such alternative hypotheses before one is warranted in making the inference. Thus one infers, from the premise that a given hypothesis would provide a 'better' explanation for the evidence than would any other hypothesis, to the conclusion that the given hypothesis is true.[6]

Might this form of induction help? Not if Chisholm is right. In considering the problem of inferring what is indirectly evident from what is directly evident — a problem that parallels our present concern — Chisholm claims that hypothetical induction, as well as deduction, enumerative induction, and induction by analogy are of no help. It is because of this, that he adopts 'critical cognitivism' which proposes epistemic principles that are neither deductive nor inductive. He states his objection to hypothetical induction when discussing the problem of other minds, where the problem is not to infer the indirectly evident from the directly evident, but rather to infer something unobserved about a person's mental states from his observed behavior. Nevertheless, if sound, his objection is easily transformable to apply to the problem of inferring what is nonbasic from what is basic.

7. CHISHOLM'S OBJECTION TO THE USE OF HYPOTHETICAL INDUCTION: HOW TO JUSTIFY BRIDGE LAWS

Chisholm considers an example of trying to use hypothetical induction to justify a claim about a person's state of depression or about his thoughts. He says,

The 'hypothesis' that Jones is now depressed, or that he is thinking about a horse, will be put forward as the most likely explanation of certain other things we know — presumably, certain facts about Jones's present behavior and demeanor. But in order to construct an inductive argument in which the hypothesis that Jones is depressed, or that he is thinking of a horse, *is* thus to be confirmed, we must have access to a premise telling us what some of the consequences of Jone's depression, or some of the consequences of his thinking about a horse, are likely to be. And how are we to justify *this* premise if we are not entitled to make use of any information about Jone's depression or thoughts? The only possible way of finding the premise our hypothetical induction requires is to appeal to still another induction — this time an argument from analogy.[7]

And, of course, as Chisholm concludes, analogical induction will not help. We can add that neither deduction nor enumerative induction will help either. So, if Chisholm is right, hypothetical induction, either alone or combined with deduction and with other forms of induction, fails to solve the problem of other minds. And, for exactly parallel reasons, it fails to provide a way to infer the nonbasic from the basic.

8. REPLY TO CHISHOLM'S OBJECTION: WHAT AN EXPLANATORY HYPOTHESIS INDUCES

The weakness of Chisholm's argument against the use of hypothetical induction lies in his claim that the only way to justify the additional premise that relates the explaining hypothesis to what it explains is by some other form of induction. It is at this point that H. Kyburg attacks the argument. He does so by stating an example closer to our present interests that concerns how someone must use hypothetical induction to justify a nonbasic hypothesis such as H = 'There is a cat on the roof now.' This hypothesis is supposed to explain a basic-report such as O_1 = 'I am now taking there to be a cat on the roof.' In order for the explanation to succeed, we need the additional statement relating H to some basic-report. Let us follow Kyburg and use:

R   if H (There is a cat on the roof during time interval Δt), then C (Practically always, when I take myself to be looking toward the roof during Δt, under what I take to appropriate conditions of illumination and perspective and health, I take something to be a cat on the roof).[8]

Here hypothesis C is a generalization from basic-reports, and let us agree with Kyburg, for now, that C is justified by enumerative inductive from 'observed' instances, that is, from appropriate basic-reports. Then generalization C is explained by hypothesis H conjoined with R, and basic-report O_1 is explained by H and R and basic-report O_2 = 'I am now taking myself to be looking toward the roof, under what I take to be appropriate conditions of illumination and perspective and health.' Then on the assumption that H provides the best explanations of C and O_1, we can conclude, following Harman, that it is reasonable that H is true.

Chisholm's objection to this example, of course, is that even if we grant that H can be justified in this way, H does not explain either C or O_1 unless R is justified, and there is no way to justify R by means of premises that are only basic-reports and analytic sentences. Kyburg's reply to this seems to be that C is an analytic consequence of H, and so R is analytic.[9] Thus R need not be justified by deduction or induction, and, furthermore, it is allowed as a premise with basic-reports. Unfortunately, R is not analytic, nor is a related principle, P^*, that Kyburg takes to be analytic. It is clearly possible that H is true and that a Cartesian malicious demon fools everyone when they look at this roof into believing that they see a dog, instead of a cat, on the roof, no matter what else they believe. Thus this way to avoid Chisholm's objection fails.

Nevertheless, Chisholm's claim about the justification of R is mistaken, as is his objection. To see this, let us assume that the relevant form of hypothetical induction is the following somewhat simplistic form:

(1)   Basic-reports, b_1, b_2, ..., b_n, are to be explained for s at t.

(2)   Hypothesis, X, explains b_1, b_2, ..., b_n better at t than any hypothesis that conflicts with X.

Therefore

(3)   It is probable, for s at t, that X is true.

This argument form clearly differs from any valid deductive form, the form of simple inductive inference, and the form of induction by analogy. Using this form, Chisholm would make his objection by letting $n = 1$, $b_1 = O_1$ ('I am now taking there to be a cat on the roof',) and $X = H$ ('There is a cat on the roof now'). This leaves R unjustified. But his mistake is in failing to realize that an explaining hypothesis or theory, can be interpreted to include both the theoretical postulates, such as H, and also the bridge laws or correspondence rules of the theory, such as R. Thus we can substitute (H-and-R) for X in the preceding argument form, and thereby justify R as well as H by hypothetical induction.

9. A NEW OBJECTION: NO WAY TO JUSTIFY WHICH HYPOTHESIS IS BEST

Chisholm's objection fails, but another remains to be considered. Our present concern is whether some deductive or inductive argument form warrants inferences from premises that are either basic-reports or analytic to non-basic conclusions. But it is dubious that any instantiations of premises (1) and (2) of the preceding argument form are basic-reports. So hypothetical induction will not provide the inferences we seek.

The premise of this objection is correct, but its conclusion does not follow from it. Another is needed to the effect that either premise (1) or (2) is not justifiable by deductive or inductive inference from premises that are either basic-reports or analytic. This additional premise is not trivial. It is at least possible that premise (1) is deducible from certain facts about a basic-report, such as that it is certain for someone at some time, which in turn, might be entailed by some sort of basic-report. But to justify the second premise requires justifying that hypothesis X is superior to certain conflicting hypotheses regarding features such as scope, simplicity, and economy. But it seems quite unlikely that such a claim is justifiable by any series of inferences, whether deductive or inductive, from premises which include only basic-reports and analytic sentences. So we have some reason to think that hypothetical induction, combined with deduction, enumerative induction, and induction by analogy, fails to provide the desired inferences. Thus it may seem that our best hope would be to find a viable form of inference that is neither deductive nor inductive, because the three forms of induction we have examined seem to encompass all species of induction. This new search takes us to Chisholm's 'critical cognitivism.'

10. CHISHOLM'S EPISTEMIC PRINCIPLES AND INFERENCES FROM DIRECTLY TO INDIRECTLY EVIDENT

What distinguishes critical cognitivism from its rivals, according to Chisholm, is that it alone proposes a set of epistemic principles in addition to deductive and inductive principles. As can be seen by examining the nine examples Chisholm first proposed, there are three sorts of these epistemic principles. One sort provides a factual, nonepistemic sufficient condition for something being evident for a person, s, at a time, t. And since this condition concerns only what Chisholm calls 'self-presenting states' for s at t, whatever is inferred to be evident by this sort of principle is what Chisholm calls 'the directly evident', or, in my terminology, 'the initially evident'. One example stated by Chisholm is:

> Necessarily, for any S and any t, if S thinks at t that he perceives something that is red, then it is evident to S at t that he then thinks he perceives something that is red.[10]

Epistemic principles of the second sort are the most important for our purposes, because they function to provide inferences from premises constituted solely of what is directly evident or analytic to conclusions stating that something else is acceptable, reasonable, or evident. And, I suppose, what can be inferred as having one of these epistemic statuses by use of this second sort of rule, but not by use of the first, is indirectly or inferentially acceptable, reasonable, or evident. An example of this sort of principle is Chisholm's first formulation of his principle B, which is equivalent to:

$B1$ If S believes that he is perceiving something to have a property F, then it is reasonable for S that he is perceiving something to be F, and that something is F.[11]

Notice that the antecedent of $B1$ concerns only a 'self-presenting state', or, linguistically, a basic-report, which meets the requirement that it is to consist of only basic-reports and analytic sentences. Principle $B1$, then, might well be the sort of principle we need to supplement deductive and inductive rules.

However, as we shall see, Chisholm's own amended versions of *B1* include an epistemic clause in their antecedents and so seem not to qualify as this sort of principle.

In both the first and second sorts of principles, the antecedent is supposed to be factual and nonepistemic, while the consequent is epistemic. But in principles of the third sort, both antecedent and consequent include epistemic claims, because they state that certain statements having a certain epistemic status affect the epistemic status of other sentences. Consider Chisholm's principle *G*:

G   If the conjunction of all those propositions *e*, such that *e* is acceptable for *S* at *t* tends to confirm *h*, then *h* has some presumption in its favor for *S* at *t*.[12]

Let us concentrate on principle *B1* as a prime example of the sort of non-deductive, noninductive epistemic principle that, according to Chisholm, provides the desired link between the directly evident and the indirectly evident, the basic and the nonbasic. Our primary concern will be to judge whether it is reasonable to adopt a set of principles for *B1*. Crucial to this decision will be the task of seeing whether *B1*, or at least one of its amended versions, survives attempts to provide counterexamples.

11. CRITICAL EXAMINATION OF EPISTEMIC PRINCIPLE *B1*

As stated, principle *B1* is inadequate, as H. Heidelberger has shown. Assume that *B1* has the form: 'If *P*, then *Q* and *R*.' Then Heidelberger's strategy is to discover a statement, *S* such that (*P-and-S*) does not imply either *Q* or *R*. So *P* implies neither *Q* nor *R*. Heidelberger creates his counter example by letting *F* be the property of being yellow, and *S* = '*s* knows at *t* that *U*', where *U* = 'There is a yellow light shining on the object *s* sees, a moment ago there was no colored light shining on the object, and at that time *s* perceived the object to be white.' Surely, given that *s* knows all this, it is at least not reasonable fo for him that he is perceiving something yellow or that something is yellow, regardless of whether he now believes that he is now perceiving something to be yellow. So *B1* must either be amended or abandoned.[13]

12. EXAMINATION OF A CHISHOLMIAN AMENDMENT TO *B1*

Chisholm later agrees with Heidelberger's criticism of *B1* and proposes an amendment to avoid the preceding counterexample. His idea is to propose a statement to be conjoined with the antecedent of *B1* that is not true in the situation imagined by Heidelberger. Chisholm's newest clause is something like:

> (2)   For any conjunction, c, of statements that are acceptable for s at t, it is false that, necessarily, if what is entailed by c is exactly what is evident for s at t, then, at t, it is more reasonable for s to believe that he is *not* perceiving something to be P than to believe that he is perceiving something to be P.

Chisholm proposes, in effect, that in *every* situation where s believes $V =$ 'I am perceiving something to be F (yellow)', but it is not reasonable for him to believe that he is perceiving something to be P, there is some conjunction of statements that are acceptable for him and that would justify the denial of P if that conjunction should be s's total evidence for V at t. What results is principle $B2$. [14]

In the situation that provides a counterexample to $B1$, statement U, which is evident for s, would provide the desired conjunction. Thus, that situation causes no problem for $B2$. It is, however, implausible to think that there is always such a conjunction to block the undesirable inference. Consider a second situation, like the previous one, with one exception. Assume that U is true, but s has conveniently forgotten about a moment ago and refuses to allow the many people who have been with him to tell him their views, which are, unanimously, that the object is white and the light is now yellow. In short, he forgets what is epistemically bothersome, and intentionally keeps himself from easily obtainable evidence. It would seem, then, that U is not acceptable for s at t because he lacks any evidence that favors it. Indeed, we can assume that the only evidence he has that is relevant to U counts against it, because it consists only of a basic-report about s's perceptual belief, and a basic-report about his experience of something yellow. So here U does not falsity clause (2) of $B2$. Furthermore, in this situation it is plausible that no conjunction concocted from these two basic-reports and any other sentences acceptable for s at t would, by itself, make it more reasonable for s to believe that he is *not* perceiving something to be yellow than to be agnostic about that claim. So by avoiding what would make U acceptable for him at t, s would be able to infer, by means of $B2$, that it is reasonable, for him at t, that he is perceiving something to be yellow. But, again, that would be incorrect. So Chisholm's latest amendment fails.

I believe that the counterexamples to $B1$ and $B2$ justify our concluding that Chisholm's critical cognitivism, with its epistemic rules, fails to provide what warrants inferences from the basic to the nonbasic. Of course, Chisholm could try other amendments, but, after trying several others myself and finding none to be plausible, I see no hope for finding a viable replacement for *B1* and *B2*.

At this point it might seem that we should conclude that no nonbasic statements are acceptable or probable relative to basic-reports, because neither deduction, induction, nor Chisholm's epistemic rules warrant te desired inferences. However, Heidelberger suggests a way to avoid this conclusion when he considers ways that Chisholm might change his principle to avoid objections. One of his suggestions is that Chisholm should use principles that, unlike *B1* and *B2*, are not conditional in form. That is, instead of proposing principles of the form:

> If q, then p is (probable, acceptable, highly credible, reasonable, evident, certain) for s at t,

Chisholm might try one with the following form:

> q makes p (probable, acceptable, highly credible, reasonable, evident, certain) for s at t.[15]

The latter sort, unlike the former, is consistent with the claim that it is false that if q and r, then p is (probable, acceptable, etc.) for s at t. Thus principles of the second sort avoid all the preceding counterexamples to Chisholm's *B1* and its kin.

Heidelberger's suggestion takes us to a different interpretation of 'p is probable *relative* to q,' namely, when it means: 'p is probable, *given* q,' or, identically, 'the probability of p, *given* q, is greater than .5' (that is, 'pr (p/q) > .5'). I shall continue to use 'p is probable *relative* to q' as ambiguous, because of having two quite different interpretations. On this second interpretation, then, it is clear that the claim that p is probable relative to q is not falsified by the claim that p is not probable relative to q and r (that is, 'Pr$(p/q \cdot r)$ < .5'), and so none of the previous problems for *B1* or *B2* arise. This is because it is a theorem of the probability calculus that Pr(p/q) = [Pr$(p/q \cdot r)$ × Pr(r/q)] + [Pr$(p/q \cdot \bar{r})$ × Pr$(\bar{r}/q)$], and this allows Pr(p/q) to be much larger than Pr$(p/q \cdot r)$. Nevertheless, the question remains whether, for p = 'I am now perceiving something that is F,' there is an appropriate set of basic-reports, q, for which Pr$_{s,t}$ $(Tpst/Tqst)$ > .5.

I should note two points here. The first is that '$Tpst$' is 'p' 'eternalized' to s at t. It can be read as either 'p is true of person, s, at time, t,' or as 'At t, s is perceiving something that is F.' I 'eternalize' reports in these ways so that we can include them in probability sentences. However, having noted this, I shall from here on usually talk of the probability of reports; but, when I do this, I should be understood to be discussing the probability of their eternalized versions. The second point is that by 'Pr$_{s,t}$ (p/q) = n' I mean, following

Carnap, that the degree of confirmation of p, for s at t, given $q = n$.[16]

13. ON PRINCIPLES FOR INFERRING CONDITIONAL PROBABILITIES

I propose that we begin by looking for a principle of the following form:

> If e is s's evidence for p at t, and e has property G, then $\Pr_{s,t}(p/q)$ > .5.

That is, we should search for some characteristic of s's evidence, e, such that if e has the characteristic, then p is probable, for s at t, given e. Although the proceding principle is a conditional and thereby allows us to detach its consequent when the antecedent is satisfied, the previous problems for Chisholm's principles do not arise because the consequent states a relative probability rather than one that is absolute (for example, $\Pr(p) > .5$).

Chisholm might propose that we can formulate the principle we desire merely by adapting his original $B1$ to the second interpretation of 'p is probable relative to q.' That is, he might propose something like:

> $BR1$ If $e = \{$'s believes at t that he is perceiving something that is F'$\}$, then $\Pr(p/e) > .5$ (where p is an observation-report of the form: 'At t, s is perceiving something that is F').

However, I propose that we relativize the probability statement in $BR1$ to person s and time t, and also that we add to the evidence set what is considered to be foundational evidence by the theory that R. Firth calls the 'traditional empiricist theory of evidence,' namely, some appropriate report about sensory experience.[17] One reason for this addition is, as Heidelberger notes, "that men are capable of believing almost anything, about what they perceive or remember no less than about anything else."[18] And, for added insurance, let us also require that s believe with certainty that he and the conditions relevant to perceiving something that is F are normal. A new candidate, which embodies all these changes, and thus combines Chisholm's 'taking criterion' with the 'empiricist criterion,' is:

> $BR2$ If set $e = \{$'I now believe with certainty that I am now perceiving something that is F,' 'I am now having an experience of something that is F,' 'I now believe with certainty that I and the conditions relevant to my seeing something that is F are normal'$\}$, and p is an observation-report of the form: 'I am now perceiving something that is F,' then $\Pr_{s,t}(Tpst/Test) > .5$.

Here a problem confronts us. How are we to evaluate $BR2$, especially without a set of principles for ordering probabilities, both relative and absolute?

The best approach, I find, is to proceed as follows. We know from the probability calculus that:

$$\text{Pr}_{s,t}(p) \geqslant \text{Pr}_{s,t}(p/q) \times \text{Pr}_{s,t}(q).$$

Thus we can arrive at a statement about the absolute probability of p, if we have a way to find the value of $\text{Pr}(q)$. Here I want to introduce, without comment, a principle similar to one I have argued for elsewhere, namely:

H For any basic-report, b, *if* (1) at t, s understands and believes b with certainty, and (2) for any basic-report, r, that, at t, s understands and believes with certainty, $\text{Pr}_{s,t}(Tbst/Trst) \geqslant \text{Pr}_{s,t}(Tbst/Z)$, where Z is a simple tautology, *then* b is certain for s at t [that is, $\text{Pr}_{s,t}(Tbst) = 1$].[19]

H allows us to conclude that for any basic-report, b, that satisfies its antecedent, $\text{Pr}_{s,t}(b) = 1$. So whenever the three statements in set e meet the antecedent of H, then, individually and conjointly, the probabilities of their eternalized versions, for s at t, equals one. Thus, given H, whenever an observation-report, p, satisfies the antecedent of $BR2$, and s's evidence for it, e, satisfies H, then $\text{Pr}_{s,t}(p) > .5$, provided that $BR2$ is true. Therefore, if we can find a situation where both antecedents are met but it is unreasonable to conclude that the degree of confirmation of p, for s at t, is greater than .5, then we will have reason to reject $BR2$. This is how we shall test $BR2$.

Let us assume that the antecedents of H and $BR2$ are met by certain members of s's evidence set, e_1, in a particular situation, namely:

$S1$ (1) $e_1 = \{b_1^1, b_2^1, b_3^1\}$, where $b_1^1 = $ 'I now believe with certainty that I am now seeing something that is yellow,' $b_2^1 = $ 'I am now having a visual experience of something yellow,' and $b_3^1 = $ 'I now believe with certainty that I and the conditions relevant to my seeing something to be yellow are normal';

      (2)   at t, s understands and believes with certainty the conjunction of b_1^1, b_2^1, b_3^1;

      (3)   for $q = (b_1^1 \cdot b_2^1 \cdot b_3^1)$, and for any basic-report, r, that s understands and believes with certainty at t, $\text{Pr}_{s,t}(Tqst/Trst) \geqslant \text{Pr}_{s,t}(Tqst/Z)$.

The crucial question, then, is whether we can further elaborate the situation described above in such a way that it is clearly implausible that the degree of confirmation of observation-report p_1, for s at t, is high. One obvious way to begin is by injecting into the situation that irrationally obstinate person, s, with the conveniently poor memory, who, as we saw, played havoc with Chisholm's principle, $B2$. Does he also provide a reason to reject $BR2$?

14. OBJECTION TO PRINCIPLE *RB2*: REFUSING TO EVALUATE
RATIONALLY

Our obstinate friend causes less of a problem for *BR2* than he did for *B2*. This is because in situation S_1, p_1 is supposed to be probable relative to a set of basic-reports that include more than the one found in *B2*, namely, *s*'s belief-report, b_1^1. In S_2, the set also contains his report about his visual experience and his conviction that everything relevant to his seeing color is normal. Nevertheless, *s*'s refusal to listen to the testimony of others, and his convenient forgetting that just a moment ago he had an expereince of the object before him as white, surely seem to require that we not conclude that p_1 is highly confirmed for *s* at *t*. This becomes even clearer, if we make, as I suggest we should, the following assumption:

   A   If *e* is *s*'s evidence for *p* at *t*, and $\mathrm{Pr}_{s,t}$ (*Test*) = 1, and $\mathrm{Pr}_{s,t}$ (*Tpst/ Test*) > .5, then *p* is acceptable (highly credible) for *s* at *t*.

My reason for assuming *A* is that if *s*'s evidence *e* satisfies the antecedent of *A*, then $\mathrm{Pr}_{s,t}$ (*e*) = 1 and so it follows that $\mathrm{Pr}_{s,t}$ (*p*) > .5. And, importantly, the latter is derivable using only $\mathrm{Pr}_{s,t}$ (*p/e*) > .5 and the probability of *s*'s evidence at *t*. That is, only what is available to *s* at *t* is needed to derive $\mathrm{Pr}_{s,t}$ (*p*) > .5 from $\mathrm{Pr}_{s,t}$ (*p/e*) > .5, as would not be true if $\mathrm{Pr}_{s,t}$ (*p*) > .5, but $\mathrm{Pr}_{s,t}$ (*p/e*) $\times$ $\mathrm{Pr}_{s,t}$ (*e*) < .5. That seems sufficient for acceptability.[20]

Given *A*, with *H* and *BR2*, p_1 is acceptable for our dogmatic believer, *s*. And that is implausible, especially if we emphasize that *s* is intentionally avoiding listening to those around him, and is avoiding trying to remember the details of his experience a moment ago. We should, then, reject *BR2* as we did *B1* and *B2*.

An obvious move at this point is to specify more fully what is to be in *s*'s evidence set if we are to produce a sufficient condition for p_1's being highly confirmed, and, according to *A*, p_1's being acceptable, for *s* at *t*. What we would like to ensure is that *s* be trying to do everything within his power to receive and evaluate fairly all the available evidence that is relevant to p_1's being true of him at *t*. Let us, then, add a fourth basic-report to *s*'s evidence set:

   b_4^1 I am not trying hard to evaluate rationally, and I believe I am now evaluating rationally, all evidence (including any about the past) now available to me that is relevant to my now seeing something to be yellow, or to my present visual perceptual conditions being normal, or to my canons of evidence being reasonable.

Then with $e_2 = \{b_1^1, b_2^1, b_3^1, b_4^1\}$ and with situation *S1* amended to include b_4^1

and e_2, we have situation S2. Note that I have included in b_4^1 a clause about trying hard to use reasonable canons of evidence. I added this because a person could be quite open and rational about everything except his own, irrationally idiosyncratic canons of evidence which he refuses to reconsider. For example, such a person might obstinately consider only 'direct' testimony from God to be evidence relevant to p_1. Thus he could meet all the other requirements of situation S2, and intentionally avoid the contrary testimony of others. Once again we would have a person for whom p_1 would not be highly confirmed at t, and p_1 would not be acceptable at t.

Is situation S2 sufficient for p_1 being highly confirmed for s at t? There is some reason to think it is. I say this in spite of the fact that it is still possible in situation S2 that, in spite of his understandingly and firmly believing that he is trying to be rational and open, s may still be blocking out relevant evidence and fooling himself about the present observation conditions and the rationality of his canons of evidence. But the point behind S2 is that it is epistemically certain for s at t that he has the relevant beliefs and experiences, and that he is trying hard to be rational in obtaining and assessing evidence and in choosing his canons of evidence. I find nothing more we can ask of him at this time. In having the relevant beliefs, and in trying to be rational, he is doing everything in his power at this time. He seems to deserve the minor epistemic honors of having p_1 be probable (that is, highly confirmed for him at t), and p be acceptable for him at t.

There is, nevertheless, still one way this person might be irrational. We must rule out this possibility if we are to have a sufficient condition for p_1 being highly confirmed for s at t. It is clearly possible that, although s fully believes that he is trying mightily to consider everything epistemically relevant to p_1, he overlooks one of his own basic-reports, b_5, which he understandingly and fully believes, and $\text{Pr}_{s,t}(p_1/b_5) < .5$. In this situation, we should not infer that p_1 is acceptable for s at t in S2, if we find such a basic-report that fits with situation S2. So if we find one, then S2 is not sufficient for p_1 being highly confirmed. Consider, the following:

b_5^1 I now believe I remember that the object now before me looked and was white just a moment ago, and I am now having an experience of a color that is the same color that I saw a moment ago.

I find it plausible that $\text{Pr}_{s,t}(p_1/b_5) < .5$., that s fully believes b_5^1 in situation S_2, and that, because of this, p_1 is not highly confirmed for s at t. Consequently, we must add a fourth clause to the description of the relevant situation so that it does not include s's understandingly and firmly believing any basic-report like b_5^1. We can guarantee this by requiring that no basic-report that s believes in this way at t is 'negatively relevant' to p_1. That is, we want to require that for any such basic-report, r, the probability of p_1, given r, is no less than that of p_1, given any simple tautology. This, of course, allows s to believe many basic-reports such as 'I now believe that $2 + 2 = 4$,' that are neither negatively or positively relevant to p_1. What results is $S3$ whose fourth clause is:

> (4)   for any basic-report, r, that s understands and believes with certainty at t, $\mathrm{Pr}_{s,t} (Tp_1 st/Trst) \geq \mathrm{Pr}_{s,t} (Tp_1 st/Z)$, where Z is a simple tautology.

I submit that $S3$ is sufficient for p_1 being probable, that is, highly confirmed for s at t. To bolster my claim, let me point out that $S3$ is only said to be sufficient for p_1 having a degree of confirmation greater than one half for the person s at the time t. This is a very weak claim. It requires no more than that the degree of confirmation of p_1 for s at t is some miniscule amount greater than that of its denial, and it is compatible with p_1 being disconfirmed for s at all times other than t. Thus this claim implies no more than that $S3$ gives a minute edge in confirmation to p_1 over its denial for one person, s, at one time, t. This extremely weak claim seems quite plausible.

15. PROPOSAL FOR A PRINCIPLE FOR INFERRING CONDITIONAL PROBABILITIES: BR3

We have been testing epistemic principles of the form:

> If R, then $\mathrm{Pr}_{s,t} (p/c) > .5$,

where e consists of eternalized basic-reports and p is an eternalized observation-report. We have done this indirectly for each principle by describing a situation that instantiates its antecedent and also that of principle H. Thus, if both H and the principle we are testing are correct, then some observation-report is probable (highly confirmed) for some person at time, whenever one situation instantiates the antecedents of both principles. I have argued that we may accept situation $S3$ as sufficient for p_1 being highly confirmed for s at t. Consequently, we should be able to extract from $S3$ a general principle of the above form that is also acceptable. We can do this by doing two things: first, replacing 'yellow' by the variable, 'F', in the basic-reports, b_1^1, b_2^1, b_3^1, and b_4^1, and in the observation-report, p_1, to form sentence variables, b_1, b_2, b_3, b_4, and p; and, second, removing from $S3$ what is required only for the instantiation of principle H. What results is:

> $BR3$ If (1) $e = \{b_1, b_2, b_3, b_4\}$, where b_1 through b_4 are basic-reports, and p is an observation-report of the form: 'I am now perceiving

something that is F;' and (2) for any basic-report, r, that s understands and believes with certainty at t, $\mathrm{Pr}_{s,t}$ $(Tpst/Trst) \geqslant \mathrm{Pr}_{s,t}$ $(Tpst/Z)$, where Z is a simple tautology, *then* $\mathrm{Pr}_{s,t}$ $(Tpst/Test) >$ .5 (that is, p being true of s at t is highly confirmed, for s at t, given that the reports in e are true of s at t).

I claim that the preceding discussion provides reason sufficient to warrant the acceptance of *BR3*. I also claim it is clear that the antecedent of *BR3* is often satisfied by someone. Consider a situation where no one is anywhere near s at t, and s has no beliefs or experiences at t that are negatively relevant to p_1. This is often true when, for example, someone first notices the bright yellow color of a flower when walking alone through a woods while mediating. Because there are so many of these situations, it is reasonable to conclude that for some instantiations of 'e' and 'p' in *BR3*, some sentences of the form $\mathrm{Pr}_{s,t}$ $(p/e) > .5$ are true. Moreover, I claim, in some of these situations that instantiate the antecedent of *BR3* — perhaps where the stroller is somewhat philosophically inclined — we find someone who is convinced about all four basic-reports that constitute evidence set, e, and believes no basic-reports that are negatively relevant to them. That is, in effect, not only does he fully believe that he is having an experience of something yellow, and that he believes he is seeing something yellow, but also, after some reflection, he becomes convinced that he and the relevant perceptual condition are normal, and that he has tried as hard as he can to be rational. So, by principles *BR3* and H, we can further conclude that at that time it is probable and, by principle A, acceptable for this person that he is seeing something that is yellow.

16. CONCLUSION

If all I have said above should be correct, then the inability of foundationalists to provide an inference from basic-premises to nonbasic conclusions would not be fatal to a foundationalist who allows only basic-reports at the foundation of justification. This is because when we understand 'p is probable relative to basic evidence, e', as a relative probability statement, not only do Heidelberger-type objections not apply, but principle *BR3* seems to provide a sufficient condition for when such relative probability statements are true. In addition, we would have a means for justifying observation-reports 'absolutely' when the only evidence for them is basic-reports. Yet, to avoid sounding too optimistic about how to get widespread justification from a restricted base, let me conclude by cautioning that the task of establishing a foundational theory that allows for the justification of claims about unperceived physical objects, the past, the future, and other minds, is barely begun by providing a way to justify observation-reports. What remains is a much larger and more difficult task.

NOTES

[1] See my 'Foundational versus Nonfoundational Theories of Empirical Justification,' in Pappas and Swain, eds., *Essays on Knowledge and Justification* (Ithaca, N.Y.: Cornell University Press, 1978), pp. 229–252.

[2] For a more detailed examination of subjunctive analyses of physical-object statements, see my *Perception, Common Sense, and Science*, (New Haven: Yale University Press, 1975), pp. 121–123.

[3] A. Plantinga, *God and Other Minds* (Ithaca, N.Y.: Cornell University Press, 1967) p. 251.

[4] *Ibid.*

[5] For problems for mixing probabilistic and nonprobabilistic premises, see P. Suppes 'Probabilistic Inference and the Concept of Total Evidence,' in J. Hintikka and P. Suppes, eds., *Aspects of Inductive Logic* (Amsterdam: North Holland Publishing Co., 1966), pp. 49–50.

[6] G. Harman, 'The Inference to the Best Explanation,' *The Philosophical Review* 74 (1965), 89.

[7] R. Chisholm, *Theory of Knowledge* (Englewood Cliffs, N.J.: Prentice-Hall, Inc., 1977, 2nd edition), p. 129.

[8] See H. Kyburg, 'On a Certain Form of Philosophical Argument,' *American Philosophical Quarterly* 7 (1970), p. 233.

[9] *Ibid.*

[10] R. Chisholm, 'On the Nature of Empirical Evidence,' in *Empirical Knowledge* (Englewood Cliffs, N.J.: Prentice-Hall, Inc., 1973), p. 242.

[11] See Chisholm, *Theory of Knowledge*, 1st edition, p. 45.

[12] See Chisholm, *Theory of Knowledge*, 2nd edition, pp. 82–83.

[13] See H. Heidelberger, 'Chisholm's Epistemic Principles,' *Nous* 3 (1969), 73–75.

[14] See Chisholm, *Theory of Knowledge*, 2nd edition, p. 76. The definitions needed to unpack Chisholm's statement of the principle so it closely resembles *B2* are on pp. 135–136. For an earlier, extremely complex revision of *B1*, see 'On the Nature of Empirical Evidence,' p. 244.

[15] See Heidelberger, 'Chisholm's Epistemic Principles,' pp. 75–78.

[16] See R. Carnap, 'Inductive Logic and Rational Decisions,' in R. Carnap and R. Jeffrey eds., *Studies in Inductive Logic and Probability* (Berkeley: University of California Press, 1971), p. 25.

[17] See R. Firth, 'Ultimate Evidence,' *The Journal of Philosophy* 53 (1956); reprinted in R. Swartz, ed., *Perceiving, Sensing, and Knowing* (Berkeley: University of California Press, 1976), pp. 486–496.

[18] Heidelberger, p. 81.

[19] See my 'On the Certainty of Reports about What is Given', *Nous*, Vol. XII, 2, (May,

1978), for a defense of a similar principle, namely, *H3*. The reason for clause (2) will become apparent when a similar clause in principle *BR3* is discussed.

[20] It may seem that principle *A* generates the lottery paradox, but this paradox arises only where what Kyburg calls the 'conjunction principle' applies. (See H. Kyburg, 'Conjunctivitis,' in M. Swain, ed., *Induction, Acceptance, and Rational Belief* (Dordrecht: D. Reidel Publishing Co., 1970), p. 53.) I maintain that the conjunction principle applies to what is acceptable to use conjointly as evidence, but not to what is merely acceptable to believe.

MARK PASTIN

THE NEED FOR EPISTEMOLOGY: PROBLEMATIC
REALISM DEFENDED

Epistemology, as I see it, is centrally concerned with the conditions under which statements (propositions, sentences, claims, whatever) are warranted — in a familiar, restricted sense of warranted; rationally as opposed to ethically, aesthetically, legally or otherwise warranted — for a person, and with the concept of warrant. This outlook presupposes that understanding of warrant conditions and of the concept of warrant are essential to understanding the nature of knowledge, which is the defining topic for epistemology. (Note: Despite this, I hold that warrant or justification is not necessary for knowledge.[1]) The other concepts requisite to understanding knowledge, e.g., the concepts of belief, truth, or process of inference, are properly investigated by metaphysics and philosophical psychology. This concern with warrant has recently been challenged. One thrust is that with fuller understanding of the semantic, syntactic, and perhaps psychological character of statements, there will be no interesting residue of issues to be explored in terms of a concept of epistemic warrant. A second thrust is that the Gettier problem, and problems arising from the operation of social factors in knowledge attribution, show that the concept of warrant does not help explain the nature of knowledge. Appeals to reliability, discrimination among alternatives, and causation, rather than warrant, are the fashion. I contend that both thrusts miss the mark. I parry the first thrust here by offering an account, to which I give the dusty label 'Problematic Realism', of the relations between epistemic features and other features of empirical statements.[2] The second thrust is treated in a sequel to this essay on the role of social factors in knowledge attributed.[3]

1. A QUESTION

I begin exploring the relations between epistemic and other features of empirical, or logically contingent, statements with the question: Are all epistemic facts dependent on non-epistemic facts? The first step in considering this question is to probe what 'dependent on' means. The idea is fairly straightforward. Just as the color of a medium-sized physical object is a function of the microstructural character of the object and its environment (including the perceiver), so epistemic facts might be a function of non-epistemic facts,

151

George S. Pappas (ed.), Justification and Knowledge, 151–168.
Copyright © 1979 by D. Reidel Publishing Company.

facts which can be perspicuously stated in language which does not employ 'warrant', any of its near synonyms, or expressions explainable only in terms of 'warrant' or its near synonyms. If this idea, when sharpened and solidified, is sound, then there would be a sense in which concern with warrant conditions and the concept of warrant is secondary. For warrant conditions and the concept of warrant would divide the world in a way that is less useful in the explanation of certain data of interest, even data epistemically formulated, than some other conceptualization of the world, perhaps in terms of semantic, syntactic, or psychological categories. To see if there is something to this line, I shall try to sharpen and give content to the idea that epistemic facts depend on, are a function of, or, in the jargon I prefer, supervene on, non-epistemic facts.

It would be impossible in the space of this essay to explore the many senses in which one type of fact can be said to supervene on another. I shall distinguish one sense that is useful in formulating a manageable version of our initial question, which is now phrased 'Do all epistemic facts supervene on non-epistemic facts?' The epistemic facts of interest are of two forms, those of the form 'that statement P is warranted for person S at time t' (warrant conditions) and those of the form 'that statement P warrants statement Q for person S at time t' (warrant relations). These are abbreviated respectively '$W(P/S,t)$' and '$W(P,Q/S,t)$'. While I shall not here explore the concepts of warrant employed, I offer some brief comments.[4] To say that a statement is warranted for a person at a time is to say the minimal good thing about the statement, that it is better off than its denial, from an epistemic viewpoint. I prefer to explicate '$W(P/S,t)$' as 'S would believe P at t were S's beliefs ideal (in specified respects $1-n$) at t',[5] but this account is not presupposed. To say that statement P warrants statement Q for S at t is to say that P's being warranted for S at t, in the specified minimal sense, suffices for Q to be warranted for S at t in the same sense. A gloss: $W(P,Q/S,t)$ iff (a) $W(P/S,t)$ and $W(Q/S,t)$, and (b) $W(Q/S,t)$ would be the case even if *only* statements necessary to $W(P/S,t)$ being the case were warranted for S at t. The *non*-epistemic facts to be considered will pertain to statements P and Q, person S, and time t, and will be named by expressions of the form '$Fn(P,Q/S,t)$' – 'fact n concerning P, Q, S, and t'.

With these preliminaries we characterize a sense in which a warranting relation supervenes on a non-epistemic fact.

> $W(P,Q/S,t)$ *supervenes on* $Fn(P,Q/S,t)$ iff (a) it is epistemically necessary that, if both $W(P/S,t)$ and $Fn(P,Q/S,t)$ obtain, then $W(Q/S,t)$ obtains, and (b) it is not epistemically necessary that if $W(P/S,t)$ obtains, then $W(Q/S,t)$ obtains.

(I restrict the characterization of supervenience to warrant *relations* because extension to warrant *conditions* involves complications not germane to my line of argument.) The expression 'it is epistemically necessary that' is stipulated to mean 'it follows from true warrant principles that'. The point of referring to what follows from true warrant principles is to avoid disputes over the sort of necessity, if any, appropriate to relations among epistemic and non-epistemic facts. Consider an arguably plausible example of a warranting relation supervening on a non-epistemic fact: Suppose that P is warranted for S at t *and* P entails Q (perhaps in a restricted sense – requiring that Q is not 'conceptually richer than' P or that the entailment is 'psychologically real'). These facts together, not separately, may allow deduction of '$W(Q/S,t)$' from true warrant principles.

Is there reason to think that warranting relations sometimes, or always, supervene on non-epistemic facts? In favor of the existential claim is the fact that it does seem that deductive or inductive relations between statements are bases of some warranting relations. In favor of the universal claim is the idea that to explain a warranting relation between statements for a person at a time, it seems necessary to appeal to *some* non-epistemic relation, perhaps not a logical (deductive or inductive) relation, but a psychological, statistical or some other sort of relation. That is, a philosophically adequate defense of a claimed warranting relation of P to Q for S at t seems to require citing of non-epistemic facts involving P, Q, S and t.

I shall not challenge the existential claim since allowing that some warranting relations supervene on non-epistemic facts hardly supports a claimed superfluity of epistemology. However, if *all* warranting relations supervened on non-epistemic facts, one might seriously argue the superfluity of epistemology, at least with respect to the category of warranting relations. For, it might be contended, all that would have to be added to a full account of the non-epistemic facts in order to explain warranting relations is the set of warrant principles constituting epistemic necessity, a set of principles which may be no more (or less) interesting than principles explaining the supervenience of macro-properties of physical objects on their micro-properties. Whatever the merits of this contention, or a suitably refined version of it, it fails because universal supervenience can not be maintained.

I have argued that certain warranting relations involved in perceptual knowledge can not be viewed as supervening on non-epistemic facts in our sense of supervenience.[6] The argument is simple but requires too much background epistemology to lay out fully here. The argument presupposes (1) that there is a distinction between those empirical statements which are *self*-warranted, warranted independent of inferential relations, and the other empirical statements warranted for a person at a time, (2) that there is correlated with this distinction a subject-matter difference between self-warranted and non-self-warranted empirical statements, and (3) that the warrant of non-self-warranted empirical statements is dependent on warranting by self-warranted empirical statements. (3) provokes the question: How do self-warranted empirical statements (hereafter, *basic* statements) warrant non-self-warranted empirical statements (hereafter, *non-basic* statements)? The argument is by exhaustion of cases that no non-epistemic relation between such statements suffices to account for this type of warranting. Basic statements clearly do not deductively warrant all other empirical statements. Nor can basic empirical statements inductively warrant all non-basic empirical statements — at least if induction is restricted to familiar forms of reasoning from sample to population. The problem is that such inductive warranting presupposes a *warranted* correlation between statements which have one type of subject-matter (and are basic) and statements which have a distinct subject-matter (and are non-basic) as the ground for further warrant extension. And it is precisely this sort of warranting relation for which we seek a *non-epistemic* basis. This pushes us towards 'special' warranting principles, principles appealed to only to bridge this basic/non-basic gap. These include principles of perceptual taking, principles of abductive inference (including so-called inference-to-the-best-explanation), and principles of inference from effect to cause (including Lockean similiarity principles). It is argued that these principles fail to ground supervenience of basic/non-basic warranting for one of two reasons: Either the principles themselves presuppose warranting relations of this kind, or the principles state epistemic rather than non-epistemic facts. Principles of inference from effect to cause and some principles of abductive inference are open to the first objection — How does the required correlation between effect and cause or data and that which is inferred to become warranted? Principles of abductive inference, along with principles of perceptual taking, are open to the second objection. It is clear that an essential part of being the best explanation is being an explanation that in some sense maximizes warrant, and that to understand when warrant is maximized one must understand basic/non-basic warranting relations. In fact, principles of inference to the best explanation are often formulated in explicitly epistemic terms — the conclusion of the inference being that there is reason to hold that . . . . Principles of perceptual taking are also formulated in explicitly epistemic terms, thus providing no basis of non-epistemic facts on which basic/non-basic warranting supervenes. This sketch is not intended to finally convince, but to suggest the structure of reasoning which, hopefully, does convince.

There are other reasons for doubting *universal* supervenience of warranting relations on non-epistemic facts. These reasons concern projectability problems. The facet of these problems relevant here is this: There is no feature of the truth conditions or non-epistemically characterized inferential relations of statements involving 'green' versus 'grue' which explains why inductive inferences on 'green', but not those on 'grue', yield warranted conclusions. That is, there is nothing in the truth-conditions or non-epistemically characterized inferential relations of 'green' and 'grue' statements which allows derivation of '$a_n + 1$ *is green* is warranted for S at t' as opposed to '$a_n + 1$ *is grue* is warranted for S at t' from 'a_1 *to* a_n *are green* (*grue*) is warranted for S at t' and non-epistemic facts concerning a_1 to a_n are green (grue), $a_n + 1$ is green (grue), S, and t. Of course, if we hold that there actually is a difference in warranting ability of 'green' and 'grue' statements, this surely will be reflected in our warranting principles, arguably allowing appropriate derivations of the above sort. This point forces attention to the notion of a warrant *principle*, employed in explaining epistemic necessity and supervenience. If we are generous enough in counting principles as warrant principles, then allowing that there is an epistemic truth may insure universal supervenience.

A distinction between *general* and *specific* warrant principles will prove helpful. The basic idea is that general warrant principles are principles that belong to a theory for the expressions '$W(\_\_/\_\_,\_\_)$' and '$W(\_\_,\_\_/\_\_,\_\_)$', whereas specific warrant principles are concerned with warrant conditions and relations specific to certain non-epistemic expressions. The issue of supervenience, and related claims of epistemic superfluity, can be viewed in terms of whether all warrant principles are general — in which case both universal supervenience and related claims of epistemic superfluity would be justified. We can clarify matters by not distinguishing general and specific warrant principles *per se*, but instead considering warrant principles general or specific *with respect to specified statements,* or, more accurately, sentences with which the statements are made. Warrant principles general with respect to sentences $P_1, \ldots, P_n$ can be formulated without employing non-logical constituents of $P_1, \ldots, P_n$. If we take names to be uniquely satisfiable predicate functions, warrant principles general with respect to $P_1, \ldots, P_n$ are those which can be formulated without employing the predicate functions that occur in $P_1, \ldots, P_n$ and without restriction to a class of predicate functions that include those occurring in $P_1, \ldots, P_n$. Some principles, not necessarily true, which satisfy this characterization with respect to P, Q, R are: (1) $W(P/S,t) \rightarrow W(P,P/S,t)$; (2) $W(P,Q/S,t) \rightarrow W(Q,P/S,t)$, where P is the 'total evidence' for Q; (3) $W(PvQ,R/S,t) \rightarrow \{W(P,R/S,t) \ v \ W(Q,R/S,t)\}$; and (4) $\forall S \ \forall t \ \{[W(P/S,t) \ \& \ P_r(Q/P) > n] \rightarrow W(Q/S,t)\}$. (If n varies with P,Q, then (4) does not qualify as general with respect to P,Q). The perceptual taking principle 'If S takes himself to perceive that x has *proper or common sensible* $\emptyset$, then that x has $\emptyset$ is warranted for S' does not stand as a general warrant principle with respect to sentences containing predicate functions for proper or common sensibles. Warrant principles not general with respect to $P_1, \ldots, P_n$ are specific to these sentences.

The class of general warrant principles of interest is that of principles general with respect to sentences not having an epistemological subject matter, i.e., sentences not containing epistemic predicate functions. These warrant principles — *fully general* warrant principles — express basic truths concerning warrant conditions and relations, and, crucially for us, are those properly taken to give content to the notions of epistemic necessity and supervenience. All other warrant principles belong to theories for the sentences, or the non-epistemic components of sentences, to which they are specific. I have argued that it is reasonable to regard these specific warrant principles as meaning-constitutive for the relevant sentences,[7] but that claim is not presently at issue. The key point here concerns the discussion of projectability problems, and basic/non-basic perceptual warranting. We noted that, if we are generous enough in what we count as warrant principles, then we obviously will be able to derive that $a_n + 1$ *is green* is warranted for S from appropriate factual and epistemic premises (and also that *a is round* is warranted for S when S takes himself to perceive that a is round). What we can *not* do is make such derivations in terms of *fully general* warrant principles, in terms of a theory of warrant conditions and relations. We must appeal to warrant principles *specific to the* non-epistemic sentences (or predicate functions) involved, to a theory of these *non-epistemic* sentences. *A theory of non-epistemic sentences (or predicate functions) adequate to the warrant conditions and relations of the sentences must include principles explicitly addressing the warrant conditions and relations of the sentences.* In this sense epistemology not only is not superfluous but pervades *all* theorizing concerning non-epistemic matters.

2. PROBLEMATIC REALISM / THE UPWARD BOUND

The first block in the structure of Problematic Realism is to note the above point, that theories of non-epistemic sentences must account for the warrant conditions and relations of these sentences. Next we must consider how much theories for non-epistemic sentences should say about epistemic matters, and the effect of this epistemic content on the rest of the theories' content. Consideration of these points will add substance to Problematic Realism.

How much should theories for non-epistemic sentences (sentences composed of non-epistemic predicate functions) say about warrant conditions and relations? The answer which I think correct is that such theories should, whatever else we take to be the proper goals of such theories, 'fully determine' the warrant conditions and relations of non-epistemic sentences. This answer sets an upward bound, I call it 'epistemic completeness', on what can be expected in terms of epistemic content from theories for non-epistemic sentences. I spend some time clarifying the goal of epistemic completeness, and then argue that it is not an unreasonable goal.

For starters we can say that a theory for non-epistemic sentences $P_1, \ldots, P_n$, combined with a general theory of warrant and relevant non-epistemic background information, should allow derivation of the warrant conditions and relations of $P_1, \ldots, P_n$. This approximation suggests that three factors are relevant to determination of the warrant conditions and relations of a non-epistemic sentence. These are: (a) basic facts, including epistemic information, which constitute a theory for the non-epistemic sentence; (b) facts formulated in non-epistemic terms concerning the conditions of use of the sentence; and (c) principles of warrant that constitute a theory of warrant conditions and relations and thus are general, in the defined sense, with respect to the non-epistemic sentence under consideration. This allows a second approximate statement of our goal: A theory for non-epistemic sentences $P_1, \ldots, P_n$ should provide sufficient information *of type (a)* to allow derivation, when combined with full information of types (b) and (c), of the warrant conditions and relations of $P_1, \ldots, P_n$. Since each of $P_1, \ldots, P_n$ has warranting relations to many other sentences, we must be clear about which of these relations are encompassed by the goal of epistemic completeness. I shall restrict attention to warrant relations *among the sentences $P_1, \ldots, P_n$* with the caveat that ideally $P_1, \ldots, P_n$ is a broad enough set of sentences to be closed under the relevant warranting relations.

Some further jargon is useful. 'T' is a theory or set of theories encompassing at least sentences $P_1, \ldots, P_n$. Where 'S' and 't' continue to be respectively person and time variables, '$D(T,S,t)$' is a true description of S's condition at t and is stated in non-epistemic terms in language compatible with that in which T is stated. '$WP(T,P_1, \ldots, P_n)$' states true warrant principles which are general with respect to $P_1, \ldots, P_n$ and are formulated in language compatible with that of T and $D(T,S,t)$. In assessing the epistemic completeness of T we are concerned with the warrant conditions and relations of $P_1, \ldots, P_n$. In other words, we are concerned with sentences of the forms 'α warrants β for S at t' and 'α is warranted for S at t', where α and β are either one of $P_1, \ldots, P_n$ or logical compounds of $P_1, \ldots, P_n$. True sentences of these forms are the warrant sentences true of S at t and involving $P_1, \ldots, P_n$.

The statement of our goal of epistemic completeness is as follows:

> T is epistemically complete for $P_1, \ldots, P_n$ iff $\forall S \ \forall t$, if W is a warrant sentence true of S at t involving only $P_1, \ldots, P_n$, then there are $D(T, S, t)$ and $WP(T, P_1, \ldots, P_n)$ which conjointly with T logically entail W.

Less succinctly: T is epistemically complet for $P_1, \ldots, P_n$ iff every warrant sentence formulated in terms of $P_1, \ldots, P_n$ and true of some person S and time t is logically entailed by the conjunction of T, a true description in non-epistemic terms of S's condition at t, and warrant principles general with respect to $P_1, \ldots, P_n$. T must supply epistemic information which, when added to general warrant principles and non-epistemic information about S at t, determines the warrant conditions and relations of $P_1, \ldots, P_n$. This goal requires considerable further explication. We have just touched on the notions of warrant and warranting and on the distinction between warrant principles general with respect to sentences and warrant princeiples specific to the sentences. The notion of logical entailment employed in statement of the goal requires specification. T, the non-epistemic information about S at t, the true general warrant principles, and the warrant sentences involving $P_1, \ldots, P_n$ are to be formulated in mutually compatible language so that the warrant sentences are deducible via inferences authorized in the language from the other components. It is not clear exactly what inferences are to be authorized in this language, but the inferences must be authorized by deductive principles formulable in non-epistemic terms. How broadly 'deductive principles' is to be interpreted is not an argumentative issue provided that the propositional, quantificational, and set-theoretic resources usually employed in formally presenting theories are included.

The point of stating this goal of epistemic completeness is to have an upward bound on *how much* epistemic information is to be included in a theory of non-epistemic sentences (or predicate functions) given that the theory must, in accordance with the first conclusion embodied in Problematic Realism, include some epistemic information. I approach this issue by considering objections that can be raised to taking epistemic completeness as an appropriate goal.

Several plausible objections to setting epistemic completeness as a goal can be raised. First, if epistemic information is to be part of a theory of certain non-epistemic sentences, then surely 'having this information' is in some sense part of understanding the sentences. But we can apparently fully understand a sentence without knowing all of its warrant conditions and relations, and we often find new ways to determine whether a sentence, which we fully understand, is warranted. These plausible considerations are not incompatible with the goal of epistemic completeness. The apparent incompatibility rests on the idea that epistemic completeness requires that all warranting conditions and relations of a sentence be stated in a theory for the sentence. What is actually required is that the theory (or, if one thinks of theories as deductively closed, the axiomatic part of the theory), in light of what it says about a given sentence *and* related sentences, when combined with factual information and general warrant principles, determine the warrant conditions and relations of the sentence. Tolerating epistemic incompleteness is less attractive than seeking epistemic completeness. Suppose we have a theory which encompasses 'duck' and 'water'. Consider the sentence, 'That the duck is in the water is now warranted for John'. If we allow epistemic incompleteness, then, given the theory, relevant information about constituents of the sentence not encompassed by the theory, full information about John's situation stated in non-epistemic terms, and general warrant principles, the truth of this sentence may not be fixed. Assignment of either truth or falsity to this sentence would be held consistent with this body of information.

The goal of epistemic completeness is also compatible with discovery of warrant conditions and relations. On my preferred reading of '$W(P/S,t)$' this expression means that S would believe P at t were S's beliefs ideal (in specified respects $1-n$) at t.[8] This makes questions concerning warrant matters of contingent truth, subject to discovery just as other contingent truths are. But one need not adopt my reading of warrant attributions. One who takes warrant attributions to be conceptual, necessary or analytic truths can correctly point out that truths in these categories are also open to discovery.

3. THE PROBLEM OF PROBLEMATIC REALISM

The first component of Problematic Realism states that a theory of non-epistemic sentences must include information about warrant conditions and relations. I hope that consideration of the above objections contributes to the plausibility of the second component of Problematic Realism, that the epistemic information in a theory for non-epistemic sentences should suffice for the theory to be epistemically complete for the sentences. I shall say just a little about how epistemic information is incorporated in such theories. For the moment I assume that the information consists of postulates of the forms '$\forall S \ \forall t \ (W(P/S,t) \rightarrow$ ____)' and '$\forall S \ \forall t \ (W(P,Q/S,t) \rightarrow$ ____)', where P and Q are non-epistemic sentences and the blanks are filled by non-epistemic information relating to the specific sentences P and Q. Obviously, epistemic information could not actually be incorporated in theories for non-epistemic sentences in postulates of these forms, since doing so sentence by sentence would be an interminable task. Hopefully, it will be possible to incorporate postulates for predicate functions of the forms ' $\forall S \ \forall t \ \forall x \ (\ulcorner F_x \urcorner$ is warranted for S at $t \rightarrow$ _____)', and ' $\forall S, \ \forall t, \ \forall x, \ \forall y \ (\ulcorner F_x \urcorner$ warrants $\ulcorner G_y \urcorner$ for S at $t \rightarrow$ ____)', where F_x and G_x are non-epistemic predicate functions and the blanks are filled by non-epistemic information relating to the specific predicate functions F_x and G_x. These postulates would be supplemented by postulates concerning the warrant conditions and relations of sentences constructed from the basic predicate functional components. While the predicate function/componential approach is ultimately to be pursued, I view epistemic information in theories for non-epistemic sentences in terms of warrant conditions and relations for whole sentences to indicate more sharply what the problem of Problematic Realism is.

In 'Meaning and Perception' I argue that if *only* information expressed in postulates of the above forms, for whole sentences, resulted from a meaning theory, the theory could satisfy the conditions for epistemic completeness for the sentences.[9] I am not here concerned with whether the postulates are *meaning* postulates; the argument is the same whatever the status of the postulates. Rather than rehashing details of the argument, I outline the general strategy. The argument is conducted within what I call a 'strict empiricist' framework according to which the warrant of non-basic, physical sentences is based by deduction or (roughly) enumerative inductive on that of basic, sensory sentences describing a person's present or recalled sensory experiences. Working within such a framework certainly does not simplify the task of arguing epistemic completeness, and it offers some well-defined problems to consider in the arguing. It is to be argued, then, that a theory for non-epistemic, non-basic (physical, in this framework) sentences which yields postulates of the above forms (for whole, logically simple sentences) can satisfy the conditions for epistemic completeness.

Given a 'strict empiricist' framework, the key problem is in explaining how the warrant conditions and relations of non-basic sentences can be derived from the theory taken with deductive and inductive warranting relations authorized by general warrant principles. If we allow that the theory is rich in epistemic information incorporated in postulates of the forms considered above, and this must be allowed to initiate the argument, the theory will have results stating: that physical sentences warrant sensory sentences (for persons and times in such and such conditions), that sensory sentences warrant physical sentences (for persons and times and under conditions), that sub-junctive conditionals having sensory sentences as antecedents and consequents warrant physical sentences, and that physical sentences warrant these condi-tional sensory sentences. Given a *rich supply* of such results, warranting relations between physical and sensory sentences, e.g., will either directly result from postulates of the theory (in the case of fundamental basic/non-basic warranting relations) or they will result from postulates of the theory together with inductive generalizations in terms of sensory sentences. The postulates tie the physical sentence, via warranting, to certain key sensory sentences which, by their inductive, content-indifferent warranting relations, tie the physical sentence to further sensory sentences. These sensory sentences in turn warrant other physical sentences, so that a chain of warranting is established. (This chain does not depend on assuming simple transitivity of warranting). Explanation of warranting relations *among* physical sentences, and among hybrid sentences composed of both physical and sensory com-ponents, is more complicated, but the strategy is the same. That strategy is to explain the warranting relations of non-basic sentences in terms of postulates of the theory establishing basic sentences as warranting interme-diaries. More generous resources to supplement the results of a theory will generally be available in applying such a strategy within frameworks other than 'strict empiricism'.

We have already worried about the relations between postulates of a theory stating warrant conditions and relations for whole, logically simple sentences and postulates, more likely to be part of an actual theory, for sentence com-ponents and modes of composition. We return to this shortly. One may also have an opposite worry, that the above argument, the 'strict empiricist' framework within which it is framed, and, crucially, the underlying view that theories include epistemic information for *individual* sentences or sentence components embodies a discredited atomism concerning the warrant condi-tions and relations of sentences.[10] 'Strict empiricism', as cartooned here, certainly does have consequences concerning the warrant conditions and relations of individual sentences.[11] But nothing about the above strategy for establishing epistemic completeness, or the two components of Problematic Realism so far considered, depends on taking individual, logically simple sentences as the primary possessors of warrant conditions and relations. On one holistic version of Problematic Realism, a theory for non-epistemic sentences will include epistemic information only about sentences expressing all or part of a theory or of a potential belief system. If T is a minimal unit of discourse for which a theory contains epistemic information, the epistemic completeness of the theory for T can be established as above. References to warrant conditions and relations of sentences which are part of T are then interpreted as elliptical references to the warrant conditions and relations of T. A more moderate holistic version of Problematic Realism allows theories to contain epistemic information concerning both individual sentences and theories, parts of theories, or potential belief systems in which the sentences are embedded. On this version of Problematic Realism, no theory can be epistemically complete for a sentence or set of sentences unless it includes epistemic information not only about the sentence or sentences but also about the warrant conditions and relations of a larger, encompassing, epistemically significant unit of discourse. But this version also plausibly allows that individual sentences have *some* warrant conditions and relations outside of an encompassing theory. It may acknowledge that 'This is red' is warranted by 'This looks red to me'.

The above considerations turn attention from individual, logically-simple sentences to larger segments of discourse or conceptualization of which the sentences are parts. To locate the problem of Problematic Realism, we must return to the relation between whole sentences and their components. The argument for epistemic completeness bases claims of epistemic completeness of a theory for a sentence on results of the theory stating warrant conditions and relations for whole sentences. This suggests the possibility that theories which break sentences into components in distinct ways, assign different referents to sentence components, or assign different truth values to sentences, might have the same results concerning the warrant conditions and relations of whole sentences, and thus be epistemically complete for the same sentences. The last component of Problematic Realism affirms this possibility: There are significant semantical and ontological differences among sentences which are not reflected in the epistemic information, or in the empirical element of that information, in an epistemically complete theory for the sentence. The problem then is how there can be such differences which are not empirically reflected. I offer some reasons to think that there actually are such differences.

4. REALISTICALLY SPEAKING

I proceed by presenting examples intended to massage the intuitions, and then presenting a general argument for the last component of Problematic Realism. In stating the last component of Problematic Realism I refer to the *empirical element* of the epistemic information about a sentence. How, or whether, we can identify an empirical element of the results of a theory stating warrant conditions and relations for a sentence depends on how, and whether, we identify a class of basic sentences in terms of which other non-basic empirical sentences are warranted. I assume the empiricist framework of the preceding section according to which basic sentences are sensory sentences, sentences describing a person's present or recalled sensory experiences. All other empirical sentences are non-basic, and warranting proceeds by enumerative induction, deduction, and what is supplied by theoretical postulates. This is for convenience, since neither the example nor the later general argument depend on the particulars of the framework. The results of theories for sentences appealed to in sketching the argument for epistemic completeness consisted of statements of warranting relations between non-basic (physical in the sketch) sentences and simple or subjunctive conditional sensory sentences. Let us call the set of results of a theory of this kind, together with results stating warrant conditions for basic sentences, the empirical element of the theory.

Consider the sentences 'Lo, there is a dagger before me' and 'Lo, I am having a perfect dagger hallucination (so that there actually is nothing before me).' The phrase 'a perfect dagger hallucination' is specified to mean that neither I, nor anyone else, can detect that this is an hallucination through all experiences expressible in sensory sentences. These two sentences have the same warranting relations to basic sentences, and epistemically complete theories for the sentences will have the same empirical elements. But the sentences are contraries, and have components with different referents (a real dagger versus an hallucinated dagger). One may wish to dismiss this case on the ground that the notion of a perfect dagger hallucination is somehow parasitical on that of a dagger, so that the second sentence means 'I am having an experience of the sort usually caused by a real dagger but not so caused this time'. A perfect dagger hallucination claim could be warranted only for someone for whom dagger claims are warranted. So, it is contended, there is no interesting difference between our original sentences that can not be located in the empirical element of a theory for closely related sentences.

To satisfy this qualm imagine people who have conceptual schemes which allow that reality is occasionally undetectably 'gappy'. In this scheme the world is usually as it seems to be, full of cheerful, middle-sized physical objects, or, when it is not, it is at least possible in principle to find out that it is not. But in rare cases it seems that there is such and such an object when there is not, and there is, in principle, no way to find out that there is not. Imagine further that these people have words ('chairhole', 'bookhole') applicable in rare cases — although they can not *know* when 'book' as opposed to 'bookhole' is appropriate. Epistemically complete theories for 'This is a book' and 'This is a bookhole' would have the same empirical elements despite the fact that these sentences are contraries and have components with different referents.

If these cases do not convince, the philosophical literature provides two further ways of supporting my point. Various reductionist programs to translate physical and theoretical sentences into an evidentially more basic jargon would, if successful, yield translations of physical/theoretical sentences having the same warrant conditions and relations as the original sentences, but differing from the original sentences in referential import. Thus, on one reading, C. I. Lewis wished to translate (preserving identity of proposition expressed) physical sentences into conjunctions of subjunctive conditional sensory sentences. Given a successful program of this sort, epistemically complete theories for a sentence and its translation would have the same empirical elements — since the point of these programs is to translate physical/theoretical sentences into the empirical evidence relevant to them. But the sentence and its translation obviously differ in referential import. The persuasiveness of this support for my point may be lessened by doubts about the prospects of these reductionist programs.

Quine's famous examples, used first to illustrate indeterminacy of translation and later to support the theses of inscrutability and relativity of reference, seem to offer cases of sentences identically related to basic sentences, so that theories for the sentences have the same empirical elements, but having both different components (terms, predicate functions) and components with different referents. Epistemically complete theories for 'This is a rabbit', 'This is a temporal rabbit-stage', 'This is an undetached rabbitpart', and 'Rabbithood there' have the same empirical elements, even though these sentences differ in referential import and internal structure. Given the epistemic framework within which the notion of an empirical element is formulated, a question can be raised about the appropriateness of employing these cases. The empirical element of a theory for a physical/theoretical sentence consists of those statements of warranting relations between these sentences and sensory (simple or conditional) sentences. Thus a content difference between physical/theoretical and basic sentences is assumed. But, if physical/theoretical sentences and basic sentences employ the *same* terminology, and if the terminology is interpreted at least to the extent that it is taken to be unambiguous, then empirical elements of theories for physical/theoretical sentences fixes the internal structure and referential import of these sentences — *to be the same as* that of the basic sentences to which they bear warranting relations. If there is no terminological or content difference between physical/theoretical sentences and basic sentences, there is no question about the content or referential import · of physical/theoretical sentences given that of the basic sentences.

This reasoning is unsound in a way that leads us to an argument for the third component of Problematic Realism. We could object, correctly I think, to the above reasoning that there really is a terminological and content difference between basic and non-basic sentences. This would embroil us in epistemological controversy tangential to our main concerns. The fundamental point is this: *There is no reason to think that the epistemic information in a theory which is epistemically complete for certain physical/theoretical sentences suffices to determine the internal structure or referential import of the basic sentences* — however basic sentences are identified and whether or not they differ in content from physical/theoretical sentences. Basic sentences may have — I think they surely do — warrant *conditions* as well as warrant *relations*. If 'This is a chair' or 'This is a quark' are taken to be basic, they will be warranted in certain conditions — be the conditions characterized in terms of physical stimulation, sense-data, or sensings — at least when the contribution of the conditions is not defeated by warranting relations to other sentences. There is nothing in the statement of warrant conditions for basic sentences, which statement would be part of an epistemically complete theory for the basic sentences and not necessarily in the language of the basic sentences, to fix their internal structure or referential import.

Note that our reasoning on this point does not depend on a specific epistemology. I first considered epistemic completeness within a 'strict empiricist' viewpoint. This involved focusing on individual, logically simple sentences as non-basic sentences and on warranting relations based on deduction, enumerative induction, or specific postulates of a theory. We noted that nothing essential depends on focusing on individual or logically simple sentences, and sketched two holistic alternatives placing larger units of discourse at the intersection of warranting relations. But it may be suggested that the empirical element of an epistemically complete theory appears impotent with respect to questions of reference and internal structure because of an impoverished supply of warranting relations. In particular, the restriction of non-deductive warranting to inductive generalizations (and theoretical postulates) may seem too narrow. I think there are better reasons to accept certain types of inductive generalization as warrant preserving than there are to so accept other forms of non-deductive inference, including abduction and inference to the best explanation. We need not trust this surmise, for the following reason: *Any plausible epistemic view allows coherence among sentences some role in warrant determination*, although there are wide differences over how large a factor coherence is. If coherence is a significant factor in determining the warrant of a sentence, as presumably is the case for non-basic sentences, then *some maximally coherent and comprehensive systems will include the sentence while other maximally coherent and comprehensive systems will include a contrary of the sentence*. This non-uniqueness result can be avoided only by endorsing principles (that the system some preferred group accepts is *the* warrant determining system) recommended only as means of avoiding the result. Non-uniqueness can not be demonstrated without specification of possible evidence sets and warrant principles from which maximally coherent and comprehensive (and otherwise adequate) systems of sentences can be constructed. If you fill in your leading epistemic candidates for these roles, you should, unless you are too free in identifying what you like with what is warranted, be able to support this result. This epistemological non-uniqueness suffices for a degree — proportional to the extent to which equicoherent systems may include contraries — of underdetermination of referential import, truth value, and internal structure by empirical elements of epistemically complete theories.

5. SUMMARY

The position defended, Problematic Realism, consists of three theses: (1) that a theory adequate to the warrant conditions and relations of non-epistemic sentences must include principles explicitly addressing the warrant conditions and relations of the sentences; (2) that the epistemic information included in such a theory must suffice for the theory to be epistemically complete for the sentences; that is, it must *fully* determine the warrant conditions and relations of the sentences; and (3) that there are differences, *real* differences, in the internal structure (what the terms and predicate of functions are), semantics (including truth values), and referential import of non-epistemic sentences which are not reflected in that part of an epistemically complete theory which concerns the empirical evidence relevant to the sentences. In what sense are the differences referred to in (3) 'real'? Are they differences in language, differences, apparent to us upon reflection, in our conceptual schemes, or 'objective' differences not depending on how, or if, we speak or think of the world? Problematic Realism takes the differences at issue to be real in all of these senses. Declaring these differences, or anything else, 'real' does not solve any philosophical problems. It raises, or revives, some very fundamental problems. For instance, a developed Problematic Realism must explain the relations between the empirical element of the results of an epistemically complete theory and other epistemic information in that theory. If the empirical element does not distinguish 'This is a chair' and 'This is a perfect chair hallucination', how can the rest of the epistemic information in a theory do so? In accepting epistemic completeness as a reasonable goal, we are committed to holding that neither of such sentences is warrantable or that the factors which can decide one as warranted are part of an epistemically complete theory. The latter alternative, which we surely favor in some cases (e.g., physical object sentences and their 'gappy' contraries) entails that there is a determinateness to warrant attributions not traceable, given the coherence argument, through plausible warrant principles to the empirical element of a theory. (This may suggest some sort of *epistemic* conventionalism, subjectivism, or rationalism — to explain the source of determinateness). This problem arises within the realm of the epistemic information required of the theory by the first two theses of Problematic Realism. A further problem — it should be called 'Kant's fundamental problem' — is how the entire body of epistemic information, empirical element and extra-empirical information, included in an epistemically complete theory is related to the semantic, syntactic, and ontological content of the theory. This question turns the thrust, parried by the first thesis of Problematic Realism, of skepticism concerning the viability or interest of epistemology back on its source. If we are to have a unified view of the world which relates the structures of epistemic notions to the structures we posit in the world, this question must be answered with principles connecting the epistemic results of an epistemically complete theory with its non-epistemic content. We can not bypass the epistemic underdetermination argued as the third thesis of Problematic Realism. But we can aim for a consistent, systematic view of the relations of epistemic and non-epistemic information. There is yet another problem: What is the status of the very principles intended to relate epistemic and non-epistemic elements of a theory? These are good philosophical questions that must be examined if we are to finally reject Problematic Realism in favor of Fully Warranted Realism.[12]

NOTES

[1] See 'Knowledge and Reliability: A Critical Study of D. M. Armstrong's *Belief, Truth, and Knowledge*', *Metaphilosophy* (April, 1978), pp. 150–162 and 'The Multi-Perspectival Theory of Knowledge', forthcoming, *Midwest Studies in Philosophy, Vol. V, Studies in Epistemology* (Morris, Minnesota, 1980).

[2] The label 'Problematic Realism' is applied to a view somewhat resembling that defended here by Jacob Loewenberg in his essay in *Contemporary American Philosophy*, ed. by G. P. Adams and W. P. Montague II (New York, 1930), pp. 55–81. C. I. Lewis considered applying this label to his own views in 'Realism or Phenomenalism?' in *The Collected Papers of Clarence Irving Lewis*, ed. by John D. Gohenn and John L. Mothershead, Jr. (Standford, California, 1970), pp. 335–347.

[3] 'Social and Anti-Social Justification', forthcoming in an anthology of essays on Keith Lehrer's philosophy.

[4] I explore these notions in 'A Decision Procedure for Epistemology?', *Philosophical Studies* (April, 1979), pp. 257–268.

[5] What it is for a belief to be ideal in relevant respects is spelled out in 'A Decision Procedure', *ibid.*

[6] In 'Perceptual Relativity', *Philosophia* (June, 1978), pp. 341–355.

[7] In 'Meaning and Perception', *The Journal of Philosophy* (October, 1976), pp. 572–585.

[8] See 'A Decision Procedure', *op. cit.*

[9] 'Meaning and Perception', *op. cit.*

[10] This issue is pursued at length in 'Warrant and Meaning in Quine's Clothing', *The Southwestern Journal of Philosophy* (April, 1979), pp. 119–132.

[11] In 'Warrant and Meaning', *ibid.*, I point out that 'strict empiricism' can be minimally reformulated to yield a holistic empiricism that retains the main epistemic features of more traditional varieties of empiricism.

[12] I profited from the comments of temporary colleaques at the University of Michigan, especially Alvin Goldman, John Pollock, and Lawrence Sklar, and from presentation of the paper at this conference. Criticism of earlier drafts by Romane Clark and Michael Pendlebury as well as other colleaques at Indiana University is also reflected here.

WILFRID SELLARS

MORE ON GIVENNESS AND EXPLANATORY COHERENCE*

I

1. Historically, there have been two competing strands in the concept of a 'self-presenting' state of affairs, i.e., the kind of state of affairs access to which is supposed to provide empirical knowledge with its 'foundation'.

2. According to the first strand, a self-presenting state of affairs is a *fact* (an *obtaining* state of affairs) which is known to obtain, not by virtue of an act of warranted belief, but by virtue of a unique cognitive act which is more basic than that of any believing however warranted.

3. The main thrust of this position is directed against what it decries as 'representationalism,' the view that whatever other conditions they must satisfy to constitute knowledge, cognitive acts are, in the first instance, representations.

4. Representationalism can take different forms. That which is most prevalent today stresses the quasi-linguistic character of cognitive acts, the idea that they belong to a framework of signs and symbols which, whether innate or acquired, enables organisms which possess it to construct representations of themselves in their environment.

5. A more traditional form stresses a distinction between two 'modes of being' which objects and states of affairs may have: (a) actual being – roughly, the being which something has independently of being an object of thought; (b) intentional inexistence, the being something has when it is thought of, *qua* thought of – Descartes' 'representative' or 'objective' reality.

6. According to the latter form, our cognitive access to the world consists *exclusively* in the occurrence of mental acts in which objects and events have intentional in-existence. The term 'exclusively' is of the essence, for it is representationalism in the (supposedly) pejorative sense by virtue of denying that we have any other cognitive access to the world than by such acts. Whatever other features these acts may have, in no case do they involve, nor are they accompanied by what the anti-representationalist would characterize as a 'direct' cognitive access to 'the facts themselves' in their character as factual.

7. The representationalist grants, of course, that certain cognitive acts have a *special* character by virtue of which they are capable of yielding

169

George S. Pappas (ed.), Justification and Knowledge, 169–182.
Copyright © 1979 by D. Reidel Publishing Company.

knowledge of certain privileged matters of fact. The possession of this special
character would either guarantee that a representational act is true, or at least
give a high antecedent probability to the proposition that this was the case.

8. Just how this special character is to be conceived, classical representationalists found it difficult to say. As a matter of fact, careful reading of the
texts reveals that most, if not all, representationalists covertly introduced a
non-representational mode of cognitive access — interestingly enough, to
representational acts themselves. Because of this fact, Immanuel Kant might
well have been the first thorough going representationalist.

9. They took it for granted that one could 'notice,' 'compare' and 'consider' one's mental acts, and to do these things was, in effect, to have non-
representational knowledge of these acts as being what they are, e.g., a
representation of a tree. Such awareness would simply be a special case of
what anti-representationalists refer to as unmediated or direct apprehension
of matters of fact.

10. That Descartes, like Locke, covertly introduced a non-representational
element into his theory of knowledge along the above lines is, I think, clear.
He did, however, also insist that certain representational acts have, in addition
to their character as representations, a special property — which he referred
to as 'clarity and distinctness' — which plays the role described in paragraph 7
above.

11. Such a property might be called a knowledge-making property, by analogy with what in moral philosophy are called right-making characteristics.[1]

12. Of course, a coherent representationalist who argues that all cognitive
access to the world is a matter of the occurrence of representational acts need
not take clarity-*cum*-distinctness to be *the* knowledge-making property, or
even *a* knowledge-making property. In any case it seems more appropriate to
a priori knowledge than to knowledge of particular matters of fact.

13. With respect to the latter, the representationalist might propose some
mode of causal confrontation of the knowing by the known. The connection
would be a knowledge-making property of the representational act, and
would give it a cognitive virtue which other kinds of representations do not
have.

14. The contemporary representationalist who stresses the linguistic
analogy might well argue that the causal relationship between the knowing
and the known in introspective, perceptual and memory judgments is reflected
by the presence of demonstrative components in the representational act.

15. To develop this theme, however, would require the formulation of a
theory of intentionality which does justice to both the logical and the causal

dimensions of discourse about mental acts, and this topic is much too large to be more than adumbrated on the present occasion.[2]

16. Representationalists typically become touchy when asked whether our only access to the fact, when it is a fact, that an act has a knowledge-making property (whatever it might be) is by the occurrence of a further representational act. And, indeed, the question whether representationalism can be so formulated as to alleviate this touchiness is a central theme in disputes pertaining to 'foundationalism'.

17. From this perspective, the alternative to representationalism is the view that we have a direct access to the *factuality* of certain privileged facts unmediated by representational acts, whether quasi-linguistic episodes (e.g., tokens of Mentalese) or conceptual acts in which states of affairs have 'representative being' or intentional in-existence.

18. According to this alternative, our direct or non-representational access to these privileged facts (call it 'direct apprehension') provides a cognitive stratum which 'underlies,' 'supports' or 'provides a foundation for' cognitive acts of the representational category. If we call the latter 'beliefs,' then while some justified true beliefs may merit the term 'knowledge,' they rest on a foundation of direct apprehensions which are not special cases of beliefs, but belong to a radically different category.

19. According to this line of thought, then, a self-presenting state of affairs is one which is either directly apprehended, or of such a kind as to be capable of being directly apprehended should the corresponding question arise. Direct apprehension or direct apprehendibility would be a source of epistemic authority.

20. Notice that for a state of affairs to be self-presenting, as thus construed, it must obtain, i.e., be a fact rather than a mere possibility.

21. Now one who takes this line might deny that direct apprehensions themselves have intrinsic epistemic value and restrict terms of epistemic appraisal, thus 'evident' or 'warranted,' to *beliefs*, and, hence, to propositions whose epistemic status does not require that they be true.[3]

22. One might accordingly argue that the self-presentingness of self-presenting states of affairs is a 'prime mover unmoved' (to borrow Chisholm's useful metaphor[4]) of epistemic authority, i.e., that the direct apprehension or apprehendibility of a state-of-affairs is a source of evidentness or warrant, but itself neither warranted nor unwarranted.

23. Or, to put it differently, one might claim that their special relation to self-presenting *facts* is a knowledge-making property of certain *beliefs*.

24. To make this move, however, would be paradoxical, for it involves

denying that the direct apprehension of a fact is itself *knowledge*. For direct apprehension, by those who have evolved the concept, is almost invariably taken to be the very paradigm of knowledge 'properly so-called'.

25. On the other hand, to hold that an act of direct apprehension is subject to epistemic appraisal as, for example, *evident* seems to point in the direction of representationalism. How could items so sharply contrasted, as *apprehensions* and *representations* are by the anti-representationalist, both be ascribed epistemic value without equivocation. The anti-representationalist program is not without its problems.

26. The classical alternative to this conception of a self-presenting state of affairs as a fact which is either directly apprehended or capable of being directly apprehended should the appropriate question arise is, of course, that of the representationalist. According to the latter account a self-presenting state of affairs is one which is such that if the relevant person at the relevant time occurrently believes (judges) it to obtain, the believing would have high epistemic worth and, indeed, would be non-inferentially warranted or self-evident.

27. Notice, as pointed out above, that this alternative is compatible with the idea that self-presenting states of affairs *need not obtain* (be *facts*). It is also compatible with the idea that when a self-presenting state of affairs *does* obtain, it is a factor which contributes (causally) to bringing about the occurrent belief (should such arise) that it does obtain. (See paragraphs 13 to 15 above).

28. The distinctive feature of this account is that the *self-presentingness* of a self-presenting state of affairs is to be understood in terms of the idea that the *factual* category to which the state of affairs belongs, e.g., that of being one's occurrent mental state of the present moment, is an (epistemic) value-making property of the state of affairs.

29. Whereas 'direct apprehension' can masquerade as a non-value-laden term (see paragraph 24 above).

II

30. Now it seems eminently clear to me that in his excellent paper on 'Coherence, Certainty and Epistemic Priority',[5] Roderick Firth rejects the radical distinction between *beliefs* and *direct apprehensions* which is central to the first account of self-presenting states.

31. In his reconstruction of the concept of givenness the central theme is the idea that certain judgments have, in his terminology, an ultimately non-inferential warrant increasing property.

32. He alternates between speaking of 'judgments' (which I have been calling 'occurrent beliefs') and of 'statement;' but it seems clear that he is using the term 'statement' not to refer to verbal performances, but as a surrogate for 'proposition' in that sense in which propositions are *contents* of beliefs (i.e., are that which is believed). I think that he is implicitly making an analogical use of Strawson's distinction between sentences and the statements they can be used to make on particular occasions, to emphasize that judgments have the conceptual counterparts of the indexical features of statement-utterances.

33. Firth distinguishes (pp. 549–50) two modes of *inferential* warrant increasing properties which statements may have. I shall paraphrase his distinction, referring to the two kinds simply as 'the first kind' and 'the second kind'.

(1)   A statement, S, has an inferential warrant increasing property, P, of the *first* kind, if P consists in the fact that S is "validly inferable from certain other statements of a specified kind."

(2)   A statement, S, has an inferential warrant increasing property, P, of the *second* kind, if the meta-statement, 'if S has the property P, then S is likely to be true'[6] has an inferential warrant increasing property, P', of the *first* kind.

34. Firth refers to both 'deductive' and 'inductive' inference. The former is reasonably unproblematic. On the other hand he does not clearly specify the scope of 'inductive.' The example he gives is a case of what is usually called 'simple' or 'instantial' induction. Nevertheless the fact that he parenthetically ties 'inferable from' to 'coheres with'[7] leaves the door open to the possibility of expanding the scope of 'inductive inference' to include other modes of non-deductive explanatory reasoning.

35. Whether or not he is prepared to avail himself of this option – and if so, to what extent – is a matter of crucial importance, for on it hinges the ultimate significance of his distinction between inferential and non-inferential warrant increasing properties.

36. In any event, Firth illustrates inferential warrant increasing properties of the *second* kind by "the property of being believed by certain scholars," e.g., I take it, by members of the relevant academy. It belongs to the *second* kind because the meta-statement,

> If a statement, S, has the property of being believed by certain scholars, then S is likely to be true,

has the property of being inductively inferable from a statement to the effect that "these scholars have usually held correct beliefs about statements similar to S in certain respects;"[8] and this property is an inferential warrant increasing property of the *first* kind.

37. What, then, is a *non-inferential* warrant increasing property? Clearly, as far as the *extension* of the concept is concerned, it is a warrant increasing property (WP) which belongs to neither of the above two kinds. As for the *intension* of the concept, the contrast between non-inferential WP's and inferential WP's of the *first* kind is unproblematic.

38. Again, if the 'inferential' WP, P' of the meta-statement,

Statements which have P are likely to be true,

is construed as the property of having inductive support in the instantial sense, the contrast between inferential *WP*'s of the *second* kind and non-inferential *WP*'s is equally unproblematic.

39. As a matter of fact, even if one counts the acquisition of a *theory* by a substantial degree of confirmation as a variety of acquiring inductive support, the distinctions remain reasonably straightforward.

40. But suppose that P' is the property of belonging to a theory of persons as representers of themselves-in-the-world, which, although it has good explanatory power and is capable of refinement by inductive procedures, *was not* (and, indeed, could not have been) *arrived at* by inferences guided by inductive canons however broadly construed. Would P' be an *inferential* WP or an *explanatory* but not *inferential* WP?

41. It might be thought that the question as to how the theory was 'arrived at' is one which belongs to the 'order of discovery' *rather than* 'the order of justification.' But reflection on the fact that to answer a question of the form 'Is x justified in $\emptyset$-ing?' requires taking x's historical situation into account should give one pause.

42. I shall return to this theme in a moment. For the time being I note only that in the essay in question, Firth does not touch on these topics, although the issues they raise suggest possibilities which are in keeping with one aspect of his enterprise, which is, as I would put it, to reconcile as far as possible the claims of those who stress warrantedness grounded in explanatory coherence (among whom I count myself) with the claims of those who stress the non-inferential warrantedness[9] of certain empirical statements (among whom I also count myself). I shall attempt to push Firth in the direction of Firth-Bosanquet.

III

43. But before arguing the case for the primacy of the concept of explanatory

coherence in epistemic evaluation, it will be helpful to take a careful look at Firth's account of the non-inferential warrantedness of certain empirical statements. It will also help in defining our problem to examine the connection he finds between the concept of non-inferntial warrant and that of what he calls 'epistemic priority'.[10]

44. He begins by suggesting that

... the statement ... 'it looks to me as if I am seeing something red' ... has a certain degree of warrant for me because it is a statement (whether true or false) that purports to characterize (and only to characterize) the content of my present experience.

To which he adds, finding the above to be too permissive,

... a statement about my present experience can have some degree of ultimate non-inferential warrant for me only if I believe it to be true (p. 553).

45. Separating out the chaff introduced by the ambiguities of the word 'statement', this amounts to the idea that the property (P_E) of being a judgment about, and exclusively about, my present experience is a non-inferential WP.

46. This requires that the meta-judgment,

MJ$_1$ Judgments which have P_E are likely to be true,

if itself warranted, have a warrant which, *as Firth is using the term*, is non-inferential.

47. Assuming, for the moment, that MJ$_1$ *is* warranted, and having in mind the question raised in paragraph 40 above, let me provisionally characterize MJ$_1$ as a

non-inductively warranted warrant principle

and contrast it with

MJ$_2$ Judgments which are believed by certain scholars are likely to be true.

which can be characterized as an

inductively warranted warrant principle.

48. Notice that in the second passage quoted in paragraph 44, Firth refers to "degree[s] of *ultimate* non-inferential warrant" (ital. mine). What he has in mind, of course, is that while the property of being believed by certain scholars (e.g., members of the American Geographical Society) is not an *inferential* property of geographical statements, so that it would be incorrect to classify its character as a WP as its being an *inferential* WP, yet it would be equally incorrect to classify it as a *non-inferential* WP, for it owes its character as a WP to its *own* inferential property of being an inductively established sign of probable truth. Although itself a non-inferential property of geographical

statements, it *has* a higher order inferential property which is the ground of its ability to contribute warrant to geographical statements. It is by virtue of this fact that it is an inferential WP of the *second* kind. And it is in this sense that it is not an *ultimately* non-inferential WP.

49. Thus, when Firth tells us that P_E, the property of being exclusively about one's own experience of the present moment, is an *ultimately* non-inferential WP, he means that P_E is not only an inferential property of the judgments in question, but that, unlike being believed by members of the A.G.S., it is not a WP by virtue of itself having an inferential property.

50. In other words, Firth is committed to the idea that MJ_1, which characterizes P_E as a WP, either itself has no WP or, if it does, has a WP which is non-inferential.

51. Since, however, Firth does not press the question as to whether MJ_1 does or does not have a WP, the possibility arises that he is emphasizing that it does not belong in the same box as MJ_2, i.e., that its WP (if it has one) is not *inductive*. This would leave open the possibility that its WP, if any, is either non-inferential, or inferential but non-inductively so (cf. paragraph 47).

52. These considerations make it clear that the question '*Does* MJ_1 have a WP?' or, to put the matter bluntly, 'Is there any *reason* to accept MJ_1?' can no longer be deferred.

53. A negative answer would, on the face of it, bring to shipwreck the enterprise of making sense of the epistemic evaluation of empirical propositions. On the other hand, an affirmative answer would immediately raise the question '*What* WP does MJ_1 have?' or '*What* reason is there to accept MJ_1?'

54. And to these questions the only available answers, given the Firthian context in which they arise, are: (1) it is self-evident or axiomatic that it is reasonable to accept MJ_1; (2) it is reasonable to accept MJ_1 *because* if it is false, no empirical statements are warranted.

55. Both of these answers would turn us aside with a stone instead of the bread which, in spite of all the dialectical niceties, we intuitively feel must be there. Self-evidence is too atomistic an interpretation of the authority of epistemic principles; while the second answer — which amounts to the old slogan 'This or nothing' — is too weak, in that we do seem to have some insight into *why* something like the epistemic principles so lovingly polished by Firth and Chisholm are true. What has gone wrong?

IV

56. Firth formulates what he calls "the central thesis of epistemic priority"

as "the thesis that some statements have some degree of warrant which is independent of (and in this sense 'prior to') the warrant (if any) which they derive from other statements".[11] He thinks that this thesis is correct, and concludes that "Lewis has always been right in maintaining that the major task of a theory of empirical knowledge is to show how it is possible . . . for statements that have independent non-inferential warrant to serve as the ground of all of the rest of empirical knowledge".[12]

57. Now it is clear that some principles which assert that a certain property of empirical statements is a WP are themselves statements which belong to the content of empirical knowledge thus

MJ$_2$ Statements which are accepted by the A.G.S. are likely to be true

is not only a *criterion* for assessing geographical knowledge claims; it is itself an empirical statement and, indeed, an inductively confirmed knowledge claim in its own right.

58. But what of MJ$_1$? And what of such principles[13] as

MJ$_3$ If a person ostensibly perceives (without ground for doubt) something to be $\emptyset$ (for appropriate values of $\emptyset$) then it is likely to be true that he perceives something to be $\emptyset$.

MJ$_4$ If a person ostensibly remembers (without ground for doubt) having ostensibly perceived something to be $\emptyset$ (for appropriate values of $\emptyset$) then it is likely to be true that he remembers ostensibly perceiving something to be $\emptyset$.

Might not these also be *both* principles which provide criteria for adjudicating certain empirical knowledge claims *and* empirical knowledge claims in their own right?[14]

59. Now if an affirmative response took the form of a claim that MJ$_1$, MJ$_3$ and MJ$_4$ are *empirically confirmed* knowledge claims — thus putting them in a box with MJ$_2$ — a sensitive nerve would be touched. Would not such a claim involve a vicious circularity?

60. Since it is obvious that they cannot be empirical generalizations which owe their epistemic authority to confirmation by instances, one might look for a less direct mode of confirmation by experience.

61. Even if indirectly, however, an appeal must ultimately be made to the fruits of introspection, perception and memory. Sooner or later we would be confronted by such pairs of statements as

It is reasonable to accept MJ$_1$, MJ$_3$ and MJ$_4$ because they are elements in a theory T which coheres with our introspections, perceptions and memories. Our ostensible introspections, perceptions and memories are likely to be true because they fall under MJ_1, MJ_3 and MJ_4.

62. How, we are inclined to expostulate, could it be reasonable (at t) to accept T *because* it is supported by our introspective, perceptual and memory judgments (IPM judgments), if it is *because* they fall under MJ_1, MJ_3 and MJ_4 that it is reasonable to accept these IPM judgments?

63. Consider

Jones accepts T for the reason that IPM judgments support T;

Jones accepts IPM judgments for the reason that they fall under T. This would seem to be no more rational on Jones's part than the situation described by

Jones saves money in order to maintain his bank account;

Jones maintains his bank account in order to facilitate his saving money.

64. We might say that in these two cases Jones is being unreasonable because his motivation is circular. They can be compared to cases in which a person is unreasonable because acting from a self-contradictory intention. Of course, the circle must not be too small (or the contradiction too blatant) if the concept of such a case is to be coherent.

65. To be distinguished from such 'subjective' unreasonableness is the objective ungroundedness[15] which would obtain if the following *per impossible* were true:

What makes it reasonable for Jones to accept T is *simply* the fact that T is supported by the IPM judgments which it is reasonable for Jones to accept.

What makes it reasonable for Jones to accept these IPM judgments is *simply* the fact that they are likely to be true by virtue of falling under T, which it is reasonable for Jones to accept.

66. It should therefore be clear, if it was not already, that what we were groping for in paragraph 58 was a way in which it could be *independently* reasonable to accept MJ_1, MJ_3 and MJ_4 in spite of the fact that a ground for accepting them is the fact that they belong to T, which we suppose to be an empirically well-confirmed theory.

67. I think that such a way can be found by following a strategy developed in two essays on the reaonsbleness of accepting inductive hypotheses.[16] As a matter of fact, the following considerations are necessary to round out the argument of those essays.

68. Such an expanded account might well be called 'Epistemic Evaluation

as Vindication'. Its central theme would be that achieving a certain end or goal can be (deductively) shown to require a certain integrated system of means. For the purposes of this necessarily schematic essay, the end can be characterized as that of being in a *general* position, so far as in us lies, to *act*, i.e., to bring about changes in ourselves and our environment in order to realize *specific* purposes or intentions.

69. In the above-mentioned essays I argued that among the necessary means to this end is the espousal of certain patterns of reasoning, specifically those involved in the establishing of statistical hypotheses, laws and theories.

70. Although I did have *something* to say about how these various patterns of reasoning are interrelated, I treated each 'mode of probabilification' as though it stood on its own feet and said relatively little about how these dimensions of *'prima facie'* reasonableness combine and interact to generate probabilities 'all things considered'.[17]

71. And, in particular, I had nothing to say about the probability of observation statements — though it is obvious that the probability of an inductive hypothesis is a function of the probability of the observational premises which are mustered to support it.

72. In the language of the present essay, I had nothing to say about the probability which attaches to ostensible introspections, perceptions and memories (IPM judgments).

73. If challenged, I would have appealed to something like PJ_1, PJ_3 and PJ_4 and argued that they are true. If asked why it is reasonable to accept them, I would have argued that they are elements in a conceptual framework which defines what it is to be a finite knower in a world one never made.

74. In short I would have appealed to a more encompassing version of what I have been calling theory T.

75. To be one who makes epistemic appraisals is to be in this framework. And to be in this framework is to appreciate the interplay of the reasonablenesses of inductive hypotheses and of IPM judgments.

76. Now in the case of particular theories, e.g., the corpuscular theory of light, one can imagine that one gets into the conceptual framework of the theory by a process of inductive reasoning. One *entertains* the framework and finds it inductively reasonable to espouse it. One espouses it *for the reason that* it is inductively reasonable to do so, and one is *being reasonable* in so doing.

77. But can one espouse theory T *for the reason that* it is inductively reasonable to do so, and be *reasonable* in so doing? We have already seen that the answer is 'No!'.

78. Clearly we must distinguish the question 'How did we get into the

framework?' from the question 'Granted that we are in the framework, how can we justify accepting it?' In neither case, however, is the answer 'by inductive reasoning' appropriate.

79. Presumably the question 'How did we get into the framework?' has a causal answer, a special application of evolutionary theory to the emergence of beings capable of conceptually representing the world of which they have come to be a part.

80. As to the second question, the answer, according to the proposed strategy, lies in the necessary connection between being in the framework of epistemic evaluation and being agents. It is this connection which constitutes the objective ground for the reasonableness of accepting *something like* theory T.

81. I say 'something like' theory T, for we are now at the moment of truth and must get down to specifies. Thus, what does all of the above metaphysical chatter about frameworks have to do with the rationality of accepting MJ_1, MJ_3 and MJ_4?

82. The answer is that since agency, to be effective, involves having reliable cognitive maps of ourselves and our environment, the concept of effective agency involves that of our IPM judgments being likely to be true, i.e., to be correct mappings[18] of ourselves and our circumstances.

83. Notice, then, that if the above argument is sound, it is reasonable to accept

MJ_5 IPM judgments are likely to be true,

simply on the ground that unless they *are* likely to be true, the concept of effective agency has no application.

84. Now for the linchpin. We must carefully distinguish between having good reason to accept MJ_5 and having good reason to accept a proposed *explanation* of *why* IPM judgments are likely to be true.

85. To explain why IPM judgments are likely to be true *does* involve finding inductive support for hypotheses concerning the mechanisms involved and how they evolved in response to evolutionary pressures. And *this* obviously presupposes the reasonableness of accepting IPM judgments.

86. To borrow a Firthian locution, MJ_5 is epistemically prior to the reasonableness of particular IPM judgments, whereas particular IPM judgments are epistemically prior to *explanations* of the likely truth of IPM judgments.

87. Some twenty-two years ago I wrote

If I reject the framework of traditional empiricism, it is not because I want to say that empirical knowledge has *no* foundation. For to put it this way is to accept that it is really 'empirical knowledge so-called,' and to be put in a box with rumors and hoaxes.

There is clearly *some* point to the picture of knowledge as resting on a level of propositions — observation reports — which do not rest on other propositions in the same way as other propositions rest on them. On the other hand, I do wish to insist that the metaphor of 'foundation' is misleading in that it keeps us from seeing that if there is a logical dimension in which other empirical propositions rest on observation reports, there is another logical dimension in which the latter rest on the former.[19]

To the extent that this passage was one of my notorious promissory notes, I hope that the present essay provides *some* of the cash.

88. I will conclude by rounding out the considerations advanced in paragraphs 85–6. They explain why I wrote in paragraph 80 that there is an objective ground for accepting 'something like' theory T; for, as it exists at any one time, theory T is a complex which includes MJ_5 *and* attempts to explain *why* IPM judgments are likely to be true. The latter enterprise is still unfinished business.

89. It is in the former respect that it constitutes the conceptual framework which spells out the 'explanatory coherence' which is the ultimate criterion of truth.[20]

NOTES

[*] This paper is a revised version of the central argument of 'Givenness and Explanatory Coherence', *The Journal of Philosophy,* 70 (1973).

[1] Compare Chisholm, *Perception*, pp. 30-32.

[2] I have, however, discussed it at length on a number of occasions, thus *Science and Metaphysics*, chapters 3–5; most recently in *Naturalism and Ontology*, Ridgeview Press, 1979, chapters 4–5.

[3] Otherwise put, 'to states of affairs whose epistemic status does not require that they obtain'. Compare the preceding paragraph.

[4] *Theory of Knowledge* (2nd edition), p. 25.

[5] *The Journal of Philosophy,* 61, 1964.

[6] Firth writes 'true' where I have put 'likely to be true' — but that is simply a symptom of his lack of concern for inferential warrant increasing properties of the *second* kind.

[7] P. 550, 1. 3.

[8] P. 550.

[9] A warrantedness, however, which may be *inferential* in *something like* Firth's account of inferential WP's of the *second* kind.

[10] Pp. 553 ff.

[11] P. 553.

[12] P. 556.

[13] Adapted from Chisholm's principles B and D, *Theory of Knowledge*, 2nd ed., pp. 80–1.

[14] After all, can it not be argued that law-like statements are both empirical hypotheses *and* material rules of inference?

[15] It is important to distinguish between two possible constructions of 'It is reasonable for Jones to do A *because* A-ing would bring about X. Thus

R₁   The fact that A-ing would bring about X makes it reasonable for Jones to do A.

R₂   It is reasonable for Jones to do A for the reason that by A-ing he (himself) would bring about X.

In R₁ what is reasonable is simply the doing of A, and the fact that A would bring about X is the *ground* of this reasonableness. In R₂ what is reasonable is the doing of A *with a certain intention or purpose*, i.e., that of bringing about X by doing A.

[16] 'Induction as Vindication', in *Philosophy of Science* **31** (1964), reprinted in *Essays in Philosophy and its History*, Dordrecht, 1974; and 'Are There Non-deductive Logics?' in *Essays in Honor of C. G. Hempel* (ed. by N. Rescher) Dordrecht (1970).

[17] After all, my philosophical purpose was to exhibit inductive reasoning as a form of practical reasoning, and by so doing to throw light on the very concept of probability.

[18] May I call them pictures?

[19] 'Empiricism and the Philosophy of Mind,' in *Minnesota Studies in the Philosophy of Science, Vol. I* (ed. by H. Feigl and M. Scriven), Minneapolis, 1956; reprinted with minor alterations in *Science, Perception and Reality*, London, 1963. The passage occurs on page 170 of *SPR*.

[20] I have, of course, neglected in this essay the equally important and no less difficult topic of deductive reasonableness.

NANCY C. KELSIK

BIBLIOGRAPHY

This bibliography covers books and articles published primarily within the past twenty-five years. It focuses on material dealing with the analysis of factual knowledge and with theories of epistemic justification. Some attempt has been made to include important reviews of books, but no attempt has been made to include every review of every book. Most of the literature on epistemic logic has not been included, nor has the extensive literature on probability and inductive inference been covered. For the latter, the reader might consult the bibliographical essay prepared by Ralph Slaght in *Induction, Acceptance and Rational Belief*, ed. Marshall Swain (Reidel: 1970).

BOOKS

1. Aaron, Richard I. *Knowing and The Function of Reason.* London: Oxford University Press, 1971.
2. Ackermann, Robert J. *Belief and Knowledge.* New York: Doubleday, 1972.
3. Armstrong, David M. *Perception and The Physical World.* London: Routledge and Kegan Paul, 1961.
4. Armstrong, David M. *Belief, Truth and Knowledge.* London: Cambridge University Press, 1973.
5. Aune, Bruce. *Knowledge, Mind, and Nature.* New York: Random House, 1967.
6. Austin, J. L. *Philosophical Papers.* London: Oxford University Press, 1961.
7. Ayer, A. J. *The Foundation of Empirical Knowledge.* London and New York: Macmillan, 1940.
8. Ayer A. J. *The Problems of Knowledge.* London and New York: Macmillan, 1956.
9. Butchvarov, Panayot. *The Concept of Knowledge.* Evanston: Northwestern University Press, 1970.
10. Capaldi, Nicholas. *Human Knowledge: A Philosophical Analysis of Its Meaning and Scope.* New York: Pegasus, 1969.
11. Chisholm Roderick M. *Perceiving.* Ithaca: Cornell University Press, 1957.
12. Chisholm, Roderick M. *Theory of Knowledge*, 2nd ed. Englewood Cliffs: Prentice-Hall, 1976.
13. Chisholm, Roderick M. and Swartz, Robert, eds., *Empirical Knowledge.* Englewood Cliffs: Prentice-Hall, 1973.
14. Cornman, James W., *Scepticism, Justification and Explanation*, (Dordrecht: D. Reidel), forthcoming.
15. Danto, Arthur. *Analytical Philosophy of Knowledge.* Cambridge: Cambridge University Press, 1968.

George S. Pappas (ed.), Justification and Knowledge, 183–211.
Copyright © 1979 by D. Reidel Publishing Company.

16. Dretske, Fred I. *Seeing and Knowing*. Chicago: University of Chicago Press, and London: Routledge and Kegan Paul, 1969.
17. Eames, Elizabeth Ramsden. *Bertrand Russell's Theory of Knowledge*. London: George Allen and Unwin, 1969.
18. Feyerabend, Paul. *Against Method: Outline of an Anarchistic Theory of Knowledge*. London: New Left Books, 1975.
19. Fogelin, Robert. *Evidence and Meaning*. London: Routledge and Kegan Paul, 1967.
20. Ginet, Carl. *Knowledge, Perception and Memory*. Dordrecht: Reidel, 1975.
21 Griffiths, A. Phillips, ed. *Knowledge and Belief*. London: Oxford University Press, 1967.
22. Hamlyn, David W. *The Theory of Knowledge*. New York: Doubleday, 1970.
23. Harman, Gilbert. *Thought*. Princeton: Princeton University Press, 1973.
24. Hill, Thomas English. *Contemporary Theories of Knowledge*. New York: Macmillan, 1961.
25. Hintikka, Jaakko. *Knowledge and Belief*. Ithaca: Cornell University Press, 1962.
26. Hintikka, Jaakko. *Models for Modalities*. Dordrecht: Reidel, 1969.
27. Jackson Frank. *Perception, A Representative Theory*. Cambridge: Cambridge University Press, 1977.
28. Johnson, Oliver. *The Problem of Knowledge*. Atlantic Highlands: Humanities, 1974.
29. Kekes, John. *A Justification of Rationality*. Albany: University of New York Press, 1976.
30. Landesman, Charles, ed. *The Foundations of Knowledge*. Englewood Cliffs: Prentice Hall, 1970.
31. Lehrer, Keith. *Knowledge*. New York: Oxford University Press, 1974.
32. Lehrer, Keith, ed. *Analysis and Metaphysics*. Dordrecht: Reidel, 1975.
33. Lehrer, Keith and James W. Cornman. *Philosophical Problems and Arguments*, 2nd ed. New York: Macmillan, 1974. Chapter 2.
34. Levensky, Mark, ed. *Human Factual Knowledge*. Englewood Cliffs: Prentice Hall, 1971.
35. Lewis, C. I. *An Analysis of Knowledge and Valuation*. La Salle: Open Court, 1946.
36. Locke, Don. *Perception and Our Knowledge of the External World*. London: Routledge and Kegan Paul, 1967.
37. Malcolm, Norman. *Knowledge and Certainty*. Englewood Cliffs: Prentice-Hall, 1963.
38. Martin, R. M. *Belief, Existence, and Meaning*. New York: New York University Press, 1969.
39. Moore, G. E. *Some Main Problems of Philosophy*. London: George Allen and Unwin, 1953.
40. Moore, G. E. *Philosophical Papers*. London: George Allen and Unsin. 1959.
41. Moore, G. E. *The Commonplace Book, 1919–1935*, ed. Casimir Lewy. London: George Allen and Unwin, 1963.
42. Morton, Adam. *A Guide through the Theory of Knowledge*. Encino, California: Dickenson, 1977.
43. Pappas, George and Swain, Marshall, eds. *Essays on Knowledge and Justification*. Ithaca: Cornell University Press, 1978.

44. Pears, David. *What is Knowledge?* New York: Harper and Row, 1971.
45. Pollock, John. *Knowledge and Justification.* Princeton: Princeton University Press, 1974.
46. Popper, Karl, *Objective Knowledge.* London: Oxford University Press, 1972.
47. Price, H. H. *Belief.* London: George Allen and Unwin, 1969.
48. Prichard, H. A. *Knowledge and Perception.* London: Oxford University Press, 1950.
49. Quine, W. V. O. *Ontological Relativity.* New York: Columbia University Press, 1969.
50. Quine, W. V. O. *The Roots of Reference.* La Salle: Open Court, 1973.
51. Quine, W. V. O., and J. S. Ullian. *The Web of Belief.* New York: Random House, 1978. 2nd ed.
52. Quinton, A. *The Nature of Things.* London: Routledge and Kegan Paul, 1973.
53. Rescher, Nicholas. *Topics in Philosophical Analysis.* Dordrecht: Reidel, 1969.
54. Rescher, Nicholas, ed. *Studies in The Theory of Knowledge.* American *Philosophical Quarterly* Monograph Series, Number 4. Oxford: Basil Blackwell, 1970.
55. Rescher, Nicholas. *Coherence Theory of Truth.* London: Oxford University Press, 1973.
56. Rescher Nicholas. *Conceptual Idealism.* London: Oxford University Press, 1973.
57. Rescher Nicholas. *Plausible Reasoning: An Introduction to the Theory and Practice of Plausibilistic Inference.* Assen: Van Gorcum, 1976.
58. Rescher Nicholas. *Methodological Pragmatism.* New York: New York University Press, 1977.
59. Rescher Nicholas, ed. *Studies in Epistemology.* American Philosophical *Quarterly* Monograph Series, Number 9. Oxford: Basil Blackwell, 1975.
60. Roth, Michael D. and Galis, Leon, eds. *Knowing: Essays in the Theory of Knowledge.* New York: Random House, 1970.
61. Russell, Bertrand. *The Problems of Philosophy.* London: Oxford University Press, 1912.
62. Russell, Bertrand. *Knowledge of the External World.* London: George Allen and Unwin, 1914.
63. Russell Bertrand. *Outline of Philosophy.* London: George Allen and Unwin, 1927.
64. Russell Betrand. *Meaning and Truth.* London: George Allen and Unwin, 1940.
65. Russell, Bertrand. *Human Knowledge: Its scope and Limits.* London: George Allen and Unwin, 1948.
66. Ryle, Gilbert. *The Concept of Mind.* London: Hutchinson, 1949. Chapter 2.
67. Scheffler, Israel. *Conditions of Knowledge.* Chicago: Scott, Foresman, 1965.
68. Scheffler, Israel. *Science and Subjectivity.* Indianapolis: Bobbs-Merrill, 1967.
69. Sellars, Wilfrid. *Science, Perception and Reality.* New York: Humanities, 1963.
70. Sellars, Wilfrid. *Science and Metaphysics.* New York: Humanities, 1967.
71. Sellars, Wilfrid. *Philosophical Perspectives.* Springfield, Illinois: Charles Thomas Publishers, 1968.
72. Slote, Michael Anthony. *Reason and Scepticism.* London: George Allen and Unwin, 1970.
73. Steiner, Mark. *Mathematical Knowledge.* Ithaca: Cornell University Press, 1975.
74. Stroll, Avrum, ed. *Epistemology: New Essays In The Theory of Knowledge.* New York: Harper and Row, 1967.

75. Swain, Marshall, ed. *Induction, Acceptance, and Rational Belief.* Dordrecht: Reidel, 1970.
76. Swartz, Robert J., ed. *Perceiving, Sensing, And Knowing.* New York: Doubleday Anchor, 1965.
77. Unger, Peter. *Ignorance.* London: Oxford University Press, 1975.
78. Von Wright, G., ed. *Problems in the Theory of Knowledge.* The Hague: Martinus Nijhoff, 1972.
79. Will, F. A. *Induction and Justification.* Ithaca: Cornell University Press, 1974.
80. Williams, Michael. *Groundless Belief.* New Haven: Yale University Press, 1977.
81. Wittgenstein, Ludwig. *On Certainty.* Oxford: Basil Blackwell, 1969.
82. Wolgast, Elizabeth. *Paradoxes of Knowledge.* Ithaca: Cornell University Press, 1978.
83. Woozley, Anthony D. *Theory of Knowledge.* London: Hutchinson University Library, 1949, Chapter VIII.

ARTICLES

84. Aaron, Richard I., 'Feeling Sure,' *Proceedings of the Aristotelian Society,* **30** (1956), 1–13.
85. Abate, Charles J., 'A Reconsideration of Justified True Belief,' *Kinesis,* **5** (1973), 87–91.
86. Abate, Charles J., 'Has Dretske Really Refuted Skepticism?' *Auslegung,* **4** (1977), 169–175.
87. Abbott, W. R., 'What Knowledge Is Not,' *Analysis,* **31** (1971), 143–144.
88. Abelson, Raziel, 'Knowledge and Belief,' *Journal of Philosophy,* **65** (1968), 733–737.
89. Achinstein, Peter, 'Concepts of Evidence,' *Mind,* **87** (1978), 22–45.
90. Ackerman, Terence F., 'Defeasibility Modified,' *Philosophical Studies,* **26** (1974), 431–435.
91. Adams, E. M., 'On Knowing That,' *Philosophical Quarterly,* **8** (1958), 300–306.
92. Agassi, Joseph, 'Privileged Access,' *Inquiry,* **12** (1969), 420–426.
93. Agassi, Joseph, 'Positive Evidence as a Social Institution,' *Philosophia,* **1** (1971), 143–157.
94. Airaksinen, T., 'Five Types of Knowledge', *American Philosophical Quarterly,* **15** (1978), 263–274.
95. Aldrich, Virgil C., 'Review of Dretske, *Seeing and Knowing*', *Journal of Philosophy,* **67** (1970), 995–1006.
96. Almeder, Robert F., 'Defeasibility and Skepticism,' *Australiasian Journal of Philosophy,* **51** (1973), 238–244.
97. Almeder, Robert F., 'Common Sense and the Foundation of Knowledge,' *Man and World,* **7** (1974), 254–270.
98. Almeder, Robert F., 'Truth and Evidence,' *Philosophical Quarterly,* **24** (1974), 365–368.
99. Almeder, Robert F., 'Defending Gettier Counter-Examples,' *Australasian Journal of Philosophy,* **53** (1975), 58–60.
100. Almeder, Robert F., 'The Epistemological Realism of Charles Peirce,' *Transactions*

of the Charles S. Peirce Society, **11** (1975), 3–17.

101. Almeder, Robert F., 'Fallibilism and the Ultimate Irreversible Opinion,' *American Philosophical Quarterly,* Monograph Series, 9 (1975), 33–54.
102. Almeder, Robert F., 'Seeing the Truth: A Reply,' *Philosophical Quarterly,* **26** (1976), 163–165.
103. Almeder, Robert F., and Arrington, Robert, 'Mannison on Inexplicable Knowledge and Belief,' *Australasian Journal of Philosophy,* **55** (1977), 87–90.
104. Alston, William P., 'Varieties of Privileged Access,' *American Philosophical Quarterly,* **8** (1971), 223–241.
105. Alston, William P., 'Has Foundationalism Been Refuted?' *Philosophical Studies,* **29** (1976), 287–305.
106. Alston, William P., 'Self Warrant: A Neglected From of Privileged Access,' *American Philosophical Quarterly,* **13** (1976), 257–272.
107. Alston, William P., 'Two Types of Foundationalism,' *Journal of Philosophy,* **85** (1976), 165–185.
108. Ammerman, Robert, 'A Note on "Knowing That",' *Analysis,* **17** (1956), 30–32.
109. Anderson, Alan Ross, 'On Professor Martin's Beliefs,' *Journal of Philosophy,* **59** (1962), 600–607.
110. Anderson, Kent C., 'A Note on Knowledge,' *Mind,* **86** (1977), 249–251.
111. Annis, David B., 'A Note on Lehrer's Proof That Knowledge Entails Belief,' *Analysis,* **29** (1969), 207–208.
112. Annis, David B., 'Knowledge and Defeasibility,' *Philosophical Studies,* **24** (1973), 199–202. Reprinted in Pappas and Swain, [43].
113. Annis, David B., 'Epistemic Justification,' *Philosophia,* **6** (1976), 259–266.
114. Annis, David B., 'Knowledge, Belief and Rationality,' *Journal of Philosophy,* **74** (1977), 217–225.
115. Annis, David B., 'A Contextualist Theory of Justification,' *American Philosophical Quarterly,* **15** (1978), 213–219.
116. Armstrong, David M., 'Is Introspective Knowledge Incorrigible?' *Philosophical Review,* **72** (1963), 417–432.
117. Armstrong, David M., 'Does Knowledge Entail Belief,' *Proceedings of the Aristotelian Society,* **70** (1969–1970), 21–36.
118. Armstrong, David M., and J. H. Scobell, 'Knowledge and Belief,' *Analysis,* **13** (1953), 111–117.
119. Arner, Douglas, 'On Knowing,' *Philosophical Review,* **68** (1959), 84–92.
120. Audi, Robert, 'The Limits of Self-Knowledge,' *Canadian Journal of Philosophy,* **4** (1974), 253–267.
121. Audi, Robert, 'The Epistemological Authority of the First-Person,' *The Personalist,* **56** (1975), 5–15.
122. Audi, Robert, 'Epistemic Disavowals and Self-Deception,' *The Personalist,* **57** (1976), 378–385.
123. Aune, Bruce, 'Knowing and Merely Thinking,' *Philosophical Studies,* **12** (1960), 53–58.
124. Aune, Bruce, 'Two Theories of Scientific Knowledge,' *Critica,* **5** (1971), 3–16.
125. Aune, Bruce, 'Remarks on an Argument by Chisholm,' *Philosophical Studies,* **23** (1972), 327–334.
126. Austin, John L., 'Other Minds,' *Proceedings of the Aristotelian Society,* Supple-

mentary volume, **20** (1946), 76–116.

127. Ayer, A. J., 'Knowledge, Belief, and Evidence,' *Danish Yearbook of Philosophy,* 1 (1964), 18–19.

128. Bailey, George, 'Pappas, Incorrigibility and Science,' *Philosophical Studies,* (forthcoming).

129. Bambrough, Renford, 'Foundations,' *Analysis,* **30** (1970), 190–197.

130. Barker, John, 'Knowledge and Causation,' *Southern Journal of Philosophy,* **10** (1972), 313–321.

131. Barker, John, 'Knowledge, Ignorance and Presupposition,' *Analysis,* **35** (1974), 33–45.

132. Barker, John, 'A Note on Knowledge and Belief,' *Canadian Journal of Philosophy,* **5** (1975), 143–144.

133. Barker, John, 'A Paradox of Knowing Whether,' *Mind,* **84** (1975), 281–283.

134. Barker, John, 'Socratic Ignorance Vindicated,' *Philosophical Studies,* **28** (1975), 71–75.

135. Barker, John, 'Audi on Epistemic Disavowals,' *The Personalist,* **57** (1976), 376–377.

136. Barker, John, 'What You Don't Know Won't Hurt You?' *American Philosophical Quarterly,* **13** (1976), 303–308.

137. Barnes, Gerald W., 'Unger's Defense of Scepticism,' *Philosophical Studies,* **24** (1973), 119–124.

138. Barnes, W. H. F., 'Knowing,' *Philosophical Review,* **72** (1963), 3–16.

139. Bearsley, Patrick J., 'Another Look at the First Principles of Knowledge,' *The Thomist,* **36** (1972), 566–598.

140. Benfield, D., 'The *A Priori–A Posteriori* Distinction,' *Philosophy and Phenomenological Research,* **35** (1975), 151–166.

141. Benfield, D., 'Levin on Knowing *a priori,*' *Journal of Critical Analysis,* **6** (1976), 35–37.

142. Benfield, D., 'The *A Priori* and the Self-Evident: A Reply to Mr. Casullo's The Definition of *A Priori* Knowledge,' *Philosophy and Phenomenological Research,* **38** (1977), 224–227.

143. Beversluis, John, ' "I Know": An Illocutionary Analysis,' *Southern Journal of Philosophy,* **9** (1971), 345–352.

144. Binkley, R., 'Critical Notice: Lehrer's *Knowledge,*' *Canadian Journal of Philosophy,* **7** (1977), 841–851.

145. Black, Carolyn, 'Knowledge Without Belief,' *Analysis,* **31** (1971), 152–158.

146. Black, Carolyn, 'Taking,' *Theoria,* **40** (1974), 66–75.

147. Black, Max, 'Saying and Disbelieving,' *Analysis,* **13** (1952), 25–33.

148. Black, Max, 'An Immoderate Skepticism, Some Comments on Professor Unger's Paper,' *Philosophic Exchange,* **1** (1974), 157–159.

149. Blose, B. L., 'What Never Occurred to Jones: A Comment on the Analysis of Knowledge,' *Philosophical Studies,* **31** (1977), 205–209.

150. Bode, James, 'Knowledge and the Evidential Condition,' *Philosophical Studies,* **31** (1977), 337–344.

151. Boër, Steven, and Lycan, William, 'Knowing Who,' *Philosophical Studies,* **28** (1975), 299–344.

152. Bon Jour, Laurence, 'The Coherence Theory of Empirical Knowledge,' *Philo-*

sophical Studies, **30** (1976), 281–312.

153. Bon Jour, Laurence, 'Rescher's Idealistic Pragmatism,' *Review of Metaphysics,* **29** (1976), 702–726.

154. Bonney, W. L., 'Mr. Deutscher on Saying and Disbelieving,' *Analysis,* **25** (1964), 17–20.

155. Boyd, R., 'Realism, Underdetermination, and a Causal Theory of Evidence,' *Nous,* **7** (1973), 1–12.

156. Bradie, Michael, 'Supererogatory Evidence,' *Southwestern Journal of Philosophy,* **6** (1975), 109–120.

157. Braine, D., 'The Nature of Knowledge,' *Proceedings of the Aristotelian Society,* Supplementary Volume XLVI (1972), 139–170.

158. Braithwaite, R. B., 'The Nature of Believing,' *Proceedings of the Aristotelian Society,* **33** (1933), 129–146.

159. Brown, D. G., 'Knowing How and Knowing That, What?' in Pitcher and Wood, eds., *Ryle,* New York: Doubleday (1970), 213–249.

160. Brown, H., 'Idealism, Empiricism and Materialism,' *New Scholasticism,* **47** (1973), 311–323.

161. Brown, R., 'Self-Justifying Statements,' *Journal of Philosophy,* **62** (1965), 145–150.

162. Broyles, J. E., 'Knowledge and Mistake,' *Mind,* **78** (1969), 198–211.

163. Buchanan, Allen, 'Basic Knowledge,' *Philosophy and Phenomenological Research,* **37** (1976), 101–108.

164. Burkholder, Peter M., 'Knowing in the Strong Sense,' *Tulane Studies in Philosophy,* **17** (1968), 1–12.

165. Byrd, M., 'Knowledge and True Belief in Hintikka's Epistemic Logic,' *Journal of Philosophical Logic,* **2** (1973), 181–192.

166. Campbell, C. A., 'Towards a Definition of Belief,' *Philosophical Quarterly,* **17** (1967), 204–220.

167. Canfield, J., ' "I Know that I am in Pain" is Senseless,' in Lehrer, ed., *Analysis and Metaphysics,* Dordrecht: Reidel, (1975).

169. Cargile, James, 'On Believing You Believe,' *Analysis,* **27** (1967), 177–183.

170. Cargile, James, 'A Note on "Iterated Knowings",' *Analysis,* **30** (1970), 151–155.

171. Cargile, James, 'On Near Knowledge,' *Analysis,* **31** (1971), 145–152.

172. Cargile, James, 'In Reply To A Defense of Scepticism,' *Philosophical Review,* **81** (1972), 229–236. Reprinted in Pappas and Swain [43].

173. Carl, W., and Horstman, R., 'Knowing and Claiming,' *Ratio,* **14** (1972), 155–171.

174. Carmichael, P. A. 'Knowing,' *Journal of Philosophy,* **56** (1959), 341–351.

175. Carrier, L. S., 'An Analysis of Empirical Knowledge,' *Southern Journal of Philosophy,* **9** (1971), 3–11.

176. Carrier, L. S., 'Scepticism Made Certain,' *Journal of Philosophy,* **71** (1974), 140–151.

177. Carrier, L. S., 'The Causal Theory of Knowledge,' *Philosophia,* **6** (1976), 237–258.

178. Carrier, L. S., 'The Irreducibility of Knowledge,' *Logique et Analyse,* **20** (1977), 167–176.

179. Carter, Randolph, 'Lehrer's Fourth Condition for Knowing,' *Philosophical Studies,* **31** (1977), 327–335.

180. Castañeda, Hector-Neri, 'Review of Hintikka,' *Journal of Symbolic Logic,* **29** (1964), 132–134.
181. Castañeda, Hector-Neri, 'Review of Malcolm,' *Review of Metaphysics,* **18** (1965), 508–547.
182. Castañeda, Hector-Neri, ' "He": A Study in the Logic of Self-Consciousness,' *Ratio,* **8** (1966), 130–157.
183. Castañeda, Hector-Neri, 'Indicators and Quasi-Indicators,' *American Philosophical Quarterly,* **4** (1967), 85–100.
184. Castañeda, Hector-Neri, 'On The Logic of Self-Knowledge,' *Nous,* **1** (1967), 9–21.
185. Castañeda, Hector-Neri, 'On The Logic of Attributions of Self-Knowledge To Others,' *Journal of Philosophy,* **65** (1968), 439–456.
186. Castañeda, Hector-Neri, 'On Knowing (or Believing) That One Knows (or Believes),' *Synthese,* **21** (1970), 187–203.
187. Casullo, Albert, 'The Definition of *A Priori* Knowledge,' *Philosophy and Phenomenological Research,* **38** (1977), 220–224.
188. Chalmers, A., 'On Learning From Our Mistakes,' *British Journal of Philosophy of Science,* **24** (1973), 164–173.
189. Chandler, J. H., 'Incorrigibility and Classification,' *Australasian Journal of Philosophy,* **48** (1970), 101–106.
190. Chisholm, Roderick, 'Sentences About Believing,' *Proceedings of the Aristotelian Society,* **56** (1956), 125–148.
191. Chisholm, Roderick, 'Epistemic Statements and the Ethics of Belief,' *Philosophy and Phenomenological Research,* **16** (1956), 447–460.
192. Chisholm, Roderick, ' "Appear", "Take", and "Evident",' *Journal of Philosophy,* **53** (1956), 722–734. Reprinted in Swartz, [76].
193. Chisholm, Roderick, 'Evidence as Justification,' *Journal of Philosophy,* **58** (1961), 739–748.
194. Chisholm, Roderick, 'The Logic of Knowing,' *Journal of Philosophy,* **60** (1963), 773–795.
195. Chisholm, Roderick, 'Notes on the Logic of Believing,' *Philosophy and Phenomenological Research,* **24** (1963), 195–201.
196. Chisholm, Roderick, 'A Note on Saying: A Reply to Mr. Landesman,' *Analysis,* **24** (1964), 182–184.
197. Chisholm, Roderick, 'The Ethics of Requirement,' *American Philosophical Quarterly,* **1** (1964), 147–153.
198. Chisholm, Roderick, 'J. L. Austin's *Philosophical Papers,*' *Mind,* **73** (1964), 1–26.
199. Chisholm, Roderick, 'Theory of Knowledge,' in R. Chisholm, *et al, Philosophy,* Englewood Cliffs: Prentice-Hall, (1964), 243–344.
200. Chisholm, Roderick, 'The Foundation of Empirical Statements,' in K. Ajdukiewicz, ed., *The Foundations of Statements and Decisions,* Polish Scientific Publishers, (1965). Reprinted in Roth and Galis, [60].
201. Chisholm, Roderick, 'The Principles of Epistemic Appraisals,' in F. C. Donmeyer, ed., *Current Philosophical Issues: Essays in Honor of C. J. Ducasse,* Springfield, Illinois: Charles Thomas (1966), 87–104.
202. Chisholm, Roderick, 'Identity Through Possible Worlds: Some Questions,' *Nous,* **1** (1967), 1–8.

203. Chisholm, Roderick, 'On A Principle of Epistemic Preferability,' *Philosophy and Phenomenological Research*, **30** (1969), 294–301.
204. Chisholm, Roderick, 'Lewis' Ethics of Belief,' in P. A. Schilpp, ed., *The Philosophy of C. I. Lewis*, LaSalle: Open Court, (1969).
205. Chisholm, Roderick, 'On the Nature of Empirical Evidence,' L. Foster and J. Swanson, eds., *Experience and Theory*, Amherst: University of Massachusetts Press, (1970), 103–134. An amended version of this paper, with the same title, appears in Chisholm and Swartz, eds., *Empirical Knowledge*, [13]. The paper appears with still further amendments in Pappas and Swain, eds., [43].
206. Chisholm, Roderick, 'Knowledge and Belief. *De Dicto* and *De Re*,' *Philosophical Studies*, **29** (1976), 1–20.
207. Chisholm, Roderick, 'Comments and Replies,' *Philosophia*, **7** (1978), 597–636.
208. Chisholm, Roderick and Sosa, Ernest, 'On the Logic of "Intrinsically Better",' *American Philosophical Quarterly*, **3** (1966), 244–249.
209. Chisholm, Roderick and Keim, R., 'A System of Epistemic Logic,' *Ratio*, **14** (1972), 99–115.
210. Clark, Michael, 'Knowledge and Grounds: A Comment on Gettier's Paper,' *Analysis*, **24** (1964), 24–48.
211. Clark, Romane, 'Comments on Hintikka,' in Care and Grimm, eds., *Perception and Personal Identity*, Cleveland: Case Western Reserve Press, (1969).
212. Clark, Romane, 'Old Foundations For A Logic of Perception,' *Synthese*, **33** (1976), 75–99.
213. Clark, T., 'The Legacy of Scepticism,' *Journal of Philosophy*, **69** (1972), 754–769.
214. Coady, C., 'Testimony and Observation,' *American Philosophical Quarterly*, **10** (1973), 149–155.
215. Coburn, Robert C., 'Knowing and Believing,' *Philosophical Review*, **80** (1971), 236–243.
216. Coder, David, 'Thalberg's Defense of Justified True Belief,' *Journal of Philosophy*, **67** (1970), 424–425.
217. Coder, David, 'Naturalizing the Gettier Argument,' *Philosophical Studies*, **26** (1974), 111–118.
218. Cohen, L. Jonathan, 'Claims to Knowledge,' *Proceedings of the Aristotelian Society*, **36** (1962), 63–75.
219. Cohen, L. Jonathan, 'More About Knowing and Feeling Sure,' *Analysis*, **27** (1966), 11–16.
220. Cole, Richard, 'Knowing Imperfectly,' *Southwestern Journal of Philosophy*, **5** (1974), 69–75.
221. Collier, K., 'Contra the Causal Theory of Knowing,' *Philosophical Studies*, **24** (1973), 350–351.
222. Collins, Arthur, W., 'Unconscious Belief,' *Journal of Philosophy*, **66** (1969), 667–686.
223. Cornman, James, 'Epistemological Skepticism,' *Encyclopedia Americana*, 1971.
224. Cornman, James, 'Foundational vs. Nonfoundational Theories of Empirical Justification,' *American Philosophical Quarterly*, **14** (1977), 287–297. Reprinted in Pappas and Swain, eds., [43].
225. Cornman, James, 'On Acceptability Without Certainty,' *Journal of Philosophy*, **74** (1977), 29–47.

226. Cornman, James, 'On Knowing and Being Justified in Believing One Knows,' (unpublished).

227. Cornman, James, 'On the Certainty of Reports About What is Given,' *Nous,* **12** (1978), 93–118.

228. Craig, Edward, 'Sensory Experience and the Foundations of Knowledge,' *Synthese,* **31** (1976), 1–24.

229. Daniels, C., 'Immediate Knowledge,: Ayer, Strawson, and Shoemaker,' *Theoria,* **33** (1967), 176–178.

230. Daniels, C., 'A Few Words About Knowledge, Skepticism, and Entailment,' *Canadian Journal of Philosophy,* **8** (1978), 341–342.

231. Danto, Arthur, 'Seven Objections Against Austin's Analysis of "I know",' *Philosophical Studies,* **13** (1962), 84–91.

232. Danto, Arthur, 'On Knowing That We Know,' in Stroll [74], 32–53.

233. Darmstadter, Howard, 'Consistency of Belief,' *Journal of Philosophy,* **68** (1971), 301–310.

234. Davis, Stephen, ' "I Know" As An Explicit Performative,' *Theoria,* **30** (1964), 157–165.

235. Day, Michael, A., 'A Comment on Lehrer's Analysis of Knowledge,' *Philosophical Forum,* (Boston) **41** (1972–73), 305–306.

236. DeGeorge, Richard T., 'Reason, Truth and Context,' *Idealistic Studies,* **4** (1974), 35–49.

237. Delaney, C., 'Peirce's Critique of Foundationalism,' *The Monist,* **57** (1973), 240–251.

238. Delaney, C., 'Foundations of Empirical Knowledge-Again,' *New Scholasticism,* **50** (1976), 1–19.

239. Delaney, C., 'Sellars' Theory of Knowledge,' in C. Delaney, G. Gutting and M. Loux, *The Synoptic Vision: Wilfrid Sellars Philosophy*, (Notre Dame: University of Notre Dame Press), 1977.

240. DeSousa, Ronald Bon, 'Knowledge, Consistent Belief, and Self-Consciousness,' *Journal of Philosophy,* **67** (1970), 66–73.

241. Deutscher, Max, 'A Note on Saying and Disbelieving,' *Analysis,* **25** (1965), 63–65.

242. Deutscher, Max, 'Review of Hintikka,' *Australasian Journal of Philosophy,* **44** (1966), 145–149.

243. Deutscher, Max, 'Bonney on Saying and Disbelieving,' *Analysis,* **27** (1967), 184–186.

244. Deutscher, Max, 'Hintikka's Conception of Epistemic Logic,' *Australasian Journal of Philosophy,* **47** (1969), 205–208.

245. Deutscher, Max, 'Reasons, Regresses and Grounds,' *Australasian Journal of Philosophy,* **51** (1973), 1–16.

246. Dicker, Georges, 'Certainty Without Dogmatism: A Reply to Unger's "An Argument for Skepticism",' *Philosophic Exchange*, (1974), 161–170.

247. Dicker, Georges, 'Is There a Problem About Perception and Knowledge?' *American Philosophical Quarterly,* **15** (1978), 165–176.

248. Doig, James C., 'Danto On Knowledge,' *Review of Metaphysics,* **29** (1975), 307–321.

249. Door, Jorgen, 'Scepticism and Dogmatism,' *Inquiry,* **16** (1973), 214–220.

250. Doppelt, Gerald, 'Dretske's Conception of Perception and Knowledge,' *Philosophy of Science*, **40** (1973), 433–446.
251. Doppelt, Gerald, 'Kuhn's Epistemological Relativism: An Interpretation and Defense,' *Inquiry*, **21** (1978), 33–86.
252. Doppelt, Gerald, 'Incorrigibility. The Mental, and Materialism,' *Philosophy Research Archives*, **3** (1977).
253. Doppelt, Gerald, 'Incorrigibility and the Mental,' *Australasian Journal of Philosophy*, **56** (1978), 3–20.
254. Downes, Chauncey, 'Descriptions in Arguments,' *Analysis*, **29** (1969), 100–101.
255. Dreher, John H., 'Evidence and Justified Belief,' *Philosophical Studies*, **25** (1974), 435–439.
256. Dretske, Fred I., 'Reasons and Consequences,' *Analysis*, **28** (1968), 166–168.
257. Dretske, Fred I., 'Epistemic Operators,' *Journal of Philosophy*, **67** (1970), 1007–1023.
258. Dretske, Fred I., 'Conclusive Reasons,' *American Journal of Philosophy*, **49** (1971), 1–22. Reprinted in Pappas and Swain, eds., [43].
259. Dretske, Fred I., 'Reasons, Knowledge, and Probability,' *Philosophy of Science*, **38** (1971), 216–220.
260. Dretske, Fred I., 'Review of Slote,' *Journal of Philosophy*, **69** (1972), 47–53. Review of Slote, [72].
261. Duncan-Jones, Austin, 'Further Questions About "Know" and "Think",' *Analysis*, **5** (1938), 198–206.
262. Dunlop, C. E. M., 'Lehrer and Ellis on Incorrigibility,' *Australasian Journal of Philosophy*, **55** (1977), 201–205.
263. Eberle, Rolf A., 'A Logic of Believing, Knowing and Inferring,' *Synthese*, **26** (1974), 356–382.
264. Edington, E., 'On The Possibility of Rational Inconsistent Beliefs,' *Mind*, **77** (1968), 582–583.
265. Ellis, Brian, 'Avowals Are More Corrigible Than You Think,' *American Journal of Philosophy*, **54** (1976), 116–122.
266. Ellis, Brian, 'Replies to Sussman and Dunlop,' *American Journal of Philosophy*, **56** (1978), 171–173.
267. Ennis, Robert H., 'Enumerative Induction and Best Explanation,' *Journal of Philosophy*, **65** (1968), 523–529.
268. Ewing, A. C., 'Common Sense Propositions,' *Philosophy*, **48** (1973), 363–379.
269. Exdell, John, and Hamilton, James, 'The Incorrigibility of First Person Disavowals,' *The Personalist*, **56** (1975), 389–394.
270. Fain, Haskell and Griffiths, A. Phillips, 'On Falsely Believing That One Doesn't Know,' *American Philosophical Quarterly*, Monograph Series 6 (1972), 10–23.
271. Feldman, Fred, 'Warranting,' *Journal of Philosophy*, **73** (1976), 585–587.
272. Feldman, Fred, 'On the Analysis of Warranting,' *Synthese*, **34** (1977), 497–512.
273. Feldman, Fred, 'Final Comments on the Analysis of Warranting,' *Synthese*, **37** (1978), 465–469.
274. Feldman, Fred, and Heidelberger, Herbert, 'Tormey on Access and Incorrigibility,' *Journal of Philosophy*, **70** (1973), 297–298.
275. Feldman, Richard, 'An Alleged Defect in Gettier Counter-examples,' *Australasian Journal of Philosophy*, **52** (1974), 68–69.

276. Fetzer, James H., 'On "Epistemic Possibility",' *Philosophia*, **4** (1974), 327–335.
277. Finn, David R., 'Dretske on Reasons and Justification,' *Analysis*, **29** (1969), 101–102.
278. Firth, Roderick, 'Ultimate Evidence,' *Journal of Philosophy*, **53** (1956), 732–739. Reprinted in Swartz, [76].
279. Firth, Roderick, 'Chisholm And The Ethics of Belief,' *Philosophical Review*, **68** (1959), 493–506.
280. Firth, Roderick, 'Coherence, Certainty, and Epistemic Priority', *Journal of Philosophy*, **61** (1964), 545–557. Reprinted in Chisholm and Swartz, [13].
281. Firth, Roderick, 'The Anatomy of Certainty,' *Philosophical Review*, **76** (1967), 3–27. Reprinted in Chisholm and Swartz, [13].
282. Firth, Roderick, 'Lewis on the Given,' in P. A. Schilpp, ed., *The Philosophy of C. I. Lewis*, (LaSalle: Open Court), 1969.
283. Firth, Roderick, 'Are Epistemic Concepts Reducible to Ethical Concepts?' in A. Goldman and J. Kim, eds., *Values and Morals*, (Dordrecht: Reidel), 1978.
284. Fisher, J., 'Fallibility and Knowledge of the Future,' *Philosophy and Phenomenological Research*, **36** (1975), 44–58.
285. Fitch, G. W., 'Deducibility For Justification,' *Canadian Journal of Philosophy*, **6** (1976), 299–302.
286. Flew, Antony, 'Review of Price,' *Mind*, **79** (1970), 454–460. Review of [47].
287. Foley, R., 'Inferential Justification and the Infinite Regress,' *American Philosophical Quarterly*, **15** (1978), 311–316.
288. Follesdal, Dagfinn, 'Knowledge, Identity, and Existence,' *Theoria*, **33** (1967), 1–27.
289. Frankfurt, Harry G., 'Philosophical Certainty,' *Philosophical Review*, **71** (1962), 303–327.
290. Fumerton, R. A., 'Inferential Justification and Empiricism,' *Journal of Philosophy*, **73** (1976), 557–569.
291. Galtung, J., 'Empiricism, Criticism and Constructivism,' *Synthese*, **24** (1972), 343–372.
292. Geach, Peter T., 'On Beliefs About Oneself,' *Analysis*, **18** (1957), 23–24.
293. Geach, Peter T., 'Review of Hintikka,' *Philosophical Books*, **4**.2 (1963), 7–8. Review of [25].
294. Geach, Peter T., 'Assertion,' *Philosophical Review*, **74** (1965), 449–465.
295. Gettier, Edmund L., 'Is Justified True Belief Knowledge?' *Analysis*, **23** (1963), 121–123. Reprinted in Roth and Galis, [60].
296. Gibson, Quentin, 'Knowing The Future,' *Analysis*, **27** (1966), 59–64.
297. Ginet, Carl, 'What Must Be Added To Knowing To Obtain Knowing That One Knows?' *Synthese*, **21** (1970), 163–186.
298. Goldman, Alan H., 'Can *A Priori* Arguments Refute the Sceptic?' *Dialogue*, **13** (1974), 105–109.
299. Goldman, Alan H., 'A Note on the Conjunctivity of Knowledge,' *Analysis*, **36** (1975), 5–9.
300. Goldman, Alvin, 'A Causal Theory of Knowing,' *Journal of Philosophy*, **64** (1967), 357–372.
301. Goldman, Alvin, 'Discrimination and Perceptual Knowledge,' *Journal of Philosophy*, **73** (1976), 771–791. Reprinted in Pappas and Swain, [43].

302. Goldman, Alvin, 'Epistemics: The Regulative Theory of Cognition,' *Journal of Philosophy*, **75** (1978), 509–523.
303. Goldstick, D., 'A Contribution Towards the Development of the Causal Theory of Knowledge,' *Australasian Journal of Philosophy*, **50** (1972), 238–248.
304. Grandy, Richard, 'Grammatical Knowledge and States of Mind,' *Behaviorism*, **1** (1972), 16–21.
305. Grandy, Richard, 'On Revisiting Psychology and Reorienting Epistemology,' *Journal of Philosophy*, **75** (1978), 525–526.
306. Grant, C. K., 'Belief In and Belief That,' *12th International Congress of Philosophy*, **5** (1959), 187–194.
307. Grant, C. K., 'On a Definition of Knowledge,' *Proceedings of the Aristotelian Society*, **73** (1972–73), 157–166.
308. Griffiths, A. Phillips, 'On Belief,' *Proceedings of the Aristotelian Society* **63** (1963), 167–186.
309. Griffiths, A. Phillips, 'Belief and Reasons for Belief,' *Proceedings of the Aristotelian Society*, Supplementary Volume XLVII (1973), 53–68.
310. Gullvag, Ingemund, 'Scepticism and Absurdity,' *Inquiry*, **7** (1964), 163–190.
311. Gustafson, Donald F., 'A Note On Knowing And Believing,' *Theoria*, **31** (1965), 275–278.
312. Gustafson, Donald F., 'Absurd But Possibly True,' *Theoria*, **32** (1966), 67–71.
313. Hagner, Paul, 'Knowledge By Acquaintance,' *Philosophy and Phenomenological Research*, **29** (1969), 275–286.
314. Hall, Michael, 'Skepticism and Knowing That One Knows,' *Canadian Journal of Philosophy*, **6** (1976), 655–664.
315. Hall, Richard J., 'Chisholm's Epistemic Principles and Our Knowledge About Particular Things in the External World,' *Philosophical Studies*, **30** (1976), 29–37.
316. Hall, Richard J., 'Criticism and Revision of Chisholm's Epistemic Principle for Perception,' *Philosophia*, **7** (1978), 477–488.
317. Haller, R., 'Concerning the So-called "Munchhausen Trilemma",' *Ratio*, **16** (1974), 125–140.
318. Hamlyn, David M., 'Epistemology, History of,' in *Encyclopedia of Philosophy*, London and New York: Macmillan, 1967.
319. Hanen, M., 'Confirmation, Explanation and Acceptance,' in Lehrer, ed., *Analysis and Metaphysics*, [32].
320. Hannay, A., 'Giving the Skeptic a Good Name,' *Inquiry*, **18** (1975), 409–436.
321. Hanson, P., 'Prospects for a Causal Theory of Knowledge,' *Canadian Journal of Philosophy*, **8** (1978), 457–474.
322. Harman, Gilbert, 'How Belief Is Based Upon Inference,' *Journal of Philosophy*, **61** (1964), 353–359.
323. Harman, Gilbert, 'The Inference To The Best Explanation,' *Philosophical Review*, **74** (1965), 88–95.
324. Harman, Gilbert, 'New Implications of "Someone", I,' *Analysis*, **26** (1966), 206–208.
325. Harman, Gilbert, 'Lehrer On Knowledge,' *Journal of Philosophy*, **63** (1966), 241–247.
326. Harman, Gilbert, 'Detachment, Probability and Maximum Likelihood,' *Nous*, **1** (1967), 401–411.

327. Harman, Gilbert, 'Unger on Knowledge,' *Journal of Philosophy,* **64** (1967), 390–395.

328. Harman, Gilbert, 'Enumerative Induction As Inference to the Best Explanation,' *Journal of Philosophy,* **65** (1968), 529–533.

329. Harman, Gilbert, 'Knowledge, Inference, and Explanation,' *American Philosophical Quarterly,* **5** (1968), 164–173.

330. Harman, Gilbert, 'Knowledge, Reasons, And Causes,' *Journal of Philosophy,* **67** (1970), 841–855.

331. Harman, Gilbert, 'Induction,' in Swain, ed., [75].

332. Harman, Gilbert, 'Review of Quine and Ullian,' *Metaphilosophy,* **2** (1971), 79–81.

333. Harman, Gilbert, 'Review of Slote,' *Philosophical Review,* **81** (1972), 253–254. Review of Slote, [72].

334. Harman, Gilbert, 'Inferential Justification,' *Journal of Philosophy,* **73** (1976), 570–571.

335. Harman, Gilbert, 'Reply to Lisagor,' *Philosophical Studies,* **29** (1976), 447.

336. Harper, A. W. J., 'On Metaphysics and Epistemology,' *Dialogue,* **12** (1973), 334–335.

337. Harrison, Jonathan, 'Mr. Malcolm on "Knowledge and Belief",' *Analysis,* **13** (1952), 66–71.

338. Harrison, Jonathan, 'Does Knowing Imply Believing?' *Philosophical Quarterly,* **7** (1963), 322–332. Reprinted in Roth and Galis [60].

339. Hart, John A., and Dees, R., 'Paradox Regained: A Reply to Meyers and Stern,' *Journal of Philosophy,* **71** (1974), 367–372.

340. Hartland-Swann, J. S., 'Logical Status of "Knowing That",' *Analysis,* **16** (1955), 111–115.

341. Hartland-Swann, J. S., ' "Being Aware of" and "Knowing",' *Philosophical Quarterly,* **7** (1967), 126–135.

342. Heal, Jane, 'Common Knowledge,' *Philosophical Quarterly,* **28** (1978), 116–131.

343. Heidelberger, Herbert, 'On Defining Epistemic Expressions,' *Journal of Philosophy,* **60** (1963), 344–348.

344. Heidelberger, Herbert, 'Knowledge, Certainty, And Probability,' *Inquiry,* **6** (1963), 242–249.

345. Heidelberger, Herbert, 'Probability and Knowledge: A Reply to Miss Weyland,' *Inquiry,* **7** (1964), 417–418.

346. Heidelberger, Herbert, 'An Undefined Epistemic Term,' *Mind,* **75** (1966), 420–421.

347. Heidelberger, Herbert, 'Chisholm's Epistemic Principles,' *Nous,* **3** (1969), 73–82.

348. Heidelberger, Herbert, 'Review of Danto,' *Metaphilosophy,* **2** (1971), 58–67. Review of [15].

349. Henle, Paul, 'On The Certainty of Empirical Statements,' *Journal of Philosophy,* **44** (1947), 625–632.

350. Hilpinen, Risto, 'Knowing That One Knows And The Classical Definition of Knowledge,' *Synthese,* **21** (1970), 109–132.

351. Hilpinen, Risto, 'Knowledge And Justification,' *Ajatus,* **33** (1970), 7–39.

352. Hilpinen, Risto, 'Remarks on Personal and Impersonal Knowledge,' *Canadian Journal of Philosophy,* **7** (1977), 1–9.

353. Hinkfuss, Ian, 'A Note on Knowledge And Mistake,' *Mind,* **80** (1971), 614–615.

354. Hintikka, Jaakko, ' "Knowing Oneself" and Other Problems in Epistemic Logic,' *Theoria*, **32** (1966), 3–13.

355. Hintikka, Jaakko, 'Existence and Identity in Epistemic Contexts: A Comment on Follesdal's Paper,' *Theoria*, **33** (1967), 138–147.

356. Hintikka, Jaakko, 'Individuals, Possible Worlds, and Epistemic Logic,' *Nous*, **1** (1967), 33–62.

357. Hintikka, Jaakko, 'Epistemic Logic and the Methods of Philosophical Analysis,' *American Journal of Philosophy*, **46** (1968), 37–51.

358. Hintikka, Jaakko, 'On the Logic of Perception,' in N. Care and R. Grimm, eds., *Perception and Personal Identity* (Cleveland: Case Western Reserve Press), 1969.

359. Hintikka, Jaakko, 'Partially Transparent Senses of Knowing,' *Philosophical Studies*, **20** (1969), 4–8.

360. Hintikka, Jaakko, 'Information, Deduction, and the *A Priori*,' *Nous*, **4** (1970), 135–152.

361. Hintikka, Jaakko, 'On The Different Constructions in Terms of the Basic Epistemological Concepts: A Survey of Some Problems and Proposals,' in R. E. Olson and A. M. Paul, eds., *Contemporary Philosophy in Scandanavia* (Baltimore: The Johns Hopkins Press), 1970.

362. Hintikka, Jaakko, 'Knowledge, Belief, and Logical Consequence,' *Ajatus*, **32** (1970), 32–47.

363. Hintikka, Jaakko, ' "Knowing That One Knows" Reviewed,' *Synthese*, **21** (1970), 141–162.

364. Hintikka, Jaakko, 'Objects of Knowledge and Belief: Acquaintances and Public Figures,' *Journal of Philosophy*, **67** (1970), 869–883.

365. Hintikka, Jaakko, 'On Attributions of "Self-Knowledge",' *Journal of Philosophy*, **67**.3 (1970), 73–87.

366. Hintikka, Jaakko, 'Sosa on Propositional Attitudes *De Dicto* and *De Re*,' *Journal of Philosophy*, **68** (1971), 489–497.

367. Hirst, R. J., 'Review of Chisholm,' *Philosophical Quarterly*, **9** (1959), 366–373. Review of [11].

368. Hocutt, M., 'Is Epistemic Logic Possible?' *Notre Dame Journal of Formal Logic*, **13** (1972), 433–453.

369. Hoffman, W., 'Almeder on Truth and Evidence,' *Philosophical Quarterly*, **25** (1975), 59–61.

370. Holland, A., 'Retained Knowledge,' *Mind*, **83** (1974), 355–371.

371. Holland, A., 'Can Mannison Avoid a Causal Theory of Knowledge?' *Philosophical Quarterly*, **27** (1977), 158–161.

372. Holland, A., 'Scepticism and Causal Theories of Knowledge,' *Mind*, **86** (1977), 555–573.

373. Hooker, C. A., 'Empiricism, Perception and Conceptual Change,' *Canadian Journal of Philosophy*, **3** (1973), 59–74.

374. Hooker, Michael, 'In Defense of a Principle of Deducibility for Justification,' *Philosophical Studies*, **24** (1973), 402–405.

375. Hooker, Michael, 'Chisholm's Theory of Knowledge,' *Philosophia*, **7** (1978), 489–500.

376. Hubin, D. Clayton, 'Googols Again,' *Philosophical Forum*, (Boston), **7** (1976), 367–374.

377. Hull, Richard, 'The Forms of Argument over the Principle of Acquaintance,'
      Metaphilosophy, **4** (1973), 1–22.
378. Hullett, James, 'The Pragmatic Conception of the *A Priori* Reviewed,' *Transac-
      tions of the Peirce Society,* **9** (1973), 127–156.
379. Imlay, Robert, 'Sayward on Assertion and Belief,' *Philosophical Studies,* **19**
      (1968), 76–79.
380. Imlay, Robert, 'Chisholm's Epistemic Logic,' *Philosophy and Phenomenological
      Research,* **30** (1969), 290–293.
381. Imlay, Robert, 'Immediate Awareness,' *Dialogue,* **8** (1970), 228–242.
382. Jackson, Frank, 'On Entailment and Support,' *Nous,* **3** (1969), 345–349.
383. Jackson, Frank, 'Is There a Good Argument Against the Incorrigibility Thesis?'
      Australasian Journal of Philosophy, **51** (1973), 51–62.
384. Johnsen, Bredo, 'Knowledge,' *Philosophical Studies,* **25** (1974), 273–282.
385. Johnson, David, 'A Formulation Model of Perceptual Knowledge,' *American
      Philosophical Quarterly,* **8** (1971), 54–62.
386. Johnson, Oliver, 'Is Knowledge Defineable?' *Southern Journal of Philosophy,* **8**
      (1971), 277–286.
387. Johnson, Oliver, 'Some Problems in the Standard Analysis of Knowledge,' *South-
      ern Journal of Philosophy,* **10** (1972), 409–421.
388. Johnson, Oliver, 'Scepticism and the Standards of Rationality,' *Philosophical
      Quarterly,* **25** (1975), 336–339.
389. Johnson, Oliver, 'Mitigated Scepticism,' *Ratio,* **18** (1976), 73–84.
390. Johnson, Sidney, 'Statements and Incorrigibility,' *Mind,* **79** (1970), 600–601.
391. Jones, Michael, 'Rule R – Rejected,' *Philosophical Studies,* **24** (1973), 392–396.
392. Jones, O. R., 'Reason and Certainty,' *Philosophy,* **45** (1970), 55–58.
393. Jones, O. R., 'Knowing and Guessing – By Examples,' *Analysis,* **32** (1971), 19–
      23.
394. Jones, O. R., 'Can One Believe What One Knows?' *Philosophical Review,* **84**
      (1975), 220–235.
395. Jones, O. R., 'Knowledge, Machines and Impoverished Belief,' *Mind,* **86** (1977),
      417–422.
396. Katz, J., *et al,* 'Tacit Knowledge,' *Journal of Philosophy,* **70** (1973), 318–330.
397. Keim, R., 'Epistemic Values and Epistemic Viewpoints,' in Lehrer, ed., [32].
398. Kekes, J., 'Fallibilism and Rationality,' *American Philosophical Quarterly,* **9**
      (1972), 301–309.
399. Kekes, J., 'The Case for Scepticism,' *Philosophical Quarterly,* **25** (1975), 28–
      39.
400. Kekes, J., 'The Domain of Justification: Common Sense,' *Philosophia,* **15** (1975),
      39–56.
401. Kekes, J., 'Recent Trends and Future Prospects in Epistemology,' *Metaphilosophy,*
      8 (1977), 87–107.
402. Kellenberger, J., 'On There Being No Necessary and Sufficient Conditions For
      Knowledge,' *Mind,* **80** (1971), 599–602.
403. Klein, Peter D., 'A Proposed Definition of Propositional Knowledge,' *Journal of
      Philosophy,* **68** (1971), 471–482.
404. Klein, Peter D., 'Knowledge, Causality and Defeasibility,' *Journal of Philosophy,*
      73 (1976), 792–812.

405. Korn, Fred, 'What it Takes to Justify,' *Philosophical Quarterly,* **27** (1977), 135–139.
406. Krause, M., 'What is it to Learn a Fact?' *Journal of the Theory of Social Behavior,* **3** (1973), 91–99.
407. Kress, J. R., 'Lehrer and Paxson on Non-Basic Knowledge,' *Journal of Philosophy,* **68** (1971), 78–82.
408. Kroiter, E., 'On Defining Incorrigibility,' *Australasian Journal of Philosophy,* **50** (1972), 279–282.
409. Kyburg, Henry E., Jr., 'A Further Note on Rationality and Consistency,' *Journal of Philosophy,* **60** (1963), 463–465.
410. Lamb, James W., 'Knowledge and Justified Presumption,' *Journal of Philosophy,* **69** (1972), 123–127.
411. Lamb, James W., 'A Skeptical Paradox Concerning Epistemic Justification,' *Philosophical Studies,* **29** (1976), 319–330.
412. Landesman, Charles, 'A Note on Belief,' *Analysis,* **24** (1963), 180–182.
413. Langtry, Bruce, 'Perception and Corrigibility,' *Australasian Journal of Philosophy,* **48** (1970), 369–372.
414. Lehrer, Keith, 'Knowledge and Probability,' *Journal of Philosophy,* **61** (1964), 368–372.
415. Lehrer, Keith, 'Knowledge, Truth, and Evidence,' *Journal of Philosophy,* **61** (1964), 695. [Abstract].
416. Lehrer, Keith, 'Letter: On Knowledge and Probability,' *Journal of Philosophy,* **62** (1965), 67–68.
417. Lehrer, Keith, 'Knowledge, Truth and Evidence,' *Analysis,* **25** (1965), 168–175. Reprinted in Roth and Galis [60].
418. Lehrer, Keith, 'Belief and Knowledge,' *Philosophical Review,* **77** (1968), 491–499.
419. Lehrer, Keith, 'The Fourth Condition of Knowledge: A Defense,' *Review of Metaphysics,* **24** (1970), 122–128.
420. Lehrer, Keith, 'Believing That One Knows,' *Synthese,* **21** (1970), 133–140.
421. Lehrer, Keith, 'Justification, Explanation, and Induction,' in Swain [75].
422. Lehrer, Keith, 'Induction, Reason, and Consistency,' *The British Journal for the Philosophy of Science,* **21** (1970), 102–114.
423. Lehrer, Keith, 'Why Not Scepticism?' *The Philosophical Forum,* **2** (1971), 283–298. Reprinted in Pappas and Swain [43].
424. Lehrer, Keith, 'How Reasons Give Us Knowledge, or the Case of The Gypsy Lawyer,' *Journal of Philosophy,* **68** (1971), 311–313.
425. Lehrer, Keith, 'Review of Butchvarov,' *Journal of Philosophy,* **69** (1972), 312–318. Review of [9].
426. Lehrer, Keith, 'Evidence and Conceptual Change,' *Philosophia,* **2** (1972), 273–281.
427. Lehrer, Keith, 'Scepticism and Conceptual Change,' in Chisholm and Swartz, [13].
428. Lehrer, Keith, 'Reasonable Acceptance and Explanatory Coherence: Wilfrid Sellars on Induction,' *Nous,* **7** (1973), 81–103.
429. Lehrer, Keith, 'Truth, Evidence and Inference,' *American Philosophical Quarterly,* **11** (1974), 79–92.

430. Lehrer, Keith, 'Reason and Consistency,' in Lehrer, ed., *Analysis and Metaphysics*, [32].
431. Lehrer, Keith, 'Reply to Dr. Radford,' *Philosophical Books,* **16**.2 (1975), 6–8.
432. Lehrer, Keith, 'The Knowledge Cycle,' *Nous,* **11** (1977), 17–25.
433. Lehrer, Keith and Roelofs, R., and Swain, M., 'Reason and Evidence: An Unsolved Problem,' *Ratio,* **9** (1967), 38–48.
434. Lehrer, Keith and Paxson, Thomas, Jr., 'Knowledge: Undefeated Justified True Belief,' *Journal of Philosophy,* **66** (1969), 225–237. Reprinted in Pappas and Swain, [43].
435. Lemmon, E. J., 'Review of Hintikka,' *Philosophical Review,* **74** (1965), 381. Review of [25].
436. Lemmon, E. J., 'If I Know, Do I Know That I Know?' in Stroll. [74].
437. Lesher, James H., 'Danto on Knowledge as a Relation,' *Analysis,* **30**.4 (1970), 132–134.
438. Lesher, James H., 'Lehrer's Sceptical Hypothesis,' *Philosophical Forum,* **4** (1972–73), 299–302.
439. Levin, Michael, 'A Definition of *a priori* Knowledge,' *Journal of Critical Analysis,* **4** (1974).
440. Levin, Michael, 'Response to Benfield,' *Journal of Critical Analysis,* **6** (1976), 37–40.
441. Levy, Steven R., 'Defeasibility Theories of Knowledge,' *Canadian Journal of Philosophy,* **7** (1977), 115–123.
442. Lewis, C. I., 'The Given Element in Empirical Knowledge,' *Philosophical Review,* **61** (1952), 168–175. Reprinted in Chisholm and Swartz, [13].
443. Lewis, C. I., 'Professor Chisholm and Empiricism,' *Journal of Philosophy,* **45** (1948). Reprinted in Swartz, [76].
444. Lewis, C. I., 'The Categories of Natural Knowledge,' in P. A. Schilpp, ed., *The Philosophy of Alfred North Whitehead*, 2nd. ed., New York: Tudor, 1951, 701–744.
445. Lisagor, M., 'On Harman's Theory of Knowledge,' *Philosophical Studies,* **29** (1976), 433–439.
446. Loeb, Louis, 'Causal Theories and Causal Overdetermination,' *Journal of Philosophy,* **71** (1974), 525–544.
447. Loeb, Louis, 'On A Heady Attempt to Befiend Causal Theories of Knowledge,' *Philosophical Studies,* **29** (1976), 331–336.
448. Lowy, C., 'Gettier's Notion of Justification,' *Mind,* **87** (1978), 105–108.
449. Lucey, Kenneth, 'Counter-examples and Borderline Cases,' *The Personalist,* **57** (1976), 351–355.
450. Lucey, Kenneth, 'Scales of Epistemic Appraisal,' *Philosophical Studies,* **29** (1976), 169–179.
451. Lugg, Andrew, 'Feyerabend's Rationalism,' *Canadian Journal of Philosophy,* **7** (1977), 755–775.
452. Lycan, William G., 'Evidence One Does not Possess,' *Australasian Journal of Philosophy,* **55** (1977), 114–126.
453. Lycan, William G., and McCall, Mark, 'The Catastrophe of Defeat,' *Philosophical Studies,* **28** (1975), 147–150.
454. Mace, C. A., 'Belief,' *Proceedings of the Aristotelian Society,* **29** (1929), 227–250.

455. MacIver, A. M., 'Knowledge,' *Proceedings of the Aristotelian Society*, Supplementary Volume, **23** (1958), 1–24.
456. Malcolm, Norman, 'Certainty and Empirical Statements,' *Mind*, **51** (1942), 18–46.
457. Malcolm, Norman, 'On Knowledge and Belief,' *Analysis*, **14** (1954), 94–98.
458. Mannison, D. S., 'Danto on Hintikka,' *Philosophia*, **2** (1972), 249–255.
459. Mannison, D. S., 'Lemmon on Knowing,' *Synthese*, **26** (1974), 383–390.
460. Mannison, D. S., ' "Inexplicable Knowledge" Does Not Require Belief,' *Philosophical Quarterly*, **26** (1976), 139–148.
461. Mannison, D. S., 'Why Margolis Hasn't Defeated the Entailment Thesis,' *Canadian Journal of Philosophy*, **6** (1976), 553–559.
462. Mannison, D. S., 'Knowing and Believing: A Reply,' *Australasian Journal of Philosophy*, **55** (1977), 147–148.
463. Marc-Wogau, Konrad, 'Review of Price,' *Philosophical Review*, **81** (1972), 246–250. Review of [47].
464. Margolis, Joseph, 'Malcolm on Knowledge,' *Logique et Analyse*, **10** (1967), 192–199.
465. Margolis, Joseph, 'The Problem of Justified Belief,' *Philosophical Studies*, **23** (1972), 405–409.
466. Margolis, Joseph, 'Knowledge, Belief, and Thought,' *Ratio*, **14** (1972), 74–82.
467. Margolis, Joseph, 'Alternative Strategies for the Analysis of Knowledge,' *Canadian Journal of Philosophy*, **2** (1973), 461–469.
468. Margolis, Joseph, 'Problems Regarding the Ascription of Knowledge,' *The Personalist*, **58** (1977), 5–17.
469. Margolis, Joseph, 'Skepticism, Foundationalism and Pragmatism,' *American Philosophical Quarterly*, **14** (1977), 119–127.
470. Martin, R. M., 'On Knowing, Believing, Thinking,' *Journal of Philosophy*, **59** (1962), 586–600.
471. Martin, R. M., 'Empirically Conclusive Reasons and Skepticism,' *Philosophical Studies*, **28** (1975), 215–217.
472. Mayo, Bernard, 'A Note on Austin's Performative Theory of "Knowledge",' *Philosophical Studies*, **14** (1963), 28–31.
473. Mayo, Bernard, 'Belief and Constraint,' *Proceedings of the Aristotelian Society*, **64** (1964), 139–156. Reprinted in Griffiths, [21].
474. McGinn, Colin, '*A Priori* and *A Posteriori* Knowledge,' *Proceedings of the Aristotelian Society*, **76** (1975–76), 195–208.
475. McIntyre, Jane, 'Contemporary Empiricism,' *Philosophy in Context*, **2** (1973), 62–65.
476. McQueen, D., 'Belief and Reasons for Belief,' *Proceedings of the Aristotelian Society*, **XLVII** (1973), 69–87.
477. Meerbote, Ralf, 'The Distinction Between Derivative and Non-derivative Knowledge,' *Philosophical Studies*, **24** (1973), 192–197.
478. Meerbote, Ralf, 'Fallibilism And the Possibility of Being Mistaken,' *Philosophical Studies*, **32** (1977), 143–154.
479. Mellor, W. W., 'Knowing, Believing, and Behaving,' *Mind*, **76** (1967), 327–345.
480. Meyers, Robert G., 'Skepticism and the Criterion in Peirce,' *Transactions of the Peirce Society*, **XIV** (1978), 3–17.

202   NANCY C. KELSIK

481. Meyers, Robert G., and Stern, K., 'Knowledge Without Paradox,' *Journal of Philosophy,* **70** (1973), 147–160.
482. Miller, Dickenson S., 'Is There Not A Clear Solution of the Knowledge-Problem? I,' *Journal of Philosophy,* **34** (1937), 701–712.
483. Miller, Dickenson S., 'Is There Not A Clear Solution of the Knowledge Problem? II,' *Journal of Philosophy,* **35** (1938), 561–572.
484. Morawetz, Thomas, 'Causal Accounts of Knowledge,' *Southern Journal of Philosophy,* **12** (1974), 365–369.
485. Morawetz, 'Skepticism, Induction and the Gettier Problem,' *Journal of Critical Analysis,* **6** (1975), 9–13.
486. Morris, W., 'Knowledge as Justified Presumption,' *Journal of Philosophy,* **70** (1973), 161–165.
487. Mucciolo, L., 'Incorrigibility Revisited,' *The Personalist,* **55** (1974), 253–260.
488. Myers, Gerald E., 'Justifying Belief Assertions,' *Journal of Philosophy,* **64** (1967), 210–214.
489. Nathan, N., 'Skepticism and the Regress of Justification,' *Proceedings of Aristotelian Society,* **75** (1974–75), 77–88.
490. Nathan, N., 'What Vitiates An Infinite Regress of Justification?' *Analysis,* **37** (1977), 116–126.
491. Nathanson, S., 'Scepticism and Concept Possession,' *Southern Journal of Philosophy,* **12** (1974), 215–223.
492. Naylor, Andrew, 'On the Evidence of One's Memories,' *Analysis,* **33** (1973), 160–167.
493. Naylor, M., 'Chisholm on the Directly Evident,' *Philosophia,* **7** (1978), 423–440.
494. Nelson, J., 'Knowledge and Truth,' *Philosophical Studies,* **27** (1975), 65–72.
495. New, C. G., 'Some Implications of "Someone",' *Analysis,* **26** (1966), 62–64.
496. New, C. G., ' "Someone" Renewed,' *Analysis,* **28** (1968), 109–112.
497. Nielson, K., 'On Refusing to Play the Sceptic's Game,' *Dialogue,* **11** (1972), 348–359.
498. Oakley, I. T., 'An Argument for Skepticism Concerning Justified Belief,' *American Philosophical Quarterly,* **13** (1976), 221–228.
499. Odegard, Douglas, 'On Defining "*S* Knows that *P*",' *Philosophical Quarterly,* **15** (1965), 353–357.
500. Odegard, Douglas, 'Can a Justified Belief be False?' *Canadian Journal of Philosophy,* **6** (1976), 561–568.
501. Odegard, Douglas, 'Conclusive Reasons and Knowledge,' *Mind,* **85** (1976), 239–241.
502. Odegard, Douglas, 'Knowledge and Reflexivity,' *Dialogue,* **15** (1976), 226–240.
503. Odegard, Douglas, 'Conjunctivity, Knowledge and Paradox,' *Australasian Journal of Philosophy,* **55** (1977), 206–208.
504. Odegard, Douglas, 'A Knower's Evidence,' *American Philosophical Quarterly,* **15** (1978), 123–128.
505. Olen, Jeffrey, 'Is Undefeated Justified True Belief Knowledge?' *Analysis,* **36** (1976), 150–152.
506. Olen, Jeffrey, 'Knowledge, Probability and Nomic Connections,' *Southern Journal of Philosophy,* **15** (1977), 521–526.
507. Olin, Doris, 'Knowledge and Defeasible Justification,' *Philosophical Studies,* **30**

(1976), 129–136.

508.   Padilla, H., 'Condiciones Para Saber,' *Critica,* **5** (1971), 129–134.
509.   Pailthorp, Charles, 'Hintikka and Knowing That One Knows,' *Journal of Philosophy,* **64** (1967), 487–500.
510.   Pailthorp, Charles, 'Knowledge As Undetected Justified True Belief,' *Review of Metaphysics,* **23** (1969), 25–47.
511.   Pailthorp, Charles, 'Is Immediate Knowledge Reason Based?' *Mind* **78,** (1969), 550–566.
512.   Pailthorp, Charles, 'A Reply to Lehrer,' *Review of Metaphysics,* **24** (1970), 129–133.
513.   Palmer, Antony, 'Review of Wittgenstein,' *Mind,* **81** (1972), 453–457.
514.   Pappas, George, 'Incorrigibility, Knowledge and Justification,' *Philosophical Studies,* **24** (1974), 219–225.
515.   Pappas, George, 'Knowledge and Reasons,' *Philosophical Studies,* **25** (1974), 423–428.
516.   Pappas, George, 'Defining Incorrigibility,' *The Personalist,* **56** (1975), 395–402.
517.   Pappas, George, 'Incorrigibilism and Future Science,' *Philosophical Studies,* **28** 1975), 207–210.
518.   Pappas, George, 'Forms of Epistemological Scepticism,' in Pappas and Swain, eds., [43].
519.   Pappas, George, and Swain, Marshall, 'Some Conclusive Reasons Against "Conclusive Reasons",' *Australasian Journal of Philosophy,* **51** (1973), 72–76.
520.   Parker, S. H., 'Doxastic and Epistemic Fallibility: a Defense of Gettier,' *Dialogue,* **15** (1973), 55–57.
521.   Pastin, Mark, 'Foundationalism Redux,' *Journal of Philosophy,* **71** (1974), 709–710.
522.   Pastin, Mark, 'Modest Foundationalism and Self-Warrant,' *American Philosophical Quarterly,* monograph series, #9 (1975). Reprinted in Pappas and Swain, eds., [43].
523.   Pastin, Mark, 'Lewis' Radical Foundationalism,' *Nous,* **9** (1975), 407–420.
524.   Pastin, Mark, 'Meaning and Perception,' *Journal of Philosophy* **73** (1976) 571–585.
525.   Pastin, Mark, 'Counterfactuals in Epistemology,' *Synthese,* **34** (1977), 479–495.
526.   Pastin, Mark, 'Keith Lehrer's *Knowledge*,' *Nous,* **11** (1977), 431–437.
527.   Pastin, Mark, 'Perceptual Relativity,' *Philosophia,* **8** (1978), 341–355.
528.   Pastin, Mark, 'Warranting Reconsidered: Response to Feldman,' *Synthese,* **37** (1978), 459–464.
529.   Pastin, Mark, 'A Decision Procedure for Epistemology,' *Philosophical Studies,* forthcoming.
530.   Pastin, Mark, 'Warrant and Meaning in Quine's Clothing,' *Southwestern Journal of Philosophy,* Summer (1978).
531.   Pastin, Mark, 'Knowledge and Reliability: A Critical Study of D. M. Armstrong's *Belief, Truth and Knowledge*,' *Metaphilosophy,* **9** (1978).
532.   Pastin, Mark, 'Social and Anti-Social Justification,' forthcoming in an anthology of essays on Keith Lehrer's philosophy (ed. R. Bogdan).
533.   Paxson, Thomas D., Jr., 'Professor Swain's Account of Knowledge,' *Philosophical Studies,* **25** (1974), 57–61. Reprinted in Pappas and Swain, eds., [43].

535. Pence, Gregory E., 'Scepticism Vanquished,' *Philosophical Forum,* 4 (1972–73), 303–304.
536. Peterson, P., 'How to Infer Belief from Knowledge,' *Philosophical Studies,* 32 (1977), 203–209.
537. Place, U. T., 'The Infallibility of Our Knowledge of Our Own Beliefs,' *Analysis,* 31 (1971), 197–204.
538. Pollock, John L., 'Criteria And Our Knowledge of the Material World,' *Philosophical Review,* 76 (1967), 28–60.
539. Pollock, John L., 'What Is An Epistemological Problem?' *American Philosophical Quarterly,* 5 (1968), 183–190.
540. Pollock, John L., 'Chisholm's Definition of Knowledge,' *Philosophical Studies,* 19 1968), 72–76.
541. Pollock, John L., 'The Structure of Epistemic Justification,' *American Philosophical Quarterly Monograph,* 4 (1970), 62–78.
542. Pollock John L., 'Perceptual Knowledge,' *Philosophical Review,* 80 (1971), 287–319.
543. Popkin, Richard H., 'Scepticism,' in *Encyclopedia of Philosophy,* Volume 7, 449–461.
544. Powers, L., 'Knowledge by Deduction,' *Philosophical Review,* 87 (1978) 337–371.
545. Prado, C. G., 'Analytical Philosophy of Knowledge,' *Dialogue,* 8 (1969), 503–507.
546. Prado, C. G., 'Gaps, Beliefs, and Arthur Danto,' *The Philosophical Forum,* 2 (1971), 402–406.
547. Price, H. A., 'Some Considerations About Belief,' *Proceedings of the Aristotelian Society,* 35 (1935), 229–252.
548. Purtill, Richard L., 'Believing The Impossible,' *Ajatus* 33, (1970), 18–31.
549. Purtill, Richard L., 'Some Varieties of Epistemological Scepticism,' *Philosophia,* 1 (1971), 107–116.
550. Purtill, Richard L., 'Epistemological Scepticism Again,' *The Philosophical Forum,* 3 (1972), 138–144.
551. Putnam, Ruth Anna, 'On Empirical Knowledge,' *Boston Studies In The Philosophy of Science,* Volume IV, (1968), 392–410.
552. Quinton, Anthony, 'The Foundations of Knowledge,' in Williams and Montefiore, eds., *British Analytical Philosophy.* (London: Routledge and Kegan Paul), (1966), 55–86.
553. Quinton, Anthony, 'The Problem of Perception,' *Mind,* 64 (1955), 28–51. Reprinted in Swartz, [76].
554. Quinton, Anthony, 'Knowledge and Belief,' in *Encyclopedia of Philosophy,* Volume 4, 345–352.
555. Quinton, Anthony, 'Review of Aune,' *Mind,* 78 (1969), 442–452, Review of [5].
556. Quinton, Anthony, 'On the Definition of Knowledge,' *Teorema,* 4 (1974), 159–175.
557. Radford, Colin, 'Knowledge – By Examples,' *Analysis,* 27 (1966), 1–11. Reprinted in Roth and Galis [60].
558. Radford, Colin, 'Knowing But Not Beleving,' *Analysis,* 27 (1967), 139–140.
559. Radford, Colin, 'Knowing And Telling,' *Philosophical Review,* 78 (1969), 326–336.

560. Radford, Colin, 'Analyzing "Knows That",' *Philosophical Quarterly,* **20** (1970), 222–229.
561. Radford, Colin, 'Does Unwitting Knowledge Entail Unconscious Belief?' *Analysis,* **30** (1970), 103–107.
562. Radford, Colin, 'On Sticking To What I Don't Believe To Be The Case,' *Analysis,* **32** (1972), 170–173.
563. Radford, Colin, 'Review of Lehrer,' *Philosophical Books,* **16**.2 (1975). Review of [31].
564. Rappaport, Steven, 'Aune's Wittgenstein on the Empiricist Thesis,' *Philosophical Studies,* **24** (1973), 258–262.
565. Ravitch, Harold, 'Knowledge and the Principle of Luck,' *Philosophical Studies,* **30** (1976), 347–349.
566. Reach, Karl, 'On The Foundations of our Knowledge,' *Synthese,* **5** (1947), 83–86.
567. Reeves, Alan, 'The Foundations of Quine's Philosophy,' *Philosophical Studies,* **30** (1976), 75–94.
568. Rescher, Nicholas, 'The Problem of a Logical Theory of Belief Statements,' *Philosophy of Science,* **27** (1960), 95–98.
569. Rescher, Nicholas, 'Foundationalism, Coherentism and the Idea of Cognitive Systematization,' *Journal of Philosophy,* **71** (1974), 695–708.
570. Rescher, Nicholas, 'The Systematization of Knowledge,' *Philosophical Context,* **6** (1977), 20–42.
571. Richman, R., 'Justified True Belief as Knowledge,' *Canadian Journal of Philosophy,* **4** (1975), 435–439.
572. Ring, Merrill, 'Knowledge: The Cessation of Belief,' *American Philosophical Quarterly,* **14** (1977), 51–59.
573. Roberts, George W., 'Some Questions in Epistemology,' *Proceedings of the Aristotelian Society,* **70** (1969–1970), 37–60.
574. Robinson, Richard, 'The Concept of Knowledge,' *Mind,* **80** (1971), 17–28.
575. Robinson, William S., 'The Legend of the Given,' in H. Castañeda, ed., *Action, Knowledge and Reality,* Indianapolis: Bobbs-Merrill, 1975.
576. Rosen, Bernard, 'Chisholm On Knowledge and Principles,' *Mind,* **77** (1968), 411–416.
577. Rosenbaum, S., 'Chisholm on Evidence and Epistemic Priority,' *Philosophia,* **7** (1978), 461–476.
578. Rosenthal, S., 'C. I. Lewis and Radical Fallibilism,' *Transactions of the Peirce Society,* **8** (1972), 106–114.
579. Rosenthal, S., 'C. I. Lewis: Similitic Certitude and Epistemic Assimilation,' *Southwestern Journal of Philosophy,* **7** (1976), 55–63.
580. Ross, J., 'Religious Knowledge,' *Proceedings of the Catholic Philosophical Association,* **46** (1972), 29–42.
581. Ross, J., 'Testimonial Evidence,' in Lehrer, ed., *Analysis and Metaphysics,* [32].
582. Rowland, Jane, 'Knowing "How" and "Knowing That",' *Philosophical Review,* **67** (1958), 154–163.
583. Rozeboom, William W., 'Why I Know So Much More Than You Do,' *American Philosophical Quarterly,* **4** (1967), 257–268. Reprinted in Roth and Galis [60].
584. Ruben, David-Hillel, 'Epistemological Empiricism: The Duality of Beliefs and

Experiences Reconsidered,' *Monist,* 59 (1976), 392–403.

585. Ruben, David-Hillel, 'A Note on Justification: Its Definition and its Criteria,' *Philosophy and Phenomenological Research,* 37 (1977) 552–555.

586. Ryle, Gilbert, 'Knowing How and Knowing That,' *Proceedings of the Aristotelian Society,* 46 (1945), 1–16.

587. Rynin, David, 'Knowledge, Sensation and Certainty,' in Stroll [74].

588. Sanford, David, 'Intermediate Conclusions,' *Australasian Journal of Philosophy,* 53 (1975) 61–64.

589. Saunders, John Turk, 'Beliefs Which Are Grounds For Themselves,' *Philosophical Studies,* 16 (1965), 88–90.

590. Saunders, John Turk, 'Does Knowledge Require Grounds?' *Philosophical Studies,* 17 (1966), 7–13.

591. Saunders, John Turk, 'Thalberg's Challenge to Justification Via Deduction,' *Philosophical Studies,* 23 (1972), 358–364.

592. Saunders, John Turk, 'Persons, Criteria, and Scepticism,' *Metaphilosophy,* 4 (1973), 95–123.

593. Saunders, John Turk, and Champawat, Narayan, 'Mr. Clark's Definition Of Knowledge,' *Analysis,* 25 (1964), 8–9.

594. Sayward, Charles, 'Assertion and Belief,' *Philosophical Studies,* 17 (1966), 74–78.

595. Sayward, Charles, 'More on Assertion and Belief,' *Philosophical Studies,* 22 (1971), 20–24.

596. Scheer, R. K., 'Knowledge of the Future,' *Mind,* 80 (1971), 212–226.

597. Scheffler, Israel, 'On Ryle's Theory of Propositional Knowledge,' *Journal of Philosophy,* 65 (1968), 727–732.

598. Schick, Frederic, 'Consistency and Rationality,' *Journal of Philosophy,* 60 (1963), 5–19.

599. Schick, Frederic, 'Consistency,' *Philosophical Review,* 75 (1966), 467–495.

600. Schick, Frederic, 'Three Logics of Belief,' in Swain, ed., [75].

601. Schmidt, R., 'Knowledge Without Truth,' *Southwestern Journal of Philosophy,* 2 (1971).

602. Schmidt, R., 'Two Senses of "Knowing",' *Review of Metaphysics,* 18 (1965), 657–677.

603. Schumaker, J., 'Knowing Entails Believing,' *Philosophy Research Archives 1,* no. 1026 (1975).

604. Scott, R., 'Swain on Knowledge,' *Philosophical Studies,* 29 (1976) 419–424.

605. Sellars, Wilfrid, 'Some Problems About Belief,' *Synthese,* 19 (1968), 158–177.

606. Sellars, Wilfrid, 'Givenness and Explanatory Coherence,' *Journal of Philosophy,* 70 (1973), 612–624.

607. Sellars, William, 'Skepticism and Inquiry,' *Philosophical Forum,* (Boston) 7 (1975–76), 203–207.

608. Sesonske, Alexander, 'On Believing,' *Journal of Philosophy,* 56 (1959), 486–492.

609. Settle, Tom, 'Concerning Rationality and Scepticism,' *Philosophical Forum,* 4 (1974), 432–437.

610. Sharpe, R., 'On the Causal Theory of Knowledge,' *Ratio,* 17 (1975), 206–216.

611. Sheehan, P., 'Quine on Revision: A Critique,' *Australasian Journal of Philosophy,* 51 (1973), 95–104.

612. Shope, R., 'The Conditional Fallacy in Contemporary Philosophy,' *Journal of Philosophy*, 75 (1978), 397–413.

613. Shope, R., 'Recent Work on the Analysis of Knowledge,' *American Philosophical Quarterly*, forthcoming.

614. Shope, R., 'Knowledge and Falsity,' *Philosophical Studies*, forthcoming.

615. Sikora, R. I., 'Foundations without Certainty,' *Canadian Journal of Philosophy*, 8 (1978), 227–245.

616. Skyrms, Brian, 'The Explication of "*X* Knows that *P*",' *Journal of Philosophy*, 64 (1967), 373–389. Reprinted in Roth and Galis, [60].

617. Skyrms, Brian, 'Review of Scheffler,' *Journal of Philosophy*, 65 (1968), 794–799. Review of [68].

618. Slaght, Ralph L., 'Induction, Acceptance, and Rational Belief: A Selected Bibliography,' in Swain, ed., [75], 186–227.

619. Slaght, Ralph L., 'Is Justified True Belief Knowledge?' *Philosophy Research Archives*, 3 (1977), no. 1118.

620. Sleigh, Robert C., Jr., 'A Note on Knowledge and Probability,' *Journal of Philosophy*, 61 (1964), 478.

621. Sleigh, Robert C., Jr., 'A Note on Some Epistemic Principles of Chisholm and Martin,' *Journal of Philosophy*, 61 (1964), 216–218.

622. Sleigh, Robert C., Jr., 'A Note on an Argument of Hintikka's,' *Philosophical Studies*, 18 (1967), 12–14.

623. Sleigh, Robert C., Jr., 'On Quantifying Into Epistemic Contexts,' *Nous*, 1 (1967), 23–31.

624. Sleigh, Robert C., Jr., 'On A Proposed System of Epistemic Logic,' *Nous*, 2 (1968), 391–398.

625. Sleigh, Robert C., Jr., 'Restricted Range In Epistemic Logic,' *Journal of Philosophy*, 69 (1972), 67–77.

626. Sloman, Aaron, 'Danto on Space Research and Epistemology,' *Inquiry*, 14 (1971), 174–181. Review of [15].

627. Slote, Michael Anthony, 'Empirical Certainty And The Theory of Important Criteria,' *Inquiry*, 10 (1967), 107–132.

628. Smith, James, 'New Implications of "Someone" II,' *Analysis*, 26 (1966), 207–208.

629. Smokler, Howard, 'Review of Swain,' *Synthese*, 23 (1971), 327–334. Review of [75].

630. Smullyan, A., 'The Concept of Empirical Knowledge,' *Philosophical Review*, 65 (1956), 362–370.

631. Smullyan, A., 'Sense Content and Perceptual Assurance,' *Journal of Philosophy*, 70 (1973), 625–628.

632. Solomon, R., 'Minimal Incorrigibility,' *Australasian Journal of Philosophy*, 53 (1975), 254–256.

633. Sosa, Ernest, 'The Analysis of Knowledge that *p*,' *Analysis*, 25 (1964), 1–8.

634. Sosa, Ernest, 'Propositional Knowledge,' *Philosophical Studies*, 20 (1969), 33–43.

635. Sosa, Ernest, 'Propositional Attitudes *de dicto* and *de re*,' *Journal of Philosophy*, 67 (1970), 883–896.

636. Sosa, Ernest, Two Conceptions of Knowledge,' *The Journal of Philosophy*, 67 (1970), 59–68.

637. Sosa, Ernest, 'Rejoinder To Hintikka,' *Journal of Philosophy,* **68** (1971), 498–501.
638. Sosa, Ernest, 'On The Nature and Objects of Knowledge,' *Philosophical Review,* **81** (1972), 364–371. Review of [9].
639. Sosa, Ernest, 'The Concept of Knowledge: How Do You Know?' *American Philosophical Quarterly,* **11** (1974), 113–122. Reprinted in Pappas and Swain, eds., [43].
640. Sosa, Ernest, 'On Our Knowledge of Matters of Fact,' *Mind,* **83** (1974), 338–405.
641. Sosa, Ernest, 'Review of Lehrer,' *Journal of Philosophy,* **73** (1976), 792–801. Review of [31].
642. Sosa, Ernest, 'Thought, Inference and Knowledge: Gilbert Harman's *Thought,*' *Nous,* **11** (1977), 421–430.
643. Stalnaker, Robert C., 'Review of Hintikka,' *Journal of Philosophy,* **69** (1972), 456–460. Review of [26].
644. Steel, T., 'Knowledge and the Self-presenting,' in Lehrer, ed., *Analysis and Metaphysics,* [32].
645. Steiner, Mark, 'Platonism and the Causal Theory of Knowledge,' *Journal of Philosophy,* **70** (1973), 57–66.
646. Stevenson, J., 'On Doxastic Responsibility,' in Lehrer, ed., [32].
647. Stine, Gail, 'Hintikka on Quantification and Belief,' *Nous,* **3** (1969), 399–408.
648. Stine, Gail, 'Dretske on Knowing the Logical Consequences,' *Journal of Philosophy,* **68** (1971), 296–299.
649. Stine, Gail, 'Two Women,' *Philosophical Studies,* **23** (1972), 84–90.
650. Stine, Gail, 'Quantified Logic for Knowledge Statements,' *Journal of Philosophy,* **71** (1974), 127–140.
651. Stine, Gail, 'Intentional Inexistence,' *Journal of Philosophical Logic,* **5** (1976), 491–516.
652. Stine, Gail, 'Skepticism, Relevant Alternatives and Deductive Closure,' *Philosophical Studies,* **29** (1976), 249–260.
653. Stine, Gail, 'Review of *Analysis and Metaphysics,*' *Philosophia,* **7** (1978), 667–674. Review of [32].
654. Stine, William D., 'Dewey's Theory of Knowledge,' *The Monist,* **57** (1973), 265–277.
655. Strawson, P., 'Does Knowledge Have Foundations?' *Teorema,* **4** (1974), 99–110.
656. Streans, Isabel, 'The Grounds of Knowledge,' *Philosophy and Phenomenological Research,* **2** (1941), 359.
657. Stubbs, Anne C., 'Strawson and Scepticism,' *Philosophical Studies,* (Ireland), **21** (1973), 111–136.
658. Suchting, W. A., 'Review of Dretske,' *British Journal for the Philosophy of Science,* **21** (1970), 121–124. Review of [16].
659. Suppe, Frederick, 'Misidentification, Truth, and Knowing That,' *Philosophical Studies,* **23** (1972), 186–197.
660. Suppe, Frederick, 'Facts and Empirical Truth,' *Canadian Journal of Philosophy,* **3** (1973), 196–212.
661. Sussman, Alan, 'Semantic Analysis in the Philosophy of Mind: A Reply to Ellis,' *Australasian Journal of Philosophy,* **56** (1978), 68–71.
662. Swain, Marshall, 'Skyrms On NonDerivative Knowledge,' *Nous,* **3** (1969), 227–231.

663. Swain, Marshall, 'The Consistency of Rational Belief,' in Swain, ed., [75].
664. Swain, Marshall, 'Schick on Consistency,' *Philosophical Studies,* 21 (1970), 49–53.
665. Swain, Marshall, 'Review of Rescher,' *Journal of Philosophy,* 68 (1971), 319–324. Review of [53].
666. Swain, Marshall, 'An Alternative Analysis of Knowing,' *Synthese,* 23 (1972), 423–442.
667. Swain, Marshall, 'Knowledge, Causality, and Justification,' *Journal of Philosophy,* 69 (1972), 291–300. Reprinted in Pappas and Swain, eds., [43].
668. Swain, Marshall, 'Epistemic Defeasibility,' *American Philosophical Quarterly,* 11 (1974), 15–25. Reprinted in Pappas and Swain, eds., [43].
669. Swain, Marshall, 'Defeasibility: A Reply to R. B. Scott's "Swain on Knowledge",' *Philosophical Studies,* 29 (1976), 425–428.
670. Swain, Marshall, 'Some Revisions of Knowledge, Causality and Justification,' in Pappas and Swain, eds., [43].
671. Swain, Marshall, 'Epistemics and Epistemology,' *Journal of Philosophy,* 75 (1978), 523–525.
672. Swain, Marshall, 'Reasons, Causes and Knowledge,' *Journal of Philosophy,* 75 (1978), 229–248.
673. Swartz, Robert, 'Leibniz's Law and Belief,' *Journal of Philosophy,* 67 (1970), 122–137.
674. Taylor, Albert J., 'On Scheffler's Conditions of Knowledge,' *Educational Theory,* 20.2, (1970), 164–176.
675. Taylor, Richard, 'A Note on Knowledge and Belief,' *Analysis,* 13 (1954), 143–144.
676. Taylor, Richard, 'Knowing What One Knows,' *Analysis,* 16 (1955), 65.
677. Teller, Paul, 'Epistemic Possibility,' *Philosophia,* 2 (1972), 303–320.
678. Teller, Paul, 'Professor Fetzer on Epistemic Possibility,' *Philosophia,* 4 (1974), 337–338.
679. Thalberg, Irving, 'In Defense of Justified True Belief,' *Journal of Philosophy,* 66 (1969), 795–803.
680. Thalberg, Irving, 'Is Justification Transmissible through Deduction?' *Philosophical Studies,* 25 (1974), 347–356.
681. Thomas, L. E., 'Philosophic Doubt,' *Mind,* 64 (1955), 333–341.
682. Thompson, Manley, 'Who Knows?' *Journal of Philosophy,* 67 (1970), 856–869.
683. Tienson, John, 'On Analyzing Knowledge,' *Philosophical Studies,* 25 (1974), 289–293.
684. Tolliver, Joseph, 'Note on Swain's Causal Theory of Knowledge,' in Pappas and Swain, eds., [43].
685. Tomberlin, James, 'Knowing without Knowing that One Knows,' *Philosophia,* 2 (1972), 239–247.
686. Tomberlin, James, 'Knowledge and Implication,' *Ajatus,* 34 (1972), 133–138.
687. Tomberlin, James, 'Is Knowledge Transitive?' *Logique et Analyse,* 16 (1973), 381–384.
688. Tomberlin, James, 'A Problem with Incorrigibility,' *Philosophia,* 5 (1975), 507–512.
689. Tormey, A., 'Access, Incorrigibility and Identity,' *Journal of Philosophy,* 70 (1973), 115–128.

690.   Turner, Dan, 'Why Scepticism,' in Pappas and Swain, eds., [43].
691.   Ulm, Melvin, 'Chisholm's Fourth Axiom' *Philosophical Studies,* **27** (1975), 57–
       61.
692.   Unger, Peter, 'On Experience and the Development of the Understanding,' *American Philosophical Quarterly,* **3** (1966), 48–56.
693.   Unger, Peter, 'Experience and Factual Knowledge,' *Journal of Philosophy,* **64**
       (1967), 152–173.
694.   Unger, Peter, 'An Analysis of Factual Knowledge,' *Journal of Philosophy,* **65**
       (1968), 157–170.
695.   Unger, Peter, 'Our Knowledge of the Material World,' *American Philosophical Quarterly* Monograph Series, **4** (1970), 40–61.
696.   Unger, Peter, 'A Defense of Scepticism,' *Philosophical Review,* **80** (1971), 198–
       219. Reprinted in Pappas and Swain, eds., [43].
697.   Unger, Peter, 'Propositional Verbs and Knowledge,' *Journal of Philosophy,* **69**
       (1972), 301–312.
698.   Unger, Peter, 'On Being Given More than Scepticism,' *Journal of Philosophy,* **70**
       (1973), 628–630.
699.   Unger, Peter, 'The Wages of Scepticism,' *American Philosophical Quarterly,* **10**
       (1973), 177–187.
700.   Unger, Peter, 'An Argument for Skepticism,' *Philosophic Exchange,* **1** (1974),
       131–155.
701.   Unger, Peter, 'Two Types of Scepticism,' *Philosophical Studies,* **25** (1974), 77–
       95.
702.   Van Cleve, James, 'Probability And Certainty: A Re-examination of the Lewis-
       Reichenbach Debate,' *Philosophical Studies,* **32** (1977), 323–334.
703.   Walsh, W. H., 'Knowledge in its Social Setting,' *Mind,* **80** (1971), 321–336.
704.   Wang, Hao, 'A Question on Knowledge of Knowledge,' *Analysis,* **14** (1954), 142–
       146.
705.   Warnock, G. J., 'Claims to Knowledge,' *Proceedings of the Aristotelian Society*
       Supplementary Volume, **36** (1962), 51–63.
706.   Warnock, G. J., 'Seeing and Knowing,' *Mind,* **79** (1970), 281–287. Review of
       Dretske, [16].
707.   Watling, John, 'Inference From The Known To The Unknown,' *Proceedings of
       the Aristotelian Society,* **55** (1955), 83–108.
708.   Weiler, Gershon, 'Degrees of Knowledge,' *Philosophical Quarterly,* **15** (1965),
       317–327.
709.   Weyland, Frances, 'A Note on "Knowledge, Certainty and Probability",' *Inquiry,*
       7 (1964), 417.
710.   White, Alan R., 'On Claiming To Know,' *Philosophical Review,* **66** (1957), 180–
       192.
711.   White, Alan R., 'Review of Hintikka,' *Philosophical Quarterly,* **15** (1965), 268.
       Review of [25].
712.   White, Alan R., 'Review of Wittgenstein,' *Philosophical Books,* **II** (1970), 30–32.
       Review of [81].
713.   White, Alan R., 'Certainty,' *Proceedings of the Aristotelian Society,* Supplementary Volume, **XLVI** (1972), 1–18.
714.   White, Alan R., 'Knowledge without Conviction,' *Mind,* **86** (1977), 224–236.

715. Whiteley, C. H., 'Epistemological Strategies,' *Mind,* 78 (1969), 25–34.
716. Wilks, R., 'Professor Black on "Saying and Disbelieving",' *Analysis,* 14 (1953), 24–25.
717. Willard, Dallas, 'A Crucial Error in Epistemology,' *Mind,* 76 (1967), 513–523.
718. Williams, Michael, 'Inference, Justification and the Analysis of Knowledge,' *Journal of Philosophy,* 75 (1978), 249–263.
719. Wisdom, J. O., 'The Sceptic at Bay,' *British Journal for the Philosophy of Science,* 9 (1959), 159–163. Review of Ayer [8].
720. Wisdom, J. O., 'Epistemological Enlightenment,' *Proceedings of the American Philosophical Association,* (1971).
721. Wolgast, Elizabeth H., 'Knowing and What It Implies,' *Philosophical Review,* 80 (1971), 360–370.
722. Woozley, A. D., 'Knowing and Not Knowing,' *Proceedings of the Aristotelian Society,* 53 (1952), 151–172.
723. Wright, Maxwell, '"I Know" And Performative Utterances," *Australasian Journal of Philosophy,* 43 (1965), 35–47.
724. Wu, Kathleen G. Johnson, 'Hintikka and Defensibility,' *Ajatus,* 32 (1970), 25–31.
725. Wu, Kathleen G. Johnson, 'Hintikka and Defensibility: Some Further Remarks,' *Journal of Philosophical Logic,* 1 (1972), 259–261.
726. Wu, Kathleen G. Johnson, 'A New Approach to the Formalization of a Logic of Knowledge and Belief,' *Logique et Analyse,* 16 (1973), 513–525.
727. Zemach, Eddy M., 'Epistemic Opacity Again,' *Philosophia,* 3 (1973), 33–41.
728. Ziedins, Rudy, 'Knowledge, Belief, and Perceptual Experience,' *Australasian Journal of Philosophy,* 44 (1966), 70–88.
729. Zvara, A., 'On Claiming to Know and Feeling Sure,' *Philosophical Studies,* 24 (1973), 272–274.

NOTES ON CONTRIBUTORS

ALVIN I. GOLDMAN is professor and chairman of the philosophy department at the University of Michigan. He was formerly a member of the Institute for Advanced Study in the Behaviorial Sciences.

MARSHALL SWAIN is professor of philosophy at Ohio State University. He has also taught at the University of Pennsylvania and the University of Illinois at Chicago Circle.

GEORGE S. PAPPAS is associate professor of philosophy at Ohio State University. He has also taught at the University of Western Ontario, Denison University and the University of Texas.

KEITH LEHRER is professor of philosophy at the University of Arizona and co-editor of the *Philosophical Studies* Series. He has also taught at Wayne State University, the University of Rochester and Vanderbilt University, and been a member of the Institute for Advanced Study in the Behaviorial Sciences.

ERNEST SOSA is professor of philosophy at Brown University. He has also taught at the University of Western Ontario, the University of Michigan and the University of Texas.

JOHN POLLOCK is professor of philosophy at the University of Arizona. He has also taught at the State University of New York at Buffalo and at the University of Rochester.

JAMES W. CORNMAN was professor of philosophy at the University of Pennsylvania. He also had taught at Ohio State University and the University of Rochester, and had been a Mellon post-doctoral fellow at the University of Pittsburgh.

RODERICK M. CHISHOLM is Romeo Elton Professor of philosophy at Brown University. He has also taught at Harvard University, the University of Graz (Austria), the University of Massachusetts, and the University of Chicago.

MARK PASTIN is associate professor of philosophy at Indiana University. He has also taught at Wayne State University and the University of Michigan.

WILFRID SELLARS is University Professor of philosophy at the University of Pittsburgh. He has also taught at the University of Iowa, the University of Minnesota, and Yale University. He is co-editor, with Keith Lehrer, of the *Philosophical Studies* Series.

NANCY C. KELSIK is a doctoral candidate in philosophy at Ohio State University.

NAME INDEX

SUBJECT INDEX

PHILOSOPHICAL STUDIES SERIES
IN PHILOSOPHY

Editors:

WILFRID SELLARS, Univ. of Pittsburgh and KEITH LEHRER, Univ. of Arizona

Board of Consulting Editors:

Jonathan Bennett, Alan Gibbard, Robert Stalnaker, and Robert G. Turnbull

1. JAY F. ROSENBERG, *Linguistic Representation*, 1974. xii + 159 pp.
2. WILFRID SELLARS, *Essays in Philosophy and Its History*, 1974. xiii + 462 pp.
3. DICKINSON S. MILLER, *Philosophical Analysis and Human Welfare*, Selected Essays and Chapters from Six Decades. Edited with an Introduction by Lloyd D. Easton, 1975. x + 333 pp.
4. KEITH LEHRER (ed.), *Analysis and Metaphysics*, Essays in Honor of R. M. Chisholm. 1975.. x + 317 pp.
5. CARL GINET, *Knowledge, Perception, and Memory*, 1975. viii + 212 pp.
6. PETER H. HARE and EDWARD H. MADDEN, *Causing, Perceiving and Believing.* An Examination of the Philosophy of C. J. Ducasse. 1975. vii + 211 pp.
7. HECTOR-NERI CASTAÑEDA, *Thinking and Doing.* The Philosophical Foundations of Institutions. 1975. xviii + 366 pp.
8. JOHN L. POLLOCK, *Subjunctive Reasoning*, 1976. xi + 255 pp.
9. BRUCE AUNE, *Reason and Action*, 1977. xi + 206 pp.
10. GEORGE SCHLESINGER, *Religion and Scientific Method.* 1977, vii + 204 pp.
11. YIRMIAHU YOVEL (ed.), *Philosophy of History and Action.* Papers presented at the first Jerusalem Philosophical Encounter, December 1974. 1978. xi + 243 pp.
12. JOSEPH C. PITT, *The Philosophy of Wilfrid Sellars: Queries and Extensions,* 1978. x + 304 pp.
13. ALVIN I. GOLDMAN and JAEGWON KIM, *Values and Morals,* Essays in Honor of William Frankena, Charles Stevenson, and Richard Brandt. 1978. xviii + 332 pp.
14. MICHAEL J. LOUX, *Substance and Attribute,* A Study in Ontology. 1978. xi + 187 pp.
15. ERNEST SOSA (ed.), *The Philosophy of Nicholas Rescher: Discussion and Replies,* 1979. xi + 236 pp.
16. JEFFRIE G. MURPHY, *Retribution, Justice, and Therapy.* Essays in the Philosophy of Law. 1979. xx + 255 pp.